HISTORY AS POLICY
FRAMING THE DEBATE ON THE FUTURE OF
AUSTRALIA'S DEFENCE POLICY

HISTORY AS POLICY

FRAMING THE DEBATE ON THE FUTURE OF
AUSTRALIA'S DEFENCE POLICY

Edited by Ron Huisken and Meredith Thatcher

Published by ANU E Press
The Australian National University
Canberra ACT 0200, Australia
Email: anuepress@anu.edu.au
This title is also available online at: http://epress.anu.edu.au/hap_citation.html

National Library of Australia
Cataloguing-in-Publication entry

Title:	History as policy : framing the debate on the future of Australia's defence policy / editors, Ron Huisken, Meredith Thatcher.
Publisher:	Canberra, A.C.T. : ANU E Press, 2007.
ISBN:	9781921313554 (pbk.) 9781921313561 (online)
Series:	Canberra papers on strategy and defence ; no. 167
Subjects:	Australia–Military policy. Australia–Military policy–History. Australia–National security. Australia–Foreign relations. Australia–Defenses. Australia–Strategic aspects.
Other Authors:	Huisken, R. H. (Ronald Herman), 1946- Thatcher, Meredith Christine, 1966- Australian National University. Strategic and Defence Studies Centre.
Dewey Number:	355.03350994

All rights reserved. No part of this publication may be reproduced, stored in a retrieval system or transmitted in any form or by any means, electronic, mechanical, photocopying or otherwise, without the prior permission of the publisher.

The *Canberra Papers on Strategy and Defence* series is a collection of publications arising principally from research undertaken at the SDSC. Canberra Papers have been peer reviewed since 2006. All Canberra Papers are available for sale: visit the SDSC website at <http://rspas.anu.edu.au/sdsc/canberra_papers.php> for abstracts and prices. Electronic copies (in pdf format) of most SDSC Working Papers published since 2002 may be downloaded for free from the SDSC website at <http://rspas.anu.edu.au/sdsc/working_papers.php>. The entire Working Papers series is also available on a 'print on demand' basis.

Strategic and Defence Studies Centre Publications Program Advisory Review Panel: Emeritus Professor Paul Dibb; Professor Desmond Ball; Professor David Horner; Professor Hugh White; Professor William Tow; Professor Anthony Milner; Professor Virginia Hooker; Dr Coral Bell; Dr Pauline Kerr

Strategic and Defence Studies Centre Publications Program Editorial Board: Professor Hugh White; Dr Brendan Taylor; Dr Christian Enemark; Miss Meredith Thatcher (series editor)

Cover design by ANU E Press

This edition © 2007 ANU E Press

Contents

The Strategic and Defence Studies Centre's 40th anniversary seminar series — vii

Contributors — ix

Acronyms and Abbreviations — xv

Introduction — 1

Self-Reliant Defence: The First Cut

1. The Self-Reliant Defence of Australia: The History of an Idea, *Paul Dibb* — 11

Global Issues

2. Global Change and Strategic Priorities, *Coral Bell* — 29

3. Restoring Utility to Armed Force in the 21st Century, *Robert O'Neill* — 49

4. The Rise of China: History as Policy, *Wang Gungwu* — 61

5. Whither the United States and Unipolarity?, *Ron Huisken* — 67

Regional Issues

6. The 'Arc of Instability': The History of an Idea, *Graeme Dobell* — 85

7. Jihadism and 'The Battle of Ideas' in Indonesia: Critiquing Australian Counterterrorism, *Greg Fealy* — 105

8. Security Cooperation in the Asia-Pacific Region, *Brendan Taylor* — 117

Australian Strategic and Defence Issues

9. The Challenge of Coherence: Strategic Guidance, Capability, and Budgets, *Mark Thomson* — 131

10. The Higher Command Structure for Joint ADF Operations, *David Horner* — 143

11. Four Decades of the Defence of Australia: Reflections on Australian Defence Policy over the Past 40 Years, *Hugh White* — 163

Index — 189

The Strategic and Defence Studies Centre's 40th anniversary seminar series

The Strategic and Defence Studies Centre is a research centre within the Research School of Pacific and Asian Studies in the College of Asia and the Pacific at The Australian National University in Canberra, the country's capital.

In the second half of 2006, the Centre marked the fortieth anniversary of its founding in 1966 with a series of three seminars (and a dinner) under the theme of *History as Policy*.

Held on 8 August 2006 at the Boat House by the Lake in Canberra (<http://www.boathousebythelake.com.au/>), the dinner was addressed by Professor Wang Gungwu, who gave a masterly sketch of the strategic implications of the rise of China, drawing on his deep knowledge of China's history. Guests included the current Chief of the Defence Force, Air Chief Marshal Angus Houston, the then Secretary of Defence, Ric Smith, and other key figures from the policy world, the intelligence community, and the media. Also in attendance were colleagues from The Australian National University, including the Convenor of the College of Asia and the Pacific, Professor Robin Jeffrey.

Boeing Holdings Australia Ltd continued a long tradition of support to the Centre by generously sponsoring the seminar series and the dinner (which was attended by Paul Gargette, its Vice President of Operations and Business Integration).

The three anniversary seminars were held on 15 August, 14 September and 10 October 2007 at University House on the grounds of The Australian National University (<http://www.anu.edu.au/unihouse/>).

Speakers at the first seminar on *Global Strategic Issues* were Robert O'Neill ('Changing concepts of the nature of security and the role of armed force'), Hugh White ('Predictions and policy'), Coral Bell ('The evolution of the international system'), and Ron Huisken ('Whither the United States?').

Speakers at the second seminar on *Regional Security Issues* were Alan Dupont ('Transnational security issues'), Graeme Dobell ('The arc of instability'), Greg Fealy ('Western counterterrorism in Southeast Asia: Is the 'war of ideas' a fallacy?'), and Brendan Taylor ('Security cooperation in the Asia-Pacific region').

Speakers at the final seminar on *Australia Strategic and Defence Issues* were Paul Dibb ('The Defence of Australia: the history of an idea'), Mark Thomson ('The challenge of coherence: Strategic guidance, force structure and budgets'), David Horner ('The higher command structure for joint ADF operations'), and Hugh White ('Summing Up: Seeing the future in the past').

The papers were of a high standard and prompted much discussion. They provided a stimulating opportunity to reflect on the contribution which the Strategic and Defence Studies Centre has made—to The Australian National University, to Canberra's strategic policy community, to the national debate, and to the wider study of strategic issues—and to foreshadow some of the work to be done in the years ahead.

***

In its study of (and work on) strategic issues, the Centre is fortunate to have thriving doctoral and masters programs, the latter currently under the excellent direction of Dr Robert Ayson. (Details of the Graduate Studies in Strategy and Defence (GSSD) program can be viewed at <http://rspas.anu.edu.au/gssd/>.) Graduates from both programs have gone on to forge successful careers either within or beyond academic circles.

The substantial volume of high-quality work undertaken within the Strategic and Defence Studies Centre would have proved impossible without the dedication of the Centre's academic and support staff, Visiting Fellows, and other researchers and guests who have graced its corridors over the past forty years. Its continued success has also been due to the assistance of numerous colleagues within the ANU academic community.

This volume forms part of the Canberra Papers on Strategy and Defence collection. Visit the Centre's website at <http://rspas.anu.edu.au/sdsc/> for further details about the Centre's history, staff, and location, and also about its output, including analysis and research items, seminar and academic programs, and its extensive publications collection.

Contributors

Coral Bell is a Visiting Fellow at the Strategic and Defence Studies Centre, The Australian National University. She has held numerous postings during her long and distinguished career, including within the Diplomatic Service and as Professor of International Politics at the University of Sussex. She was awarded an Order of Australia in 2005. Her research interests are mainly in crisis management and the interaction of strategic, economic and diplomatic factors in international politics, especially as they affect US and Australian foreign policies. Her articles have appeared in a number of leading international journals, such as *Foreign Affairs*, *The National Interest* and *The American Interest*. Recent publications have included *Living with Giants: Finding Australia's place in a more complex world,* and *A World Out of Balance: American Power and International Politics in the Twenty-First Century*. She also contributed 'The International System and Changing Strategic Norms' in (eds) R. Ayson and D. Ball, *Strategy and Security in the Asia-Pacific*. Her next paper (to be published in early 2008 by the Lowy Institute for International Policy) is *The End of the Vasco da Gama Era: The next landscape of world politics*.

Paul Dibb is Emeritus Professor and Chairman of the Board at the Strategic and Defence Studies Centre, The Australian National University. He was formerly a Deputy Secretary of Defence, and Director of the Australian Joint Intelligence Organisation. His research interests are Australian defence policy, regional security, and alliance relationships, and his publications reflect these interests. They include *The Soviet Union: The Incomplete Superpower*; *Towards a New Balance of Power in Asia*; (with Robert D. Blackwill) *America's Asian Alliances*; and *Essays on Australian Defence*. He also contributed 'America and the Asia-Pacific Region' in (eds) R. Ayson and D. Ball, *Strategy and Security in the Asia-Pacific*. His articles have appeared in a range of leading international journals, including *Survival*, *Orbis* and *Washington Quarterly*. He was also the author of the highly-influential 1986 *Review of Australia's Defence Capabilities*.

Graeme Dobell is one of the Australian Broadcasting Corporation's most experienced reporters of Asia Pacific affairs. Previously the ABC's Southeast Asia radio correspondent in Singapore, he is now the Canberra-based Foreign Affairs and Defence Correspondent for Radio Australia, reporting also for ABC radio news and current affairs programs. He joined the ABC in 1975 and has concentrated mostly on reporting politics and international affairs, serving as a correspondent in Europe, America and throughout Asia and the Pacific. Since 1985, Graeme Dobell has focused on reporting the affairs of the Asia Pacific region and has covered the APEC summits and the security dialogue of the ASEAN Regional Forum. Assignments in his career as a correspondent have included the Falklands War, coups in Fiji, Thailand and the Philippines, Beijing after the crushing of the pro-democracy movement in Tiananmen Square and the return of Hong Kong to China. He is the author of *Australia Finds Home—The Choices and Chances of an Asia Pacific Journey*, a 400 page book on Australia's relationship with the Asia Pacific, published by ABC Books.

Greg Fealy is Fellow and Senior Lecturer, Indonesian Politics, in the Department of Political and Social Change (a joint appointment with the Faculty of Asian Studies) at The Australian National University. He has held various positions, including as a Visiting Professor in Indonesian Politics at the Johns Hopkins School of Advanced International Studies; as a lecturer in Southeast Asian History at Monash University; as an Indonesia analyst with the Australian Government; and as a consultant on Indonesian civil society and election programs. His research interests are Indonesian politics, modern Islamic political history, Islam and civil society, and the impact of globalisation on religion and culture in Southeast Asia. Recently, he has examined transnational Islamist and neo-revivalist movements in Indonesia, as well as terrorism in Southeast Asia and trends in contemporary Islamic politics. Three co-edited publications include (with V. Hooker) *Voices of Islam in Southeast Asia: A Contemporary Sourcebook*; (with A. Borgu) *Local Jihad: Radical Islam and terrorism in Indonesia*; and (with A. Bubalo) *Joining the Caravan? The Middle East, Islamism and Indonesia*. He contributed 'Half a Century of Violent Jihad in Indonesia: an Historical and Ideological Comparison of Darul Islam and Jema'ah Islamiyah', in (eds) M. Vicziany and D. Wright-Neville, *Islamic Terrorism in Indonesia: Myths and Realities*; and 'Islamisation and politics in Southeast Asia: The contrasting case of Malaysia and Indonesia', in (eds) N. Lahoud and A. Johns, *Islam in World Politics*.

Wang Gungwu is Professor at the National University of Singapore, and Emeritus Professor at The Australian National University (where he was Professor and Head of the (then) Department of Far Eastern History, and Director of the Research School of Pacific Studies). He has taught at the University of Malaya and was Vice-Chancellor of the University of Hong Kong between 1986 and 1995. He has held high-level positions in other institutions, including as a former President of the Australian Academy of the Humanities; Foreign Honorary Member of the American Academy of Arts and Science; and Honorary Member of the Chinese Academy of Social Science. Appointments in Singapore include Chairman of the East Asian Institute, the Institute of Southeast Asian Studies and the Lee Kuan Yew School of Public Policy; and Vice-Chairman of the Chinese Heritage Centre. He has been awarded a CBE along with numerous academic and cultural prizes. A prolific and respected author, his books (in English) since 1995 have included *The Chinese Way*; *China's Position in International Relations*; *China and Southeast Asia: Myths, Threats, and Culture*; *The Chinese Overseas: From Earthbound China to the Quest for Autonomy*; *Don't Leave Home: Migration and the Chinese*; *Anglo-Chinese Encounters since 1800: War, Trade, Science and Governance*; and *Divided China: Preparing for Reunification 883–947*. In 2004 he was the subject of Gregor Benton's *Diasporic Chinese Ventures: The Life and Work of Wang Gungwu*.

David Horner is Professor of Australian Defence History at the Strategic and Defence Studies Centre, The Australian National University, and Official Historian Peacekeeping and Post-Cold War Operations. He served for 25 years in the Australian Regular Army, including active service in South Vietnam. Since 1994 he has been editor of the Army History Series and, from 1998 to 2002, was head of the Australian Army's Land Warfare Studies Centre. His research interests include Australian defence history, particularly strategy, command, intelligence and operations and current defence issues. Currently, he heads the joint ANU-Australian War Memorial's major project on the Official History of Australian Peacekeeping and Post-Cold War Operations. He is also an adviser to television programs and a highly-regarded author whose volumes include *High Command, Australia and Allied Strategy, 1939-1945*; *The Gunners: A History of Australian Artillery*; *Inside the War Cabinet: Directing Australia's War Effort, 1939-1945*; (with D. Ball) *Breaking the Codes: Australia's*

KGB Network; *Blamey: The Commander-in-Chief*; *Defence Supremo: Sir Frederick Shedden and the Making of Australian Defence Policy*; 'Making the Australian Defence Force' (Volume 4 of *The Australian Centenary History of Defence*); and *Strategic Command: General Sir John Wilton and Australia's Asian Wars*.

Ron Huisken is Senior Fellow at the Strategic and Defence Studies Centre, The Australian National University. He has held a variety of research and teaching positions in Australia and overseas, together with assignments in the United Nations and the Australian Public Service. He spent a number of years with the Stockholm International Peace Research Institute working particularly on military expenditures, naval forces and nuclear arms control. At the UN Department of Disarmament Affairs, he played a key role in producing a landmark study on the relationships between disarmament and development. In government in Australia, he worked predominantly on arms control issues with the Department of Foreign Affairs and Trade and on alliance management questions with the Department of Defence. He also served as deputy Chief of Mission in the Australian embassy in Bonn in 1990–94. He returned to academia in 2001 where his research interests include East Asian security, alliance politics, and proliferation. His publications include (with F. Barnaby) *Arms Uncontrolled; The Origin of the Strategic Cruise Missile*; and *The Road to War on Iraq*.

Robert O'Neill is currently Planning Director of the United States Studies Centre of the University of Sydney. He is a widely respected authority in the field of strategic studies who has served in the Australian Regular Army, and taught military history at the Royal Military College of Australia. During periods spent in the United Kindgom, he has been director of the International Institute for Strategic Studies in London, Chichele Professor of the History of War at the University of Oxford and a Fellow of All Souls College. He has held many prominent appointments, including as Chairman of the Council of the IISS (1996–2001), Chairman of Trustees of the Imperial War Museum, London (1998–2001), Chairman of the Council of the Centre for Defence Studies, King's College, London (1991–96), and Chairman of the Sir Robert Menzies Centre for Australian Studies in the University of London (1990–96). He is also a former director of both the International Peace Academy, New York, and the Ditchley Foundation, Oxfordshire, and a former member of the Canberra Commission on the Elimination of Nuclear Weapons established by the Australian Government in 1995–96. On retirement from the University of Oxford in 2001 he became

Chairman of the Council of the Australian Strategic Policy Institute in Canberra until 2005. He was also Deputy Chairman of the Board of the Graduate School of Government at University of Sydney (2003–2005) and remains a board member of the Lowy Institute for International Policy. His research interests focus on war and warfare in the past and present, and ways of resolving international tensions. While Head of the Strategic and Defence Studies Centre at ANU (1970–82), he wrote the *Official History of Australia's role in the Korean War* and he is also the former Armed Services Editor of the *Australian Dictionary of Biography* (1970–2001). He was elected a Fellow of the Academy of the Social Sciences in Australia in 1978 and awarded an Order of Australia in 1988.

Brendan Taylor is a lecturer in the Graduate Studies in Strategy and Defence program at the Strategic Defence Studies Centre, The Australian National University. He is the course coordinator for the program elective 'The US and East Asian Security'. His research interests include Northeast Asian security, American foreign policy, economic statecraft, and alliance politics. He lectures to a number of undergraduate and postgraduate classes at The Australian National University—where he coordinates Masters-level courses on 'Asia-Pacific security' and 'The US and East Asian security'—as well as to various Australian Defence Colleges and public fora. He is a member of the Australian Committee of the Council for Security Cooperation in the Asia-Pacific. His publications have appeared in such leading international journals as *Asian Security*, *Comparative Strategy*, and the *Australian Journal of International Affairs*. He also co-authored (with D. Ball and A. Milner) *Mapping Track II Institutions in New Zealand, Australia and the Asian Region*, An Independent Study Submitted to the Asia New Zealand Foundation in March 2005.

Mark Thomson began his career as an academic working in theoretical physics. As a scientist he held research and teaching posts in Australia and the United Kingdom. In the mid-1990s he joined the Department of Defence and commenced work in the Force Development and Analysis division scrutinising capability development proposals. Over the next five years he held a diverse range of jobs in the department, which saw him working on budget management, organisational change and force development. In this period, he was deployed on operations as a Civilian Truce Monitor to Bougainville in 1997 and as Political Military Advisor to the INTERFET Commander in 1999. In 2002 he joined the newly-formed Australian Strategic Policy Institute as inaugural director of the Budget and Management

Program. His research touches on a wide range of issues including Australia's defence and security budgets, links between strategy and force structure, the internal management of the Department of Defence and defence industry.

Hugh White is the Professor of Strategic Studies and the Head of the Strategic and Defence Studies Centre, The Australian National University. Before taking up that position he was the first Director of the Australian Strategic Policy Institute. He has worked in strategic policy and related fields for two decades. He has served as an intelligence analyst with the Office of National Assessments, as a journalist with the Sydney Morning Herald, and as a senior adviser on the staffs of Defence Minister Kim Beazley and Prime Minister Bob Hawke. Between 1995 and 2000 he was also Deputy Secretary for Strategy and Intelligence. He teaches 'Australian Defence and Strategic Planning' and contributes to the Graduate Studies in Strategy and Defence program's core courses. He has written on a wide range of Australian defence policy issues and is also a regular commentator in print and other media. He recently appeared on episode 5 ('Australians on the Front Line') of the ABC television program 'Difference of Opinion'. Recent publications include *Beyond the Defence of Australia: finding a new balance in Australia's defence policy* and (with E. Wainwright) *Strengthening Our Neighbour: Australia and the Future of Papua New Guinea*. He has also contributed 'The New Australia-Indonesia Strategic Relationship—A Note of Caution', in (ed.) J. Monfries, *Different Societies, Shared Futures: Australia, Indonesia and the Region*; 'Old, New or Both? Australia's Security at the Start of the New Century', in (eds) D. McDougall and P. Shearman, *Australian Security After 9/11*; and 'Australian Strategic Policy', in (eds), A. Tellis and M. Wills, *Strategic Asia 2005-06: Military Modernisation in an Era of Uncertainty*; 'The Ethics of Invasion: Jus ad Bellum and Iraq', in (eds) T. Coady and M. O'Keefe, *Righteous Violence: The Ethics and Politics of Military Intervention*; and the chapter on Defence in (eds) J. Cotton and J. Ravenhill, *Trading on Alliances: Australia in World Affairs 2001-2005*.

Acronyms and Abbreviations

ACOPS	Assistant CDF (Operations)
ADF	Australian Defence Force
ANU	The Australian National University
APEC	Asia-Pacific Economic Cooperation
ARF	ASEAN Regional Forum
ASEAN	Association of Southeast Asian Nations
BCOF	British Commonwealth Occupation Force
CDF	Chief of the Defence Force
CDFS	Chief of the Defence Force Staff
CGS	Chief of the General Staff
CDS	Chief of Defence Staff
CJFA	Commander Joint Forces Australia
COMAFV	Commander Australian Force Vietnam
COMAST	Commander Australian Theatre
COMFLOT	Commodore Flotillas
COSC	Chiefs of Staff Committee
CSCAP	Council for Security Cooperation in the Asia-Pacific
DFAT	Department of Foreign Affairs and Trade
EAS	East Asia Summit
GDP	Gross Domestic Product
HQADF	Headquarters Australian Defence Force
HQAST	Headquarters Australian Theatre
INTERFET	International Force East Timor
IISS	International Institute for Strategic Studies
JI	Jemaah Islamiyah
NATO	North Atlantic Treaty Organization
NEAT	Network of East Asian Think Tanks
PNG	Papua New Guinea
RAAF	Royal Australian Air Force
RAMSI	Regional Assistance Mission to Solomon Islands
RAN	Royal Australian Navy
SARS	Severe Acute Respiratory Syndrome
SCO	Shanghai Cooperation Organization
SDSC	Strategic and Defence Studies Centre
UN	United Nations
USMC	United States Marine Corps
VCDF	Vice Chief of the Defence Force
WMD	Weapons of Mass Destruction

Introduction

Ron Huisken

To celebrate its fortieth anniversary in 2006, the Strategic and Defence Studies Centre (SDSC), sponsored by Boeing Australia Holdings Limited, organised a series of seminars on what we judged to be some the key issues that should inform the future development of Australian defence policy.

Particularly in the first 20 years after its establishment, scholars at the SDSC played a prominent role in shaping the ideas and aspirations that eventually found official expression in *Defence of Australia* (the 1987 White Paper on the Defence of Australia) and the *Review of Australia's Defence Capabilities* (or so-called Dibb Review) that preceded it.[1] We did not select the title for our anniversary seminars out of a sense of nostalgia. Australian defence policy has never been far from the Centre's core interests. Moreover, we have a number of concerns about the manner in which adjustments to defence policy are being determined. One particular concern is the spontaneity (to characterise it politely) that has crept into defence policymaking and acquisition decisions, and the gap between declaratory policy and actual practice that has emerged as a result. A second is that much of the heated debate about expeditionary versus 'defence of Australia' capabilities seems unaware that this has long been the core dilemma confronting Australian defence planners and that there may be value in revisiting the answers arrived at in the past. And a third is the extent to which the specialist community has dissipated its energy advocating policy developments already agreed by government, while important judgements—such as whether expeditionary deployments in Australia's immediate neighbourhood and in distant theatres are equally important and probable, and call for a similar suite of capabilities—remain unexplored.

The papers assembled in this volume do not pretend to constitute a comprehensive coverage of the issues that defence policymakers need to reflect upon. Defence policy does not flow easily from a single political decision or determination. It is instead a construction, an edifice of judgements rather than a single insight. In a first step, these judgements must traverse the defining characteristics and possible sources of threat to Australian interests in the unfolding global and regional order. Judgements then have to be made about which of these threats or risks it would be appropriate and feasible for Australia to acquire military capacities to counter and which should be addressed through other policy instruments. For those residual risks where the option to use force is deemed essential, their relative importance has to be assessed before determining the broad mix of capabilities that offers the strongest fit with the spectrum of risks. Finally, the broad force structure that flows from this edifice of judgements has to be reconciled with fiscal realities, a process that may require some iterative re-visiting of core assessments further up the chain.

For some 25 years, from 1975–2000, a defence policy centred on the self-reliant 'defence of Australia' doctrine enjoyed strong political, professional and public support. This volume begins with Paul Dibb recalling how Australia gravitated toward the conviction that it could and should aspire to defend itself, and the major challenges he faced in 1985–86 when he was tasked by the then Defence Minister, Kim Beazley, to develop the general thrust of 'defence of Australia' into a coherent and affordable capabilities program for the Australian Defence Force (ADF). Dibb stresses that his report was primarily about how to structure the ADF, not about how governments might wish to use it. The author of the concluding chapter, Hugh White, has a similarly ideal pedigree to explain how 'defence of Australia' worked in practice and to address the core question of where to from here? White was the senior defence official involved for most of the 1990s in using the 'defence of Australia' doctrine to guide the allocation of ADF resources and in advising government on whether and how this core policy should be adapted in the light of new circumstances, not least the end of the Cold War.

Both authors highlight that, while expressed differently at various points in our brief history, a central dilemma for Australia's defence planners has always been where we envisaged the frontline for our defence to be, and it is this issue that has shaped the defence capabilities needed rather decisively. For a long time, this central judgement was buried under the acceptance in Australia of a semi-sovereign status, a community that deemed self-defence to be out of reach and was content to sub-contract its defence to the mother country or to our newer great and powerful friend. In other words, the frontline for Australia's defence was wherever the United Kingdom or the United States deemed it to be and, except for 1942–43, this was never close to Australia.

Having finally resolved in the mid-1970s to aspire to the self-reliant 'defence of Australia', the determination on where we should position the frontline of our defence stood exposed as central to the relevance and effectiveness of our defence capacity. 'Defence of Australia' determined that our frontline (i.e., the primary geographical determinant of our air and maritime strike capabilities in particular) should be the sea-air gap across northern Australia. This national focus did not stem from a strategic assessment that the world had improved to such an extent that the traditional deployment of Australian forces to distant battlefields could be completely discounted. Nor was there a political decision that Australia would simply no longer countenance such deployments in the future. 'Defence of Australia' included the overt judgement that the forces acquired to address this core mission would be sufficiently large and versatile to meet the other tasks that government could ask of them—including, in particular, UN or US-led operations.

White, in particular, highlights how significantly the exclusivity of the sea-air gap frontline was whittled back to accommodate secondary but formally-endorsed guidelines to the ADF to also anticipate operating on frontlines that ranged somewhat vaguely up the East Asian seaboard. These adaptations of 'defence of Australia' resulted from efforts by both Labor and Liberal Governments to anticipate the probable consequences of the end of the Cold War; the achievement by most of Australia's Southeast Asian neighbours of high and sustained rates of economic growth which eroded both our technological edge and our relative strategic weight; the later 1997–98 Asian financial crisis which saw the Association of Southeast Asian Nations (ASEAN) lose much of its coherence and launched Indonesia on the difficult road to democracy; the rise of China; the East Timor experience; and the epidemic of stability concerns among the island states of the Southwest Pacific.

The process of formal and comprehensive re-evaluations of defence policy—that is, synthesising strategy, force structure and budgets—stopped in 2000 with that year's Defence White Paper, *Defence 2000: Our Future Defence Force* (*Defence 2000*). Since then, we have seen three Defence Updates, each of which endorsed the enduring validity of *Defence 2000*. The qualifications to 'defence of Australia' endorsed up to 2000 (essentially authorising capabilities additional to the 'defence of Australia' mission) did not require the ADF to be able to operate independently beyond Australia and its most immediate neighbourhood—it was clearly specified that all such operations would be conducted with allies and/or friends. Even with this significant limitation on the desired capabilities, the Australian Government's undertaking to provide three per cent annual real growth in the defence budget (effectively ensuring that the ADF budget stayed at about two per cent of Gross Domestic Product (GDP)) meant a very tight fiscal environment for defence, with no scope for any indulgent excursions or significant mismanagement of major acquisition programs. Since 2000, of course, we have had the 11 September 2001 terrorist attacks on the United States. Endorsing the view that conventional military forces had a central role in confronting international terrorism has generated still more frontlines for the ADF—in Afghanistan and Iraq—all more distant from Australia than Southeast or even Northeast Asia.

A reasonable working assumption is that the ADF, with an annual budget of some A$20 billion—representing a relatively stable resource allocation bargain within government and a relatively stable social contract between government and the people in respect of taxation and the provision of public goods and services—is being allowed and indeed encouraged to prepare to defend Australia and its interests on too many fronts. The question, as always, remains how many frontlines can we sensibly task the ADF to defend, and on what basis do we construct the edifice of judgements that would allow us to separate the really essential frontline(s) from the merely desirable or even the important, and then to devise a logical and affordable set of force structure priorities?

The remaining essays in this volume show that if devising a coherent and affordable defence policy was difficult in the past, it is not going to be any easier in the future. In the first of several chapters on what we have termed global issues that should affect Australia's defence policy, Coral Bell takes a penetrating look at the international system a few decades hence and sees, alongside further significant population growth and a quite dramatic increase in urbanisation worldwide, up to a dozen states with a claim to the label 'major power'. As we are presently in a unipolar world, we face a complex, compressed and inherently stressful redistribution of power and influence. Two Asian states, China and India, are likely to constitute the epicentre of this transformation. Bell contends that, notwithstanding all the changes (nuclear weapons, the information and communications revolutions, and globalisation for example) that most analysts feel minimise the likelihood of hegemonial war (or one or more of these major powers resorting to force either to accelerate or retard the redistribution of power in the international system), the prospect of such a war remains the most destructive threat imaginable and its avoidance the first priority of statesmanship and diplomacy.

Bell proposes that something like the Concert of Powers that staved off hegemonial war for a century following the Napoleonic wars may be the only diplomatic institution capable of managing the crowded global leaderboard in prospect over the coming decades. In a later chapter, Brendan Taylor indirectly supports the decisive importance of the major powers consciously assuming prime responsibility for the stability of the international system. Taylor documents the luxuriant growth in multilateral security processes in the Asia Pacific but concludes that the impact of these processes has been, and will likely remain, quite marginal for a long time.

In a second chapter on global issues, Robert O'Neill takes a sobering look at the state of the campaign against international terrorism. O'Neill concludes that the first five years of this campaign have gone very badly, courtesy, in the main, of the war in Iraq. We should by now have had a far better security outlook on this front than is in fact the case. Although he considers that a number of important actors may have lost sight of the limited utility of military power, he concedes that military force will have an indispensable part to play in bringing this phenomenon under control. At the same time he is alarmed at how completely the lessons of past campaigns against irregular fighters have been forgotten, even as political and military leaders have watched the strong propensity for conventional military power to become a counterproductive blunt instrument play itself out over and over again. O'Neill offers a list of thoughtful suggestions on the capacities and qualities that the armed forces of states opposing terrorism must be funded to acquire if they are to fulfil their limited but essential role in this long campaign.

In a somewhat analogous fashion, Greg Fealy brings out the fact that beyond the battlefield, in the realm of hearts and minds, the very special challenges posed by jihadism requires policy to be guided by the most careful and nuanced analysis. Fealy focuses on Indonesia where jihadism is present but still so marginal that a military counterterrorist campaign is neither underway nor necessary. Australia is doing what it can to encourage and assist the Indonesian Government to win the 'battle of ideas' and to strengthen further the country's evident inhospitability to jihadist theology and solutions. His analyses of attitudes in Indonesia toward descriptors like fundamentalism, radicalism, extremism and jihadism mirror O'Neill's views on the complexities of the modern battlefield. It is distressingly easy to mis-diagnose the situation, to resort to generalisations, and to pursue policy settings that, at best, have no effect or, at worst, prove counterproductive, as Fealy believes may be the case with Australia's current approach to Indonesia.

In two further chapters on global issues Wang Gungwu and Ron Huisken look at China and the United States respectively. In what was initially an address to the dinner that opened the anniversary seminars, Wang reminds us that China is unique among the current crop of major powers in having experienced both the highs and lows of power and influence several times. The thrust of Wang's analysis is that China is constructing the current revival of its fortunes with great care and seriousness, and, among other things, drawing on a careful study of both its own history and that of other powers so as to minimise the risk of jeopardising the strong positive trajectory that it has achieved. While China's phenomenal development has already complicated the management of Australia's relationships with key players in the East Asian arena, it has thus far not figured prominently in the debate on Australia's defence policy.

America's resolve and capacity to continue to play a decisive role in preserving the strategic order in East Asia has always been a core issue in the formulation of Australian defence policy. Huisken tries to account for the Bush Administration's tragic decision to invade Iraq, and to identify the scope of the costs that history will attribute to this decision. While he concludes that Iraq has shortened America's 'unipolar moment' (not least because it has given China a very favourable environment in which to expand its power and influence) and probably prolonged the era of virulent terrorism, Huisken remains confident that the United States will recover its equilibrium and continue to be a decisive force in shaping the future order. Clearly, however, the United States will play a different and less dominant role than seemed would be the case just a few years ago and its allies will have to be cognisant of this fact.

On regional issues, other than the papers on jihadism in Indonesia (Fealy) and multilateral security processes in the Asia Pacific (Taylor), Graeme Dobell examines the current characterisation of the band of Melanesian states to the North and East of Australia as an 'arc of instability'. Dobell confirms the likelihood that these states will be the source of recurring politico-military challenges for Australia. He also looks into how this most proximate of external frontlines has played into the long-running debate between expeditionary versus continental forces. How strongly should geography shape Australian defence policy, and how does this arc play in the politics of alliance management with the United States? In a concluding anecdote, Dobell points to the dilemma that the capability imperatives for dealing with possible challenges in the 'arc of instability' are likely to be quite distinct, both from the 'defence of Australia' and from the 'defence of Australian interests on more distant frontlines'.

In the concluding set of chapters on Australian strategic and defence issues, Mark Thomson shows that, even when there is clear strategic guidance, strong budget discipline, and a rigorous capability development process, maintaining and developing the most effective defence force possible is an extremely complex and difficult task. If one or more of these basic ingredients is weak or missing, which Thomson believes to be currently the case, we can quickly lose our way, at great cost and in a manner that may take years to fix. David Horner sets out to explain, in non-technical terms: (1) the centrality of the command structure to the effectiveness of a defence force; and (2) the cautious, always contested, evolution of arrangements to accommodate, first, a single defence force (rather than three separate Services), then a defence doctrine (emphasising the centrality of operations in or from Australian territory), and finally, the incidence of operations far from Australia as part of international coalitions. This process is endless: the command structure is perpetually a 'work in progress'. Changes in defence policy, in technology and operational concepts will always point to adaptations that seem desirable yet challenge existing power relationships and require the prolonged negotiations, incremental steps and periods of experiment that have characterised the process to date.

Fittingly, the final chapter by Hugh White, already outlined above, concludes with the acknowledgement that the continuing authoritative text on defence policy, *Defence 2000: Our Future Defence Force*, does reflect tensions that the Ministers and senior officials who crafted it could not (or did not wish at the time) to resolve, but which have since been used to undermine the integrity of the capability development process. White acknowledges, for example, that *Defence 2000* reiterates the centrality of 'defence of Australia' to capability development while at the same time it: (1) endorses the doubt than an ADF focused on this mission will also be able to meet other demands that government may make of it; (2) proposes the development of capabilities for strategic tasks beyond the defence of Australia; and (3) states that the ADF's top-end air and maritime capabilities should also be assessed in the context of major power conflict in East Asia rather than only against the mission of defending the sea-air gap.

In short, events and interests have exposed these tensions and have rendered *Defence 2000* inadequate to the task of providing clear guidance for the development of ADF capabilities. We are therefore back to the issue of where we should position the frontline for the defence of Australia and its interests. Moreover, if prepared to bear the costs, we need to determine the priority order of those frontlines we believe we must be able to defend with military force. Alternatively, can we devise an organising principle for the ADF that moves away from the notion of frontlines without generating a different set of tensions and ambiguities?

The US military, for example, studied the transformation possibilities of the information revolution relentlessly during the 1990s, but hesitated repeatedly because of the risk that the envisaged lighter, faster, easier to deploy and support, networked forces might falter against the traditional heavy armoured forces that the United States could still encounter in the future. Eventually, confidence developed to deem this risk to be trivial, provided transformation was pursued to its full potential and included sensitive areas such as re-thinking the basic shape of military formations; command and control arrangements; and how intelligence is collected, analysed and disseminated. As we have seen, this confidence was fully justified (at least for traditional force-on-force encounters), but is a similar path feasible for Australia? Would it allow us to again say that 'one size fits all'—that a force optimised for continental defence could conduct major expeditionary operations just as well or vice versa?

Defence Update 2007 [2] offered something to each of the major schools of thought. It endorsed all the front lines in play and offered support for advocates of each of them. Continental defence and the capacity to be a decisive influence in our immediate region seemed to get top billing and thereby confirm the basic validity of *Defence 2000*. However, a military threat to the Australian continent now looks so improbable that it offers only weak guidance on the appropriate size and shape for the ADF. Therefore two other yardsticks have been given a stronger profile: making a bigger contribution to international coalitions in distant theatres like Iraq and Afghanistan; and ensuring that the ADF is qualitatively on a par or better than the best armed forces in our region. The first yardstick suggests the vice versa noted above: a robust expeditionary capability will ensure a force capable of defending Australia and of taking the initiative when necessary to address challenges to stability in our immediate region. The second yardstick looks more to an ADF that will contribute fully to Australia being taken seriously in the region in the continuous posturing for influence over the direction of regional affairs. It is worth noting that this will be a growing challenge given that Australia's relative strategic weight within the region looks set to decline inexorably.

Either yardstick (or more probably both) could transform the ADF into a force that could reasonably be portrayed in this inexact science as adequate for continental defence. Whether this latest prescription will constitute the basis for a durable consensus on defence policy between government, the military and the general public is another matter. The apparent tilt toward expeditionary capabilities could mean that the ADF will be shaped by missions over which Australia has the least political and military control. Australia has always been a quite marginal player in international coalitions and no re-balancing of effort within a basically stable overall defence effort will alter this fact. Ensuring that the capacity to take the lead in contingencies in our area of paramount defence interest gets priority over contributing to coalitions in more distant theatres will require careful discipline.

The second yardstick, which might be termed credibility, also asks for a great deal of discipline in the force development process. Comparisons with the capabilities of other military forces is an inescapable element of the defence 'game', but making it too explicit could become tantamount to delegating control over our defence budget and over the balance of capabilities within the ADF to those states in the region against whom we choose to benchmark ourselves.

Defence Update 2007 reiterated the three primary mission areas (international, regional and national) for the ADF. Can we afford, on about two per cent of GDP, to avoid having to choose between them? Can we convince ourselves that an ADF is within reach that is equally competent in each mission area? What degree of concurrency must we sensibly plan for, both within and between these mission areas? And, if we have to at least list them in priority order, what rank should be allocated to those mission areas? The debate on defence policy looks set to have a robust future. The themes in this volume are offered as a contribution to this debate.

ENDNOTES

[1] For an overview of the Centre's activities since its establishment in 1966, see (eds) Meredith Thatcher and Desmond Ball, *Essays Commemorating the 40th Anniversary of the Strategic and Defence Studies Centre (SDSC)*, Canberra Papers on Strategy and Defence, CP 165, Strategic and Defence Studies Centre, The Australian National University, Canberra, August 2006.

[2] Department of Defence, *Australia's National Security: A Defence Update 2007*, Canberra, Commonwealth of Australia, June 2007, available at <http://www.defence.gov.au/ans/2007/pdf/Defence_update.pdf>, accessed 24 October 2007.

Self-Reliant Defence: The First Cut

Chapter 1

The Self-Reliant Defence of Australia: The History of an Idea

Paul Dibb

For much of Australia's history, there has been a deeply-held view that Australia was a vulnerable country incapable of defending itself. This sense of vulnerability reflected a keen awareness that Australia was a large, sparsely populated continent rich in agricultural land and resources. The colony was located on the other side of the world from its British origins and fears of a foreign invasion surfaced at various times during the nineteenth century.[1]

As David Horner points out, from the earliest days the Australian colonists were concerned for their security and it was partly the desire for collective defence that drove the early colonial governments towards Federation in 1901. Tension, however, soon arose between two strands in Australian defence policy, later described in a shorthand way as 'fortress Australia' versus 'forward defence' (though in the early twentieth century it was the 'Australianists' versus the 'imperialists').[2] But when Japan threatened Australia with invasion in the Second World War, the fears that Australia could not defend itself without help from a large ally were starkly confirmed. After the war, this perspective led to the policy of 'forward defence' that saw Australian expeditionary forces fighting communism in Korea and Vietnam alongside the United States, as well as in Malaya with the British and in Borneo during the Confrontation. It was only during the 1970s, following America's defeat in Vietnam, that the need for the self-reliant 'defence of Australia' emerged as a serious proposition.

The purpose of this chapter, then, is not to provide a comprehensive history of the 'defence of Australia' idea. Instead it will focus on the last 30 years since the publication of the 1976 Defence White Paper *Australian Defence*, in which the government of the day moved distinctly away from 'forward defence' towards policies that required a force structure which—for the first time in Australia's history—was to be primarily driven by the need to be able to defend the continent unaided. I will address four main policy issues:

- A summary of defence policy developments leading to *Australian Defence*.
- The reasons for the Dibb Review and the new policy delivered in the 1987 *Defence of Australia*.

- The Howard Government's 2000 Defence White Paper (*Defence 2000: Our Future Defence Force*) and what elements it contained of continuity and change.
- Finally, I shall explore whether the Howard Government has now disposed of 'defence of Australia' in favour of an ADF structured primarily as an expeditionary force.

But before I begin, let me make some important clarifications. The so-called 'defence of Australia' doctrine never focused solely on the defence of the continent itself: it also envisaged Australian forces operating further afield (albeit in limited numbers) if national interests required it. And the idea of self-reliance never meant self-sufficiency. It is important to recall that major factors in the need to develop concepts for defending Australia were the British withdrawal from east of Suez and President Richard Nixon's Guam doctrine that America's friends should be able to defend themselves against all but a major attack with their own combat forces.

It is also necessary to point out that while there have been two opposing and long-standing schools of thought in Australian defence policy, sometimes leading to bitter disagreements, the fact is that neither of them seems likely to completely drop the 'defence of Australia' doctrine or, indeed, the need to be able to operate alongside the United States in certain circumstances in theatres well beyond Australia's own region. There remain, of course, important differences of priorities, but it seems unlikely that any Australian political party now will declare that the defence of Australia is not the first duty of government. The idea that Australia should be able to defend itself has taken firm root in public opinion.[3]

The Foundations of the 'Defence of Australia' Idea

One of the earliest proposals regarding Australia's defence came from Field Marshal Kitchener, who was invited by the Commonwealth Government in 1910 to prepare a memorandum on the defence of Australia. His conclusions were based around the proposal that Australia's land forces should be organised on the basis that an enemy contemplating an invasion of a sufficiently credible scale would be unable to evade British naval forces that Australia assumed would always be available. This led him to estimate the land forces required at 80 000 fighting troops, half of which would be required to secure the largest cities and to defend ports from attack, while the other half would be free to operate as a mobile striking force anywhere in Australia.[4] The First World War then intervened and during the 1920s and 1930s there was heated debate about the merits of planning for a future invasion as distinct from low-level threats (including raids.)[5]

However, the rise of Japan and the direct threat of invasion to Australia in the Second World War again put paid to any serious consideration of how Australia itself might be defended without the assistance of a great and powerful ally. The first post-war review of Australia's strategic circumstances was undertaken in 1946. It concluded that 'the size of this country demands for its defence armed forces and an industrial potential quite beyond our present capacity'.[6] There was some thought given to local defence, but it was considered that the requirements for such could be met by those forces contributing to Empire Cooperation.

In 1947, the security deriving from Australia's isolation was noted, as was the security provided by geography: 'her geographical position is such that no hostile power, without possessing command of the sea and local air superiority could successfully invade Australia.'[7] In the 1950 assessment of the basis for Australia's defence policy, geographical isolation continued to be seen as fundamental to Australia's security. During the 1950s, Australia's defence priorities were seen as having sufficient forces at all times to ensure the security of Australia, but with a greater focus on possible military activity in the Southeast Asian region and adjacent areas. It was assessed that while the line against communism was held in Indochina, defence in-depth was provided for the Australia-New Zealand main support area.[8] The strategic perception of developments in Southeast Asia, especially the communist insurgencies, largely reflected this continuing preoccupation. Three successive lines of Australian defence were envisaged: (1) support for the defence of the Indo-Chinese mainland; (2) should this fail, the implementation of contingency plans to defend Malaya; and (3) consideration for the immediate defence of the Northwest approaches to Australia depending 'on the probable form and scale of attack at any given time'.[9]

By 1959 Australia's defence planners were beginning to think in terms of shaping forces for the defence of Australia independently of allies.[10] It was stated that, in certain circumstances, 'Australia might have to rely completely on her own defensive and economic capacity for an indeterminate period'. Consequently, it was assessed that our forces should be designed primarily with the ability to act independently of allies.[11] This approach was rejected by Cabinet, which insisted that Australia should be prepared for involvement in limited war in Southeast Asia and its forces should have, as far as possible, the necessary organisation and techniques to operate effectively with major allies.[12]

It was not until the 1960s that the political leadership was even prepared to entertain tentative ideas for the defence of Australia itself. This reflected the fact that (as already mentioned) in 1967 the British Government decided on withdrawing its forces east of Suez and the 1969 statement by President Nixon that America's allies in the Pacific had to be able to defend themselves against all but a major attack. Thus the 1967 *Strategic Basis of Australian Defence Policy* recognised that Australia must be prepared to deal with situations 'which directly threaten our territorial interests and which we could not reasonably rely on receiving help from our allies'.[13]

By 1970, the Minister for Defence, Malcolm Fraser, was arguing that his aim was to achieve forces which were organised, equipped and trained for the direct defence of Australia, and for effective employment in the region of which Australia was a part.[14] The 1971 *Strategic Basis* paper thus recognised clearly that Australia needed to pursue her own security interests far more: it proposed that 'more emphasis than hitherto should be given to the continuing fundamental obligations of continental defence'.[15] Studies were undertaken on maritime air, air defence, strategic transport, and defence communications and infrastructure, and it was envisaged that in most instances we would see Australian forces operating as a joint force complementary to each other.

Elements of this new policy appeared in the 1972 public document *Australian Defence Review*, which argued for a more independent national defence capability and for self-reliance as laying 'claim to being a central feature in the future development of Australia's defence policy'.[16] The big breakthrough, however, was the 1973 *Strategic Basis of Australian Defence Policy* which set the course followed, by and large, up to the late 1980s. It asserted that Australia 'must now assume the primary responsibility for its own defence against any neighbourhood or regional threats'.[17] Recognition was given to the fundamental requirements that flowed from the enduring features of Australia's geographic circumstances. In particular, it identified the importance of capabilities for surveillance; naval and maritime air defence; long-range transport; responses to hostile landings; defence infrastructure and communication networks; comprehensive intelligence; and industrial, scientific and technological support. A comprehensive study of continental defence was also recommended.

The problem was that the Service chiefs disputed the content and direction of this assessment and its process of preparation. The newly created Defence Organisation was riven by disputes over how strategic guidance should be prepared and by whom. In 1973, the Chief of the General Staff (CGS) was carpeted by the then Defence Minister, Mr Lance Barnard, to explain why he had publicly refuted the 1973 *Strategic Basis of Australian Defence Policy* after it had been endorsed by the government (and, incidentally, not dissented from by the CGS in the Defence Committee). The classified 1974 *Defence of Australia* study, which had very limited circulation within the Defence Organisation, was so controversial that it was ordered to be destroyed by the Secretary. It examined scenarios in which Australia might be threatened by a major power and situations in which it might be directly attacked by a lesser power. The 1974 study also addressed contingencies in which Australia might be involved in military conflict with

Indonesia, either directly or through support for Papua New Guinea (PNG). It canvassed options for Australia to acquire its own nuclear weapons, even though Australia had ratified the Nuclear Non-Proliferation Treaty in 1969.

Specific requirements for the independent defence of Australia were further examined in 1975. The various threads of defence planning that had been emerging gradually during the previous decade were drawn together. In particular, the concept of a 'core force' was devised. A 'core force' would be suited to undertaking peacetime tasks, sufficiently versatile to deter or cope with a range of low-level contingencies against Australia, and with relevant skills and equipment capable of timely expansion to deter or meet a developing situation.[18]

A series of studies was proposed, beginning with the low-level contingencies which were considered credible in the short term, and subsequently moving to higher-level situations. These studies were to be guided predominantly by the physical characteristics of the country and its geography. In 1976, the value of contingency studies, in providing a sound basis for prudent defence insurance against future uncertainty, was reaffirmed and a series of possible low-level contingencies was put forward to help inform the shaping of the force structure in the Five Year Defence Program.

In the event, a clearly articulated independent Australian defence policy was not released to the public until the Fraser Government's seminal 1976 Defence White Paper, *Australian Defence*. This White Paper argued that the area of Australia's primary strategic concern was the adjacent maritime area—the countries and territories of the Southwest Pacific, PNG, Indonesia and the Southeast Asia region. It contended that, for practical purposes, the requirements and scope for Australian defence activity should be limited essentially to these areas closer to home. With regard to Australia's defence requirements, it argued that the primary requirement was for increased self-reliance:

> We no longer base our policy on the expectation that Australia's Navy or Army or Air Force will be sent abroad to fight as part of some other nation's force, supported by it. We do not rule out an Australian contribution to operations elsewhere if the requirement arose and we felt our presence would be effective, and if our forces could be spared from their national tasks. But we believe that any operations are much more likely to be in our own neighbourhood than in some distant theatre, and that our Armed Forces will be conducting joint operations together as the Australian Defence force.[19]

This was a revolutionary breakthrough in independent Australian strategic thinking. And subsequent classified defence documents confirmed the priority that should continue to be given to the independent defence of Australia. For example, the 1979 *Strategic Basis* paper emphasised the importance of Australia being able to demonstrate that it was serious and competent in defence matters, and capable of responding effectively to low-level pressures or military attacks and of timely expansion in response to more substantial threats. And the 1983 *Strategic Basis* paper gave priority to the development of military capabilities appropriate to the independent defence of Australia. It accorded priority in terms of equipment acquisition, training and infrastructure development to the requirements of contingencies considered credible in the shorter term 'including deterrence of such escalation as an enemy might be capable of'.[20]

But none of these documents (either classified or in the public domain) was able to set out in specific terms the force structure priorities for the self-reliant 'defence of Australia'. The nub of the problem, of course, was the challenge of determining what should drive Australia's force structure in the absence of a specific threat. And at the heart of this challenge was the need to specify actual force structure priorities within an affordable budget. That took almost another decade—until 1986.

The Practical Implementation of the 'Defence of Australia' Doctrine

The central issue here was not a lack of hard work. Both within the Defence Organisation and in the SDSC, there was much detailed articulation of the problems of defending Australia.[21] In fact, the largest proportion of the SDSC's work in the second half of the 1970s and in the 1980s concerned the defence of Australia. In many ways the Centre was at the forefront of the conceptual revolution in Australian defence policy from 'dependence on great and powerful friends' to 'greater self-reliance' and from 'forward defence' to 'defence of Australia'.

The first major step in this process was a conference organised by Robert O'Neill on *The Defence of Australia: Fundamental New Aspects* in October 1976, which was designed to assist policymakers struggling with the transformation of Australia's defence posture. Ross Babbage wrote about the need for revolutionary change and why Australia must now mobilise its own resources to develop an independent capability to defend itself. Desmond Ball noted that the Services were more interested in equipment questions than in any other element of defence policy. The problem he correctly identified was that Australia lacked a basic policy of sufficient clarity and cohesion to enable the resolution of competing claims. He criticised the then popular idea in Defence of a core force because, he said, it did not know what the core force would expand into in an emergency.

O'Neill wrote about the development of operational doctrine for the ADF. He produced the formative studies of the requisite command-and-control structure for a joint ADF in 'defence of Australia' contingencies, including a proposal to establish functional command arrangements.

The Department Defence too was busily undertaking contingency studies. But the three military Services and Headquarters Australian Defence Force (which was formed in 1984) struggled to reach agreement with the most senior civilian advisers about what threats they should be prepared to counter, and therefore what force structure priorities should be considered by government. In 1981, for example, as the Senior Assistant Secretary for Strategic Policy, I attended meetings in which only very generic and indicative force structure principles could be agreed upon: no consensus was reached on specific priorities for particular force structure elements.

By late 1984, the Defence Organisation had become quite dysfunctional in some respects. For well over a year the Minister's two most senior advisers, the Chief of the Defence Force (CDF) and the Secretary, had exchanged deeply antagonistic correspondence. The Defence Organisation did not even touch on any agreement about force structure priorities for the defence of Australia, which is what the Minister had directed. Instead, it was bogged down in what I can only describe as the theology of defence policy concerning such issues as intelligence warning time, the definition of lower and higher levels of contingency, the priority (or not) to be given to Australia's northern approaches, the core force, and the expansion base.

I was appointed in February 1985 as Ministerial Consultant to the Minister for Defence to resolve these issues. My terms of reference directed me to undertake a review of Australia's defence capabilities: I was asked to examine the content, priorities and rationale of defence forward planning and to advise on which capabilities were appropriate for Australia's present and future defence requirements. I was to make judgements on the appropriate balance between equipment, personnel numbers, facilities and operating costs, between current readiness and long-term investment, and between the relative priorities given to responding to various levels of possible threats. I was to look as far forward as practicable, and it was suggested that an appropriate timeframe could be the next decade. My report was to be formulated in the light of already endorsed strategic guidance.[22] It was to be completed within 12 months (and, in fact, the classified version of the report was delivered to the Minister in March 1986, with the public version being released in June 1986).

I soon recognised that this was not some sort of academic exercise: the disagreements between the military and civilian elements of Defence Headquarters were severe. My chief aim of delivering a workable policy solution would be a serious challenge. In the initial drafts, I would have to come down fairly hard in some areas in order to allow for the inevitable bounce back in negotiations with the CDF and the Secretary and their senior military and civilian advisers.

My work was to focus on the development of a clear set of force structure priorities for the self-reliant 'defence of Australia'. For over a year my team circulated drafts to the Chiefs of Staff Committee (COSC), which was augmented to include discussions with the Secretary of Defence and his chief advisers. Most months they saw and commented upon drafts written by myself and my team.[23]

The main policy differences were that the civilians tended to regard only the lowest of low-level threats as being credible for the immediate and medium term future, whereas the military was more inclined to want to structure now for high-intensity conflict. These differences undermined any possibility of agreement on force structure priorities, the expansion base and stockholding policy. Fortunately, I was able to chart a course that was strategically responsible while also pacifying to some extent and in different ways the principal protagonists. My approach was to give priority to the more credible threat, and to the lower-level threats that could arise with little warning. This clearly recognised that contingencies could escalate on the basis of current and foreseeable regional military capacity, and that we should be able to handle such escalation. At the third level of conflict there were possibilities for more substantial conventional military action—but below the level of invasion. This could only occur if regional countries developed over time the necessary capacities—an outcome that would take many years. The conclusion was that our defence priorities must ensure that the ADF had available sufficient equipment, support and trained personnel to respond to credible military situations. We also needed to take account of the possible demands of more substantial threats. The basic skills necessary for higher-level conflict should be available, to be expanded and further developed within warning time. But any tendency to prepare for unrealistically high levels of threat should be resisted.[24]

The end result was an historic document which the CDF and the Secretary jointly signed to the Minister broadly agreeing with the direction of my recommendations, but also noting of course that areas of difference remained. As the then CDF, General Sir Phillip Bennett, wrote to me in a personal letter:

> The important point is that an agreed course can now be set, and I assure you that it will have my full support in its subsequent implementation following government consideration ... I, and the Chiefs of Staff, agree the general direction of your review and the great bulk of your proposals for the future development of the Australian Defence Force.[25]

One of the most contentious issues was the size and role of the Australian Army, which was having difficulties adjusting to the post-Vietnam War era. An *Army Development Guide* had been prepared as a basis of force structure development by the Army Office. It argued that, where an enemy had lodged essentially a four brigade divisional group (including supporting troops),

Australia would require a field force comprising some 135 000 troops, and the whole Army would be some 270 000 strong.[26] The Army recognised that this was not attainable, so instead it proposed an 'Objective Force-in-Being' with a strength of 94 000 personnel to provide the firm base from which expansion for higher levels of conflict could occur, while concurrently maintaining forces committed to lower-level operations.

I had substantial reservations about this approach as it was at serious variance with the government's endorsed strategic guidance (which my terms of reference instructed me to follow). Instead, I recommended:

> The minimum number of regular infantry battalions that we require is six. A lesser number of regular battalions could be faced with an impossible operational task. A similar number of reserve battalions would also be required, to be available for early deployment from a reserve force of at least 10 battalions.[27]

The interesting question I have is whether the Army is in fact any bigger today?

In passing, let me note that there is a classified version of the *Review of Australia's Defence Capabilities* or Dibb Review which has not been released publicly. It dealt with specific contingencies in our neighbourhood, including contingencies involving Indonesia, as well as situations to do with the security of PNG. It also canvassed such issues as targets for strike operations, and specific intelligence and surveillance priorities.

The Dibb Review was a *capabilities* review that, within the context of the Australian Government's strategic policies, provided a basis and rationale for the self-reliant structure of the ADF. The Review did not make recommendations on strategic policy, and it did not canvass how the ADF should be *used* overseas. The subsequent 1987 Defence White Paper, *Defence of Australia*, which I helped to draft, set out the government's strategic priorities, including the matter of overseas operations. The White Paper is quite clear on this point. It stipulates that the government's policy of defence self-reliance 'gives priority to the ability to defend ourselves with our own resources' and that this policy 'is pursued within the framework of alliances and agreements'. It concludes by saying:

> This paper has stressed that the priority need for the Defence Force is to fulfil the national task of defending the nation. It has also dealt with the need for Australia's defence effort to take account of developments in our region of primary strategic interest, and to be capable of reacting positively to calls for military support elsewhere, should we judge that our interests require it. The Government considers that Australia can deal with both, but to do so we must be alert to priorities.[28]

So it was that Australia developed pioneering ideas of how to develop a Defence Force without a threat. They were based on two key concepts: (1) the enduring nature of Australia's strategic geography and its maritime approaches; and (2) a requirement to have a clear military technological advantage in our own region.

This was essentially capabilities-based defence planning long before its time and it carried us through the decade of the 1990s when many other countries were essentially adrift in the post-Cold War world.

The End of the 'Defence of Australia' Doctrine?

Of course, policies had subsequently to be adjusted in response to changing strategic circumstances, yet they did not basically depart from the priority to be given to the defence of Australia. The 1994 Defence White Paper, *Defending Australia*, expanded the idea of defence self-reliance when it argued that we would have to pay more attention to what it called short-warning conflicts because of potential military developments in our region. However, it continued to give priority to making our sea and air approaches an effective barrier to attack, and to ensuring that our forces were familiar with the northern operating environment and that our equipment was optimised for conditions there.

It was prescient of *Defending Australia* to observe that deployments in the Persian Gulf, Namibia, Cambodia, Somalia, Rwanda, the South Pacific and elsewhere, as well as our continual defence deployments around the region,

> have demonstrated that capabilities developed for the defence of Australia are sufficiently versatile to fulfil a wide range of other tasks. We do not need to make these activities a primary basis for our defence capability planning, because forces developed for the defence of Australia give us a sufficient range of options to meet them.[29]

Thus, there was essential continuity in Australia's defence planning for a full decade. The new government came into power in 1996, and its 1997 defence policy document stressed that defeating attacks against Australia's territory was our core force structure priority.[30] But it also stated that the next highest priority was to provide 'substantial capabilities to defend our regional strategic interests'.[31] It went on to say that 'priority will be given to the first of these tasks, but decisions will be influenced by the ability of forces to contribute to both tasks'.[32] The guidance to the ADF to provide for forces in sufficient number and with the ability to be deployed on both the local and regional level was further hampered by the definition of 'regional interests' being expanded from the immediate neighbourhood to include the wider Asia-Pacific region.

Even so, the Howard Government's *Defence 2000* did not herald dramatic change—except in the key area of defence funding. The fact was that the self-reliance idea had been undermined in the late 1980s and early 1990s by poor economic performance and reduced defence budgets. A prolonged period of so-called 'zero growth' for the defence budget and the acquisition of important new advanced technologies—particularly for the Royal Australian Air Force (RAAF) and the Royal Australian Navy (RAN)—had meant decreased funding for operating costs and personnel numbers, particularly for the Army.

Defence 2000 represented both strategic continuity and budgetary changes. It was an extremely carefully considered piece of work by the National Security Committee of Cabinet over the best part of a year. It neither walked away from the 'defence of Australia' construct nor returned to the 'forward defence' policies of previous Coalition Governments. It was different in two key areas: first, it involved unprecedented consultation with the Australian community; second, it introduced a new approach to defence planning by providing Defence with a costed defence capability plan for the development of Australia's armed forces over the next decade.

The geographical approach, however, was reassuringly familiar. *Defence 2000* asserted that Australia's most important long-term strategic objective 'is to be able to defend our territory from direct military attack'.[33] This is described as 'the bedrock of our security and the most fundamental responsibility of government'.[34] This was then followed by a series of geographical priorities (the so-called concentric circles):

- fostering the security of our immediate neighbourhood;
- promoting stability and cooperation in Southeast Asia;
- supporting strategic stability in the wider Asia-Pacific region; and
- supporting global security.

The statement is made that we have strategic interests and objectives at the global and regional levels. However, it then proceeds to give the highest priority to the interests and objectives closest to Australia because, in general, the closer any crisis is to Australia, the more important it will probably be to our security and the more likely we will be able to assist in confronting and resolving it. This in fact reflected the ADF's actual experience in East Timor the previous year, in 1999.

The force structure priorities in *Defence 2000* are classical 'defence of Australia' orthodoxy. Thus, the priority task for the ADF is the defence of Australia and we must: (1) be *self-reliant*—able to defend Australia without relying on the combat forces of other countries; (2), have a *maritime strategy*—be able to control the air and sea approaches to our continent; and (3) have *proficient land forces*—be able to defend Australia and its approaches, and also to contribute substantially to supporting the security of our immediate neighbourhood.

This final task specifically extended the force structure determinants of the ADF to the neighbourhood. It represented an important shift, yet basically at the margin, to the primary drivers of the force structure, and reflected the deterioration in strategic circumstances in our immediate neighbourhood. The Army was no longer to give priority to providing the basis for its rapid expansion to a size required for major continental-scale operations. The government's aim was to provide available land forces that could respond effectively to any credible armed lodgement on Australian territory *and* provide forces for more likely types of operations in our immediate neighbourhood.

All this was compatible with an essentially bipartisan approach to defence policy principles that had existed for more than 25 years. Having the defence of Australia and our neighbourhood requirements as the primary drivers of the ADF's force structure is eminently sensible. That still leaves niche capabilities for deployments much further afield in support of our alliances and our global interests.

But the terrorist attacks on the United States of 11 September 2001 threatened to change all that. Some immediately proclaimed the end of the 'defence of Australia' doctrine, which they described as 'discredited'. The previous Defence Minister, Senator Robert Hill, never uttered the words 'defence of Australia' in public, except in a perfunctory manner. He seemed to be much more interested in the foreign policy aspects of the Defence portfolio. For example, it is said that he argued in Cabinet in December 2005 that Australia's most important strategic priority was the Middle East—an argument that he lost.

Certainly, Hill's two *Defence Updates* in 2003 and 2005 were strong on declaratory policy and thin on strategic logic. In my view, Hill was responsible (during his four-year term as Minister for Defence) for seriously undermining the logical strategic priorities of our force structure. The 2003 document was keen to get into product differentiation by showing that the prospect of military attack on Australia had diminished. Yet that was simply raising a 'straw man', because previous Defence White Papers never counted on the likelihood of attack but, rather, on its seriousness were it to occur. Rather lamely, *Australia's National Security: A Defence Update 2003* went on to say that although ADF involvement in coalition operations further afield was somewhat more probable than in the recent past, it was likely to be 'limited to the provision of important niche capabilities'.[35]

Australia's National Security: A Defence Update 2005 emphasised the need for a bigger Army (but only by an additional 1485 regulars) and concluded, correctly, that Defence remains the primary instrument of the Australian Government in building warfighting capacity to respond to possible future threats.[36] But it failed spectacularly to explain the strategic reasoning for the acquisition of tanks, the region's largest amphibious ships, the air warfare destroyers (other than to defend the amphibious ships), and the C-17 *Globemaster* III heavy transport aircraft. Substantial parts of *Australia's National Security: A Defence Update 2005* read more like a foreign policy document, perhaps also reflecting the leanings of the then Secretary of Defence Ric Smith who was a former senior Foreign Affairs officer.

My colleague, Professor Hugh White, has sought to move beyond the 'defence of Australia' as the central organising principle of defence policy, and focus instead on maximising Australia's military capacity to protect its interests in the stability of the Asia-Pacific region in the face of conventional strategic threats. He believes that the ability to defend the continent will still be important, but the primary focus should be maximising capabilities to protect interests offshore. He claims that, if we choose well, forces designed primarily to defend Australia's wider strategic interests will provide Australia with a robust capacity to defend the continent.[37] White recognises that this will require great clarity and discipline in force planning. In my view this will be particularly the case, as he proposes that we should have forces 'maintained at a level able to operate effectively against the forces maintained by major Asian powers, and in sufficient numbers'.[38]

Hugh White's own force structure proposals concentrate on the need for high-level air and naval forces—primarily submarines and combat aircraft—and he considers that we should not be putting our money into air warfare destroyers and large amphibious ships (although he does envisage a lighter constabulary army of 12 battalions or even more).[39] With regard to what forces Australia needs for expeditionary operations, his question is whether there may be some future expeditionary operations in which we would wish to exercise 'substantive strategic weight', or whether they will all be merely diplomatic gestures?[40] His conclusion is that Australia should aim to build and sustain military capabilities that will give it 'real strategic weight in Asia' as a regional power.[41] But, significantly, he concludes his paper by recognising that Australia's relative strategic potential in Asia is 'in long-term decline'.[42]

My concern here is that these proposals are too ambitious, even unrealistic, both in terms of the resources that Australia will have available for our national defence effort, and compared with the likely economic and military growth of major Asian powers. Furthermore, the concept is potentially open-ended in its scope and could well lead to equally open-ended force structure proposals. And in my experience of the force structure development process, the ADF could be expected to focus on their expeditionary capability, leaving the defence of Australia a very poor second, irrespective of what the government of the day might claim as its policies. There would be a severe risk that the 'discipline in force planning' required by these policies might be most conspicuous by its absence.

Concluding Thoughts

The question now is whether we have lost the rationale for Australia's force structure? Have we moved away from the defence of Australia and our regional commitments as the primary drivers of the force structure to an expeditionary force primarily designed for operations alongside our US ally in places such as the Middle East? If so, and if we are not careful, this will leave us with something of a hybrid force not optimised for either contingency.

We must not become a one-shot ADF, putting all our eggs into the one basket of protecting two large amphibious ships capable of deploying about 1000 troops each. That must not become the sole operational purpose of the air warfare destroyers or the F-35 *Lightning* II joint strike fighters. In my opinion, leaving the RAN and RAAF with little, if any, independent strategic purpose other than transporting and protecting the Army is a dangerous development and strategically indefensible. In any case, what is the purpose of such an amphibious capability? It seems too modest if it is to mount an opposed landing, and too much if it is only about operating in a permissive environment.

Let me be plain. I have no problem if the primary drivers of the ADF's force structure remain the defence of Australia and credible regional contingencies. And I note here it is reported that Defence Minister Brendan Nelson's classified strategic review, considered by Cabinet in August 2006, affirmed that policy. I also support the idea of a somewhat larger Army with more light infantry. But I think we should not be cutting back on such crucial capabilities for the defence of Australia as mine warfare and anti-submarine warfare, to take two important examples. And it is about time we got on with actually implementing network-centric warfare, as distinct from constantly talking about it.[43] I also think we cannot afford to take our eye off maintaining a clear regional advantage in such high-technology capabilities as strike, air combat, and naval warfare (both surface and subsurface).

Our unique strategic geography will simply not disappear. What I have called the 'arc of instability' to our north promises to confront us with even more challenging contingencies than those we have experienced recently in East Timor and Solomon Islands. These are abiding strategic interests for Australia.

However, we need to be careful in the contemporary era about what we expect from the ADF with regard to the threat from terrorism, countering the proliferation of Weapons of Mass Destruction (WMD), and supporting regional states in difficulty. These are all activities in which Defence has a supporting rather than leading role.

Finally, the financially easy days of defence planning may soon be over for Australia. We face the prospect of a rapidly ageing population, which will create greater demands for healthcare in competition with the defence budget.[44] When our economy inevitably slows down as an ageing population erodes workforce participation, or our economy simply goes into recession, the pressure will be on to demonstrate that we have a tough-minded and intellectually rigorous force structure plan in place for the ADF. The problem is that this does not seem to be the case at the present time.

ENDNOTES

[1] See Tom Millar, *Australia in Peace and War*, Australian National University Press, Canberra, 1978, pp. 11–22.

[2] David Horner, 'Security objectives', in (ed.) F. A. Mediansky, *Australian Foreign Policy*, Macmillan, Melbourne, 1997, pp. 74–77.

[3] See Department of Defence, *Australian perspectives on defence: Report of the community consultation team*, Commonwealth of Australia, Canberra, September 2000, p. 2, available at <http://www.defence.gov.au/consultation2/cctpaper.pdf>, accessed 8 November 2007; and Ian McAlister, *Attitude matters: Public opinion in Australia towards defence and security*, Australian Strategic Policy Institute, Canberra, 2004, p. 24.

[4] Field Marshal Viscount Kitchener of Khartoum, *Memorandum on the Defence of Australia*, Commonwealth of Australia, Melbourne, 1910, p. 5.

[5] See, for example, Samuel Albert Rosa, *The Invasion of Australia*, reprinted from 'Truth' by 'The Worker' Trustees, Sydney, 1920, which proposed that Australia needed to be defended by submarines, aircraft and 'properly equipped forts' rather than by battleships and a large army. His conclusion was that Australia 'is one of the easiest countries in the world to defend'. (p. 19).

[6] Department of Defence, *Key Elements in the Triennial Reviews of Strategic Guidance since 1945*, Submission to the Parliamentary Joint Committee on Foreign Affairs and Defence, 17 February 1987, *Inquiry into the Management of Australia's Defence and National Security*, Official Hansard Report, Submissions and Incorporated Documents, Volume II, p. 3.

[7] Department of Defence, *Key Elements in the Triennial Reviews of Strategic Guidance since 1945*, pp. 3–4.

[8] Department of Defence, *Key Elements in the Triennial Reviews of Strategic Guidance since 1945*, p. 4.

[9] Department of Defence, *Key Elements in the Triennial Reviews of Strategic Guidance since 1945*, p. 6.

[10] Horner, 'Security objectives', in (ed.) F. A. Mediansky, *Australian Foreign Policy*, p. 80.

[11] Department of Defence, *Key Elements in the Triennial Reviews of Strategic Guidance since 1945*, p. 7.

[12] Horner, 'Security objectives', in (ed.) F. A. Mediansky, *Australian Foreign Policy* p. 80.

[13] Department of Defence, *Key Elements in the Triennial Reviews of Strategic Guidance since 1945*, p. 8.

[14] Address by the Honourable Malcolm Fraser, Minister for Defence to the City of Sydney Special Branch of the Liberal Party, 10 September 1970.

[15] Department of Defence, *Key Elements in the Triennial Reviews of Strategic Guidance since 1945*, p. 10.

[16] Department of Defence, *Australian Defence Review*, Australian Government Printing Service, Canberra, 1972, pp. 11 and 26.

[17] Department of Defence, *Australian Defence Review*, p. 11.

[18] Department of Defence, *Australian Defence Review*, p. 13.

[19] Department of Defence, *Australian Defence*, Australian Government Printing Service, Canberra, 1976, p. 10.

[20] Department of Defence, *Key Elements in the Triennial Reviews of Strategic Guidance since 1945*, p. 17.

[21] See, for example, (ed.) Robert O'Neill, *The defence of Australia—fundamental new aspects*, proceedings of a conference organised by the Strategic and Defence Studies Centre, The Australian National University, Canberra, 1977; J. O. Langtry and Desmond Ball, *Controlling Australia's threat environment*, Strategic and Defence Studies Centre, The Australian National University, Canberra, 1979; and Ross Babbage, *Rethinking Australia's Defence*, University of Queensland Press, St Lucia, 1980.

[22] Department of Defence, *Review of Australia's defence capabilities*, Report to the Minister for Defence by Mr Paul Dibb, Australian Government Publishing Service, Canberra, March 1986, p. xv.

[23] My team consisted of Dr Richard Brabin-Smith, Colonel Bill Crews and Mr Martin Brady. Both Brabin-Smith and Brady became Deputy Secretaries of Defence later in their careers, while Crews became Director of the Defence Intelligence Organisation.

[24] Department of Defence, *Review of Australia's Defence Capabilities*, pp. 5–6.

[25] Personal letter to Paul Dibb from General Sir Phillip Bennett, Chief of the Defence Force, dated 14 April 1986.

[26] Ross Babbage also argued that an Army 'of at least 150 000 and possibly 250 000 might well be required' to meet an intensive campaign of small scale raids on a continuing basis 'throughout large parts of the continent and against offshore territories and coastal shipping'. (Babbage, *Rethinking Australia's Defence*, p. 87).

[27] Department of Defence, *Review of Australia's Defence Capabilities*, p. 10.

[28] Department of Defence, *The Defence of Australia*, Australian Government Publishing Service, Canberra, 1987, p. 110.

[29] Department of Defence, *Defending Australia*, Australian Government Publishing Service, Canberra, 1994, p. 15.

[30] Department of Defence, *Australia's Strategic Policy*, Commonwealth of Australia, Canberra, 1997, p. 29, available at <http://www.minister.defence.gov.au/sr97/SR97.pdf>, accessed 8 November 2007.

[31] Department of Defence, *Australia's Strategic Policy*, p. 36.

[32] Department of Defence, *Australia's Strategic Policy*, p. 36.

[33] Department of Defence, *Defence 2000: Our Future Defence Force*, Commonwealth of Australia, Canberra, 2000, available at <http://www.defence.gov.au/whitepaper/docs/WPAPER.PDF>, accessed 8 November 2007, p. 30.

[34] Department of Defence, *Defence 2000: Our Future Defence Force*, p. 29.

[35] Department of Defence, *Australia's National Security: A Defence Update 2003*, Commonwealth of Australia, Canberra, 2003, p. 24, available at <http://www.defence.gov.au/ans2003/>, accessed 8 November 2007.

[36] Department of Defence, *Australia's National Security: A Defence Update 2005*, Commonwealth of Australia, Canberra, 2005, p. 26, available at <http://www.defence.gov.au/update2005/defence_update_2005.pdf>, accessed 8 November 2007.

[37] Hugh White, *Beyond the Defence of Australia*, Lowy Institute paper, no. 16, Lowy Institute for International Policy, Sydney, 2006, p. ix, available at <http://www.lowyinstitute.org/Publication.asp?pid=521>, accessed 8 November 2007.

[38] White, *Beyond the Defence of Australia*, p. 51.

[39] White, *Beyond the Defence of Australia*, pp. x, 30 and 52.

[40] White, *Beyond the Defence of Australia*, p. 55.

[41] White, *Beyond the Defence of Australia*, p. 56.

[42] White, *Beyond the Defence of Australia*, p. 57.

[43] Defence does not envisage what it calls a 'Seamless NCW Force' until 2020. See Department of Defence, *NCW Roadmap*, Commonwealth of Australia, Canberra, available at <http://www.defence.gov.au/capability/ncwi/docs/2007NCW_Roadmap.pdf2007>, accessed 8 November 2007.

[44] See the article by Ken Henry, Secretary to the Treasury, entitled 'Australia's Defence to 2045: The Macro-economic Outlook', *Defender* (Journal of the Australian Defence Association), vol. XXII, no. 3, Spring 2005, pp. 19–24.

Global Issues

Chapter 2
Global Change and Strategic Priorities

Coral Bell

The world is at present undergoing a series of profound and complex changes, adding up to a sort of slow-motion revolution (or a very fast evolution) of many dimensions. The unipolar society of states (which came into being in 1992 following the dissolution of the Soviet Union in December 1991) is transforming itself into a more historically familiar structure—a multipolar society of states. Yet the processes of both globalisation and regionalisation are also hard at work, complicating that fundamental redistribution of power. Moreover, the world is becoming more urbanised than ever before. Over 50 per cent, and probably in time, 70 or 80 per cent of its rapidly–rising population, especially in Asia, will live in cities.[1] That social transformation will accelerate another which might best be called 'the revolution of rising expectations'. The poor world is beginning to know how the rich world lives, and to ask why it should not live in some approximation of those conditions. Partly in consequence, there is also a redistribution of power within the state, away from the government and towards 'non-state actors', some very dangerous. As if all that material change were not enough, there is also an ongoing *normative shift* (a shift in the rules governing action by sovereign states) which is at least equally revolutionary and, to cap it all, a climate change process of possibly catastrophic outcomes.

Over the long term, most of the world's governments will need to rethink their strategic and diplomatic priorities in the light of this major transformation of the international context. Although the changes will not be complete or even fully visible for a decade or two, they are to my mind already casting their shadows before them. Changes in US strategic priorities, in particular, will be important not only to Australia and its region, but to the entire world.

The Unipolar Moment

The original populariser of the concept of unipolarity[2] wrote of a 'unipolar moment' and that now seems prescient enough. The remaining duration of that moment, on present evidence, is now very brief, which would mean the new multipolar power-structure being in place about a decade from now. The origin of the current unipolar phase was the dissolution of the Soviet Union, and thus the demise of the bipolar world of the Cold War, which had lasted since 1946. The new Russia had insufficient economic, diplomatic or political strength to step into the strategic shoes of the old Soviet Union; neither then did China, the European Union or any other possible candidate. So it was the absence of a peer-competitor for the United States which created the unipolar world, and it is that situation which is now changing faster than many people expected, producing the mutation back into a multipolar world.

My case for believing that the phase of unchallenged US paramountcy has already entered its twilight years[3] rests on an analysis of the factors which created and sustained it in the first place, and which are, I shall argue, currently being fairly rapidly eroded. Some of these factors are quite independent of the United States, but I shall look first at those related to it.

The unipolar world depended on three pillars: (1) the overwhelming ascendancy of the US military over that of any other sovereign state, or potential alliance of states, seen in the Pentagon as a possible rival or 'peer-competitor'; (2) its diplomatic strength, as expressed in secure alliances, and capacity to induce 'bandwagoning' by states which were not actual allies; and (3) its initially unmatched economic strength. All three of these factors seem to me to be diminishing, though at different rates.

Military Reassessment

The most paradoxical case is that of US military ascendancy. In both conventional and nuclear terms, US military power is still as great as ever, when compared to that of any other sovereign state. The trouble is that the threat now does not emanate from the armed forces of another sovereign state but from a 'non-state actor'—a loose worldwide network of jihadist cells using the strategy of asymmetric war, and the tactics mostly of urban guerrilla operations. On the evidence of Iraq, US strategies have not as yet proved very effective against such a 'non-state actor'. One particularly notable aspect of this kind of asymmetric war is the extraordinary economy of means for the jihadists, and the very heavy costs of defence against their potential attacks to almost all sovereign states, particularly the United States. The terrorist attacks of 11 September 2001 cost the jihadists hardly more than box-cutters, airline tickets and some training expenses. By contrast, the economic and direct financial costs to the United States and just about every other sovereign state in the world in the years since are as yet uncountable, but enormous. In the case of the United States, the direct costs five years after 11 September 2001 are well above US$500 billion.[4]

Moreover, the visible difficulties in Iraq of coping with an insurgency even (or especially) with the kind of weapons that the United States developed for combat with another superpower in a sense devalues US military capacity as a factor in its overall diplomatic clout. Governments still no doubt (as in Australia) reflect that if they were threatened by another sovereign state, an alliance with the United States would be a vital asset. But, while the actual threat continues to originate from the likes of al Qaeda, how useful is that alliance going to be? Some Europeans are arguing that any alliance with the United States is actively counterproductive, and may indeed invite attack by the jihadists. Yet, to my mind, although the United States and its allies are, without doubt, the high-priority targets, the jihadist campaign is in fact against the entire contemporary society of states, which they regard as a structure of injustice. Although undoubtedly exacerbated by the current conflict in Iraq, the seeds of the jihadist campaign were not sown there.

Relative Diplomatic Clout

That is one of the factors eroding the second pillar of the unipolar world—US diplomatic clout—and it is here that the rate of erosion has been most rapid. In late 2001, just after the attacks in New York and Washington, the United States gained the sympathy and the moral or diplomatic support of the entire world, except for a few Islamic societies. Yet less than two years later, by mid 2003, that sympathy had been mostly lost due to the catastrophic strategic error (to my mind) of the invasion of Iraq in March 2003. As that episode is discussed more fully below in chapters 3 and 5, I will make little further comment. The relevant point for this study is simply that the viability of an alliance depends in part on the belief among its members that the government of the leading power will make decisions that are wise and prudent, and take account of the interests of the other members. As far as the Bush Administration is concerned, that belief did not survive 2003. Conceivably, the next administration could repair some of the damage. Certainly most of the cabal of neoconservatives in policymaking circles who pushed (even before 2001) for that invasion,[5] have already been marginalised or exiled from power. Nevertheless, the Bush Administration was re-elected by an increased majority in 2004, despite the gathering US unease over Iraq. One must assume, therefore, that amorphous beliefs exist within the US populace at large that act as an undercurrent of continued support for that kind of adventurism.

Comparative Economic Strength

As to the third factor—economic strength—the trouble is not primarily misconceived policies in Washington, though they do play a role. It is that the potential 'peer-competitors' in this arena have grown so very formidable. Indeed, the real origin of the redistribution of global power seems to me to lie in the world beyond the United States. America still has a giant's strength, but a company of prospective giants has been emerging elsewhere in the world, primarily due to differential rates of demographic and economic change. Kevin Rudd, then Australia's Shadow Foreign Minister, has pointed out that this is the biggest change in the global economic system since the original rise of the United States in the nineteenth century.

Most people will be familiar with this phenomenon as it relates to China. The size of its population, its rate of economic growth over the past three decades, and the fact that its political elite seems at present to be firmly in control and to be following rational (though by no means liberal) policies, have meant that its diplomatic as well as its economic clout have grown in leaps and bounds over the past few years.

The rise of India has been, until recently, less widely noted or acknowledged. The Indian Government reformed its policies 15 years after China, and its growth rate has been less spectacular: at the end of 2005, 7.5 per cent as against China's long-term average of nearly 10 per cent. Both countries are expected to grow strongly over the foreseeable future, and India has some future advantages over China. Because of the 'one child' policy, China's population structure is more like that of Western nations than that of the rest of Asia, while India's population is younger and more conducive to rapid future economic growth. Moreover, India has a very large educated middle-class, which is English-speaking (a major advantage in the age of the Internet), and it has managed to maintain a respectable level of political democracy over the years since its sovereignty was restored. That eases its relations with the Western powers. Above all, unlike China, India has no intrinsic reason for strategic tension with the United States, Japan or Russia—an important factor which will be elaborated on later in this chapter.

The rise of China and India is not the whole story of the global redistribution of power, although it is the most dramatic aspect of that process. Several other sovereignties from what we used to call the 'Third World' have also been undergoing impressive growth, not only in population numbers but in economic strength. World population by mid-century will run, on present demographic projections to nine billion people, of whom India and China will together account for three billion. But the other major Asian powers will account together for another billion. So Australia's approximately 25 million people are on track to have about 4000 million Asian neighbours. Most Asian countries are poor but with growing middle classes, and thus have an increasing demand for all kinds of goods and commodities, such as oil. Within those totals, Muslims may number about two billion. From elsewhere in the non-West, powers like Brazil and Mexico in Latin America, are assuming a new importance. Even Africa is beginning to present some candidates for future diplomatic and strategic clout, such as Nigeria and South Africa. A number of small powers, who happen to be in possession of oil-bearing real estate, in Latin America, Africa, Central Asia or the Persian Gulf, will also benefit by an increase in diplomatic clout in the looming age of 'energy insecurity'.

Demographic Change

I readily concede that, in the past, mere population numbers have neither endowed a country with economic or diplomatic clout, nor necessarily military strength. But that was a time before the sovereignties of the non-West were endowed with competent governments, or had developed a nationalist consensus and modern means of communication and administration. Things are different now. Moreover, the conventional indices of ability to make a mark on the society of states have been joined by some new ones. Take Bangladesh for instance. Until quite recently, the country tended to be dismissed as a 'basket case', with no assets save far too many very poor people. Yet can anyone not now assume that a society of (in a few decades) about 100 million young Muslim men (with very few jobs or prospects, a growing trend towards fundamentalism, and the possibility that much of their territory may be inundated by rising sea-levels) has no means of making an impact on the society of states?

Strategic location may also be a major asset: Vietnam is already looking like a useful ally to some of the 'China hawks' in the Pentagon, for instance. Regional prestige may prove an asset, as is currently the case for South Africa, and probably will be later for several other powers, including middle powers like Australia. As noted earlier, the world is at present undergoing not only a process of the redistribution of power between its peoples, but also, simultaneously, processes of globalisation, regionalisation and normative shift. Managing the relationship between those four factors of change may need to become a diplomatic art in itself.

The social revolutions of rising populations, urbanisation, communications technology, and demands for better lives, must inevitably have major impacts on domestic politics in many Third World countries, just as they did earlier in the First World. Still, their long-term effect is as yet an enigma, as is the effect of the redistribution of power within societies. In the West, political consciousness and an emerging nationalist consensus accompanied industrialisation and rising population numbers. So sometimes did militarism and expansionist tendencies (we need think only of the history of Germany between 1870 and 1941, and also of Japan during that period (and, since 1945, within the 'Western' camp). We must not assume that the emerging powers of the non-West will follow the patterns set by their Western predecessors; but we should bear in mind that like causes do tend to produce like effects.

Great Powers and Emerging Powers

To sum up the prospects as I see them, towards the 2020s, there will be six demographic and economic giants in the world (the United States, the European Union, China, India, Russia and Japan) and six other very substantial powers (Pakistan, Indonesia, Mexico, Brazil, Nigeria and Iran); that is, 12 main players to be considered. The centre-stage of world politics will be relatively crowded. One could say, in shorthand, four super-powers and eight great powers. At least eight governments, possibly 10, will have nuclear weapons at their disposal. By mid-century, according to UN demographers, there will be 18 countries of over

100 million people, many of them achieving substantial economic growth, and thus placing increased demand on the world's resources.

The United States will be rising towards 400 million, and may still perhaps be the largest economy. The European Union will have a combined population of approximately 600 million, and may be surpassing the United States economically. Yet it will have neither the assets of military capacity nor the decisionmaking speed of a single sovereignty. China may possibly have overtaken either or both in sheer economic size, but not in respect of its people's individual prosperity. India is forecast to be the largest in population, and quite possibly the fastest growing economically. All four will be in brisk competition for some kinds of resources, especially oil. Add to that the kind of domestic sources of social tension mentioned earlier, and we certainly must expect a turbulent world—a world that will need strong diplomatic institutions if it is not to spin lethally out of control. Moreover, the remnants of the jihadist movement, at least, will probably be lingering, and most of the world's Muslims will live in South or Southeast Asia.

US Paramountcy

In that world, the policymakers in Washington are nevertheless still likely to be the decisive group in establishing the context in which the rest of the society of states makes its decisions. So all other governments must ask what will be its strategic priorities, and how will its allies and potential 'peer-competitors' make their own choices, in the light of their respective interpretations of Washington's capabilities and intentions? The most spectacular example of how fast US strategic priorities can change remains, of course, the aftermath of the 11 September 2001 terrorist attacks on US soil. In an hour or two on that traumatic day, China lost its previously pre-eminent place on the Pentagon's list of preoccupations, to be instantly replaced by the Arab world, or the Middle East, or even the Islamic world in general. At the time of writing, that set of US strategic priorities is still in effect. It will not necessarily persist, to my mind, in a multipolar world, but the process of its being modified is likely to be quite protracted.

Donald Rumsfeld's *Quadrennial Defense Review* for 2006 places the jihadists atop the threat list, ahead of the rising power of China.

It is, however, the jihadists themselves who control, at least for the present, those particular priorities. As long as they appear able to mount a major attack on the United States, especially if they continue to seem capable of acquiring a nuclear weapon (from Pakistan or Iran or maybe even Russia or North Korea), they and the Middle East area in general are likely to remain at the forefront of Washington's security preoccupations. Rumsfeld said in February 2006 that he expected the campaign against them to endure for 20 years. Washington is now labelling it 'the long war'. Nevertheless, I am going to assume, for the sake of advancing some arguments about the more distant future, that by about 2015, other possibilities will have displaced the jihadist threat at the top of the US security agenda. The most obvious is, of course, the growth of Chinese power, and its potential as a prospective 'peer–competitor', at last able to step into the long-empty shoes of the old Soviet Union.

Anyone who has been watching China's inroads into what had been regarded as secure enclaves of US influence must be struck by how adroit it has been diplomatically—far more so than the Soviet Union ever was. Moreover, China has a national asset that the Soviet Union never had: its highly efficient export economy, which creates an almost insatiable appetite for commodities of every sort (oil, coal, iron ore, wheat, rice, cotton and so on). Countries that have commodities to sell (like Australia) must thus eagerly welcome China as a diplomatic friend. And that emphasises my earlier point about the diplomatic potential of regionalism in a multipolar world, which is well illustrated by two cases: Central Asia and Latin America. Africa, in time, may become a third example.

When it was created in 1996, the grouping of China, Russia, Kazakhstan, Kyrgyzstan and Tajikistan was regarded simply as a rather unpromising Chinese effort at some regional fence-mending. This message was reinforced following 11 September 2001, as the United States rapidly established a strong new regional influence in Central Asia due to the strategic necessities of the campaign in Afghanistan. But once it became apparent, by 2002–2003, that the United States might have longer-term ambitions in Central Asia, especially in regard to its oil reserves, China and Russia developed genuine (though perhaps temporary) common interests in checking any future prospects that the United States may have of controlling resources there as they had 50 years earlier in the Middle East.

Oil

In the current world situation, with the demand for oil expected to rise steeply, and stay high long-term, because of the future needs of China and India, and other rapidly industrialising countries, every government is bound to be preoccupied with ensuring its access to oil on favourable terms if it is a net consumer, or with selling at the most favourable price, if it is a net producer. So the grouping, now named the Shanghai Cooperation Organization (SCO), quite logically invited India, Pakistan and Iran to its meeting in July 2005, and would obviously regard them as possible recruits.[6] The meeting rather tartly urged the United States to set a date for departure from its Central Asian bases, and the Uzbeks gave Washington six months notice to quit.[7]

What seems to me particularly noteworthy in that rather obscure episode is that it suggests that regional organisations may be useful diplomatic instruments for enabling middle and minor powers to rein in the ambitions of the most powerful sovereignties, not only the United States but others as they emerge. Recent events in Latin America strongly reinforce that view.

Regional Organisations

The Organization of American States, whose origin dates back to the 1890s, had, until recently, seemed rather firmly under the thumb of the United States. But forces on the left, which in the 1990s seemed to have been defeated, later regrouped and began to reassert themselves. The US-favoured candidate for the post of Secretary General of the organisation was defeated by the candidate favoured by Venezuela's President Hugo Chávez, a dedicated enemy of Washington, and a friend of Cuba's Fidel Castro. Evo Morales in Bolivia may prove an even more significant figure, since he represents the indigenous Indian population of the area. Morales has already described himself as 'Washington's worst nightmare' and has presented an agenda of social and economic demands that seem to justify that claim.

Even the two most important sovereignties of the area, Mexico and Brazil (both potential great powers), are by no means certain future friends of the United States. Mexico's President Vicente Fox, who initially was greeted by George W. Bush as his closest 'amigo', proved a disappointment to the United States during his six years in office and we are yet to see how Felipe Calderón will fare. Mexicans are no better off than when he was inaugurated, and still equally inclined to vote with their feet for life in the north. Brazil's political future is also ambiguous. The present incumbent, Lula da Silva, is a Social Democrat of sorts, but he may have difficulty in holding that line against those politically further to the left. The President of Chile, Michelle Bachelet, is the daughter of one of Salvador Allende's ministers, who was tortured during the Augusto Pinochet years, subsequently dying from a heart attack. Things have dramatically changed there.

Fidel Castro, having now survived almost 50 years of US efforts to dispose of him, may be having the last laugh, as the political and social forces he represented are reinforced in most of the region. Bush's critics can reasonably claim that the US President's obsessive concentration on the Middle East has induced a dangerous neglect of his hemispheric neighbourhood. But there is more to it than that. Washington's assertive unilateralism in the period 2001–2004 was disliked as much there as in other parts of the world. Somewhat paradoxically, Bush's rhetorical concentration on the new, virtuous US pursuit of democracy and human rights for all has actually strengthened China's diplomatic hand. The world still has governments furious about being harassed on such matters, and some have resources of great interest to China. Places like Burma, Sudan, Uzbekistan, and North Korea are 'off limits' these days for Western diplomats and trade or oil ministers wanting to pursue deals and friendships, but not for the Chinese Foreign Minister and his aides.

China's Diplomacy

The governments of such countries, as noted above, can reiterate that China's long-held policy is not to interfere in the internal affairs of other countries. They can even revive the old Chinese claim, dating from the days of the non-aligned movement, that China is the natural friend of all 'Third World' countries, their counterbalance to US demands that they should adopt its diplomatic and political norms, and its economic structure. When Bush waxes enthusiastic about the virtues of democracy, many 'Third World' policymakers are inclined to retort that the United States is not government 'by the people, for the people', but government 'by the rich, for the rich'. This almost gives them common ground with the jihadists, who also complain that the society of states presided over by the United States is a structure of injustice and hypocrisy.

One can see the way those 'Third World' resentments feed into global rivalries in the relationship between Venezuela and China. Hugo Chávez can more convincingly threaten to cut off oil supplies to the United States now that he has China as an alternative buyer—one that is promising to build oil refineries in his own territory. Iran, under increasing pressure about its nuclear ambitions, can use a similar alternative-market strategy with North Korea: oil in exchange for fissile material.

It is not in the much-discussed future of Taiwan that I see the long-term danger of conflict between China and the United States, but in that far more fundamental future contest over resources, particularly oil. The Taiwan problem can (and I think will) be settled in time by the Islanders themselves. About a million Taiwanese already work on the mainland. A lot of them marry there. Politically influential Taiwanese businessmen have already invested some US$100 billion on the mainland, and will not want to see those funds endangered. Polling on the island indicates that only about 10 per cent want a unilateral declaration of independence, and 80 per cent are opposed to even a change of name. The Taiwan lobby still operates in Congress, but is much weaker than in the past. When it proposed in February 2005 a joint resolution to restore diplomatic relations with Taiwan, the Bush Administration strongly opposed any such scheme, making it clear that it wants no change in the status quo, from either side.

One might argue that such an attitude will last only as long as Washington has its hands full in the Middle East, and also depends on China and Russia keeping North Korea as near to rational policies as can be expected. Perhaps this is the case, but I would be inclined to argue that the United States could be cautiously approaching a much larger change in its North Asia policies, a change that will be of great importance to Australia. It would in some ways resemble the policy decision outlined in the Acheson White Paper of 1949, crafted just after Mao Zedong's victory in the civil war in China. Washington had then to decide whether it was prepared to face the prospect of war with the de facto newly-created government of China, in an effort to reverse the verdict of the civil war. It decided not to, and that was at a time when China was weak to the point of utter exhaustion, after the decades-long conflict. Now that it faces a China growing strong, not only economically and diplomatically, but to some degree militarily, a similar answer seems to me to be tentatively signalled. (I do not want to seem to be overrating China's military strength in the world league. It still has very little power-projection capacity, and the Chinese 'top brass' readily admit that there is no way they could win a military encounter with the United States. On the other hand, a US analyst with very good Pentagon sources has said that China is likely to have a minimal second-strike nuclear capacity by the end of this decade, which should mean an effective one by the end of the next decade, round 2020.)[8]

The Changing US Stance

If I had to suggest a definition of the US policy whose outlines seem to me, in moments of optimism, to be emerging late in the Bush second term, I would call it 'balance plus accommodation, with a deterrent undertone'. The official statement, in which it was most clearly conveyed, was a speech by Robert Zoellick, then Deputy Secretary of State, on 21 September 2005. He is an accomplished diplomat, and naturally mixed the signals in that speech adroitly for his various audiences. (Some Australian journalists even identified it as a Cold War speech.) But let me quote what I think were the primary signals, which, judging by Beijing's reactions, seem to have been quite readily picked up by his Chinese audience:

> It is time to take our policy beyond opening doors to China's membership in the international system ... we need to urge China to become a responsible stakeholder in that system. ... Its national interest would best be served by working with us to shape the future international system ... Chinese leaders have decided that their success depends on being networked into the modern world. ... They recognize that the international system sustains their peaceful prosperity, so they work to sustain the system.[9]

Zoellick's audience contained many 'China hawks' who understood the change it was signalling, and received it coldly. No doubt the regime in Taiwan also got the message, and was chagrined. President Chen Shui-bian issued what might be accounted a defiant rejoinder in his Chinese New Year speech, putting proposals for a new constitution, and urging that Taiwan should seek a seat in the United Nations, which would of course imply that the international community had accepted the island as an independent sovereign state. Washington's reply was immediate, and as strong a rebuke as any ally has ever delivered to another. The spokesman said that the United States had not been consulted and that the proposal represented a unilateral change to the status quo and thus was totally at odds with Washington's stance. President Chen's term of office lasts until 2008, but he and his party are increasingly unpopular in Taiwan, and Ma Ying-Jeou, the former leader of the most significant opposition party, the old Kuomintang (and also former Mayor of Taipei) has been visiting the mainland, and elsewhere, and making conciliatory statements. On 2 May 2007, Ma was officially named the Kuomintang's nominee for the 2008 presidential election and it will be a nice piece of historical irony if he is elected and finally makes peace with the heirs of Mao, who are these days more Chinese nationalist than Maoist.

I will return presently to the question of what kind of global diplomatic structure the changed distribution of power in the society of states might require, but let me look first at some regional strategic and diplomatic changes in the Asia-Pacific which seem to support my hypothesis.

These changes are shaping up, as was implied earlier, as an echo of the strategy hinted in the Acheson White Paper of 1949. Its central focus was on the 'Island Chain' stretching down from Japan to Australia. Taiwan was not included in that chain, because at the time it was thought of as simply part of China. The remnants of the Kuomintang and its army had taken refuge there, but in 1949 no-one expected them to hold out for very long. The outbreak of the Korean War a year later (when US President Harry S. Truman included Taiwan in the area within US protection, along with South Korea) changed that assumption. And, for some 50 years afterward, that June 1950 definition of the US stance on the positions of Taiwan and South Korea remained central to US strategy in East Asia.

The strategic 'backstop' for the original 1949 concept, by contrast, had been on Japan and the island of Guam, and the most recent phase of US strategic and diplomatic thinking seems to return focus to these two locations. The United States is strengthening its submarine and cruise missile deployments on Guam. The US Air Force is also constructing an operations centre there to serve the entire Pacific area.[10] The strategic ties between the United States and Japan have been strengthening since 1995, and Japan has of course a good deal more to be anxious about than the United States or Australia from the re-emergence of a China that is both powerful and still dwelling on old wrongs at Japan's hands.

But the current US concept is both diplomatically and strategically more ambitious than its 1949 predecessor, since Southeast Asia and South Asia are both within its compass. The Philippines and Singapore have been successfully cultivated in terms of US naval access, and India has been more sedulously wooed by the recent US Ambassador, Robert Blackwill,[11] than any of his predecessors since the Kennedy period. China and India were at war as recently as 1962 and China still holds a swathe of what India regards as Indian territory, but the potential common strategic and diplomatic interests of the United States, Japan and India extend beyond these considerations.

The twenty-first century is taking shape in many people's minds as Asia's century, and that raises the obvious question of whether it will evolve towards one paramount power, a bipolar balance, or a 'concert of powers'. By about 2050, as noted earlier, India will have more people than China, and may be as advanced economically, and more stable politically. It has as ancient and splendid a civilisation as China. Most importantly, as already mentioned, it has no area of strategic rivalry with the United States, Japan or Russia, whereas China has sources of potential quarrel with all three: with the United States, on influence over Japan and East Asia in general; with Japan itself over the past; and with Russia, over the vast territories of the Russian Far East, which the old Tsarist Empire won from the old Chinese Empire in a series of 'unequal treaties' during the nineteenth century and which now turn out to be so rich in valuable commodities like oil. So, a great deal is implied in the notion of a common strategic interest between the United States, India and Japan, and indeed perhaps Russia as well.

Moreover, until recently, most analysts would have asserted that the United States would be very unlikely to relinquish its 'forward deployment' in East Asia, particularly its troop deployment in South Korea, and its strongly asserted strategic commitment to Taiwan. But times change, and no sensible strategist wants to fight on an unfavourable battlefield. Even Doug Bandow, a strategic commentator with very strong right-wing affiliations, a policy adviser for former US President Ronald Reagan, with connections to a number of conservative Washington think-tanks, defines the South Korean deployment as 'a commitment that costs far more than it is worth, absorbs valuable military resources, and keeps the Korean people in a dependent relationship that insults their nationhood'.[12]

The so-called 'tripwire' of US troops has been moved south, and cut by a third. If North Korea is in possession of deliverable nuclear weapons, those troops would obviously be hostages in any future military encounter. Young Koreans, especially, value friendship with China above the tie with the United States, and regard the North Koreans more as long-lost brothers than as long-term enemies. The South Korean Government has made it clear that it would resist being involved in any regional dispute (for instance, over Taiwan) and would even object to US troops based on its territory being used in any such encounter.

But Bandow, who is a realist as well as a conservative, makes it clear that there are larger considerations at work for Washington: 'As much as the United States might prefer to maintain its current dominance over every continent on earth, it cannot expect its regional dominance to last for ever.'[13] In other words, it must reassess its strategic priorities as the global distribution of power changes. And those East Asia deployments may not be as high on the list as they once were.

I would not expect any official US statement in the near future to carry any open endorsement of these views on the evolution of US policy on Northeast Asia, particularly as regards Taiwan and South Korea, although it is possible that the issue may arise in the 2008 US Presidential contest. On the whole, re-definitions are usually proclaimed only after really traumatic crisis periods such as the attacks on 11 September 2001 or the period of the Tet Offensive of 1968, which evoked Richard Nixon's Guam Doctrine of 1969. Some sudden and acute reversal of fortune on Iraq or Iran would be the likeliest candidates for an equivalent in the next few years, though one should not underrate the possibilities of the erratic leader in North Korea, with his missile firings and nuclear ambitions, or, indeed, even radical change in South Korea.

We should also bear in mind that there is an even more obvious location for changing US commitments: the Atlantic arena. The Europeans are in the enviable position of facing no serious military threat for the foreseeable future, so it is difficult to see why deployments of US land forces (109 000 at present)[14] should be stationed there, except that it provides a useful forward-staging area for Afghanistan and the Middle East. Russia, whose population may fall to 80 million by the end of this century, (as against the 250 million of the old Soviet Union) is more likely to need the strategic backing of the 600 million people of the European Union than be in any position to take them over. But the future of that relationship is too large and speculative an issue to discuss here.

New Strategic Priorities

Let me therefore return to the question I posed at the beginning of this essay. What changes in strategic priorities are necessary or desirable in the light of the emerging re-distribution of power in the world? Obviously to answer that in detail, even for the 12 or so powers which I have argued are 'likely' to be part of the central balance, would require an entire book in itself. Yet I believe one central and almost universal priority can be postulated: the necessity of avoiding hegemonial war.

By hegemonial war I mean war to determine the order of power in the world. The First and Second World Wars, and the Cold War were all hegemonial wars in that sense. So, in intent, is the present 'Jihadists' War'. The jihadists certainly want to demolish the current order of power in the world, which they regard as a structure of injustice and hypocrisy. Yet, to my mind, only a war that pits the major powers against each other would have the enormous destructive capacity of either the First or Second World Wars. It is therefore to avoiding another encounter of that sort that the society of states must devote its best efforts.

This brings my argument to a further two questions. What kind of diplomatic structure or institution has had the best historical 'track record' of avoiding hegemonial war? And can one see any possibility of anything similar being constructed in the next few decades?

The most hopeful augury for the future stability of the society of states is that there are already faint signs, even in this lame-duck period of Bush's final term of office, that Washington is beginning to develop diplomatic strategies (perhaps also military strategies and new weapon designs) for the post-unipolar world—the emerging multipolar world. I would associate the initiative not with the US President, the Vice-President or any of the hopefuls for 2008, but with the State Department and the National Security Council. I would also argue (though admittedly with thin evidence as yet) that the thoughts of some relevant policymakers seem to have turned in two historically familiar directions: the 'balance of power' and the 'concert of powers'. Dr Condoleezza Rice spoke earlier of 'a balance of power favouring freedom' and her hand must be seen in the 2006 operational signals of the building of the strategic basis of a future balance system in relations with India and Japan. Her deputy, Robert Zoellick (now President of the World Bank), ventured further, mentioning the far more controversial notion of a 'concert of powers' in his 2005 speech quoted earlier.

Not, of course, that those are the only mind-sets in Washington concerning the future of US power. There is much diversity. Even a sort of isolationism is back on the cards, with a few people arguing that it might have been better for the world if the United States had drawn away from international politics after the end of the Cold War in 1992, as it did after the end of the First World War in 1919. It would at least have meant no current Iraq War, which would have made the world a lot less distressing. Yet at the opposite end of the spectrum, even after Iraq, there are still a few unrepentant hegemonists who insist that the unipolar world can be maintained on the military plane, even if not on the economic or diplomatic planes.

The most spectacularly obvious signal of new US thinking on the future 'balance of power' was George W. Bush's trip to India in 2006, and in particular the nuclear technology agreement he signed there. I call it spectacular because it more or less drove an M1 *Abrams* tank through his previous counterproliferation line, as used against Iran and North Korea, and also put a large dent in the Nuclear Non-Proliferation Treaty, to the embarrassment of various allies including Australia—in our case because of the question of selling uranium to a power which has not signed the Treaty.

Even if Bush's Indian deal is not endorsed by Congress,[15] it will send about as clear a message to China as could well be imagined, especially as the Pentagon has also been authorised to sell advanced fighter aircraft, the F-16 *Fighting Falcon* or the F/A-18 *Hornet*, to India.[16] As mentioned earlier, China and India were at war as recently as 1962, and China still holds a large swathe of territory in the high Himalayas that India regards as Indian. But China is not willing to relinquish it, due to the territory's importance to their military control of Tibet and Xianjiang. The Bush signal to China is the old traditional warning: 'a balance of power can be constructed against your rising military capacity if you push your luck.' The renewed emphasis on the strategic relationship with Japan is, of course, a reinforcement of that message. The Indian Government has its own reasons for assuming that a great-power ally, either the United States or Russia (or preferably both) might prove quite useful in its future context, since both China and Pakistan will be substantial nuclear powers, and Persian Gulf or Central Asian or Russian oil must remain vital to its development.

Yet Beijing has also to ponder the Zoellick signal of the potentialities of a much closer relationship with the advanced Western world (a high place in a global 'concert of powers'), so one can say that there has been brought to the attention of its policymakers not only a very formidable stick (a possible 'balance of power' coalition against it), but also a very juicy carrot, one consonant with its long history of civilisation.

In some ways both those concepts are more difficult for Washington to adjust to than for Beijing. Both concepts have been regarded in the United States, ever since Woodrow Wilson's time, as amoral and discredited European diplomatic devices. He saw the failure of the Concert of Powers in 1914 as proof that the idea did not work. But the more reasonable way of interpreting that patch of history is that, after all, the Concert *did* work for 99 years, from 1815 to 1914. No other diplomatic device has had an equal level of success in preventing hegemonial war, which is the sole essential function of such a system. Moreover, the Concert achieved that record despite two great-power wars (Crimean and Franco-Prussian) and the fact that tensions between the great powers were actually stronger in the nineteenth century than they are at present, because of the long-running imperial rivalries between the British, the French, and the Russians. The Germans, fatally, entered that imperial competition by the end of the century, and so the Concert failed, and the war in 1914 (originally seen as likely to be both short and limited) destroyed that entire society of states.

However, Wilson's supposed improvement on the Concert, the League of Nations, lasted only 20 years, from 1919 until 1939, was ineffective even for that brief life, and ended in a particularly murderous hegemonial war. The United

Nations has lasted better, some 60 years now, but has been similarly ineffective in the security field. Security issues have therefore been the domain of a traditional 'balance of power' coalition, the North Atlantic Treaty Organization (NATO), which has seen off its adversary (the Soviet Union) without direct hostilities: the ultimate success for any 'balance of power' coalition. So comparing the nineteenth and twentieth century periods as a whole, one would have to judge that the two Wilsonian systems, the League of Nations and the United Nations, have fared less well, as far as the most vital issue (prevention of hegemonial war) is concerned than the two traditional systems, 'concert of powers' and 'balance of power'. Dean Acheson, Harry S. Truman's Secretary of State, was the principal architect of NATO, with substantial assistance from George Kennan and Ernest Bevin, the British Foreign Secretary of the time. They could not call their achievement by its rightful and traditional name, however, because that would have been politically tactless in view of the assumed necessity for a Wilsonian flavour in US rhetoric in the foreign policy field—a tradition all too readily audible today in the speeches of President George W. Bush.

One obvious objection to my optimism about a possible global 'concert of powers' is to argue that its predecessor was successful only because all its decisionmakers were children of one civilisation, and shared many assumptions and norms. That last point is true, but is offset to my mind by *four factors* which more than compensate for the current diversity of cultural origins. *First*, the problems which confront the current decisionmakers are vastly more global than those of the nineteenth century. No one then was worried about global warming, which is now likely to damage every society in differing degrees. *Second*, though there were transnational terrorists back then (the anarchists), they were infinitely less formidable than the current jihadists, so had far less capacity to promote solidarity in the society of states against their common adversary, a 'non-state actor'. *Third*, international communication for most of that period was slow and difficult, whereas it is now universal and instantaneous. *Fourth*, the penalties associated with war were vastly less in the nineteenth century than they are now. Then it was fought by professional armies, on distant battlefields, not (as now) by the destruction of great cities and their peoples.

Above all, however, my optimism on the issue of the prospective dominant powers finding consensus is that it is already being done, with few difficulties and not much fanfare. The grouping which began more than 30 years ago as the G7, is now the G8 with the addition of Russia, and appears likely to become the G10 with the admittance of China and India (which were invited to the 2006 summit). The group could in fact become the G12, which would be a fair approximation of a contemporary 'concert of powers'. Its preoccupations are now no longer economic, or directed to the problems of its own members, but are rather global in nature. The Gleneagles meeting of 2005 was mostly concerned with the problems of Africa and world poverty, and the 2006 meeting in St. Petersburg with the troubles of the Middle East.

I am not arguing that it will or should replace the UN Security Council, but formal structures like the United Nations are far less flexible about membership and agendas than informal ones like the old Concert of Powers or its contemporary parallel. Over time, power does recognise countervailing power, however reluctantly, and makes the necessary adjustments. However, change may need to be informally established for some time before it is incorporated into the formal structures of the society of states. In time, the UN Security Council will probably expand to reflect twenty-first century realities, but for the moment the G8+ might serve as its 'stand-in' for some purposes.

There is a strong flavour of 'forward to the past' about contemporary history. According to economic historians, China and India were probably the largest economies in the world until about 1820.[17] Afterwards, the industrialisation of the West ensured its economic dominance. But by 2020 the wheel may have come full circle, and China and India may again be the largest economies in the world. In fact, one of our most eminent experts, The Australian National University's (ANU) Professor Ross Garnaut, has said that China may make it to top place by 2010,[18] though others put it about 2040.

After the Enlightenment (in Europe at least), the idea that people would massacre each other over minor differences of religious doctrine seemed ridiculous. Yet in Iraq and Afghanistan, Sunni have been killing Shia (and vice versa) as earnestly as Protestants killed Catholics (and vice versa) in sixteenth and seventeenth century Europe. The national state, in its present form, was invented by the Europeans only four centuries ago, but they seem now to be circling back in some respects to its pre-Westphalian origins, with its peoples defining themselves not only in the larger context as Europeans, but in the smaller context as English, Scottish, Welsh, Breton, Catalan, Czech, Slovak, Bosnian, Croatian or Montenegrin, among many others. By century's end, the European Union might be less a confederation of 35 national states than a federation of 300 or so provinces, like the mini-states that nourished the composers Franz Joseph Haydn and Wolfgang Amadeus Mozart in their time. The great city which for a time was called Leningrad is now again St. Petersburg, and the present decisionmaker for all the Russians has again been welcoming the dignitaries of the rest of the world to its restored Tsarist splendours. The political structures of Europe were once exported to other continents, like Africa, to which they were not well suited. Perhaps the new changes in Europe, which reflect recognition of the identities of long-submerged tribes, might do better.

If some of the iniquities of the past have returned to haunt the twenty-first century world, there seems a kind of historic logic in hoping that one of the diplomatic institutions of the past may be able to take on the most important of the jobs dealt with quite successfully then. The task the Concert of Powers managed better and longer than its successors—the prevention of hegemonial war—is going to be the most vital problem of all in this new century, and the emerging distribution of power seems more like that of the nineteenth than the twentieth century. Then there were five dominant powers—Britain, France, Russia, Prussia and Austria—but eight other near-great powers—Spain, Italy, the Ottoman Empire, the United States and Japan towards the end of the period, and the substantial empires of Portugal, Belgium and the Netherlands. There existed therefore 13 or (adding Serbia, which proved so crucial) 14 governments whose preoccupations and ambitions needed to be considered, though not all received adequate attention. Now there are emerging 12 dominant powers or more, but by mid-century (as mentioned earlier), according to UN demographic forecasts, there will be 18 sovereignties of more than a hundred million people, and still other aspirants may be waiting in the wings.

The society of states needs to construct diplomatic arrangements between these established and emerging powers that can maintain a reasonable consensus; otherwise the risk of hegemonial war seems likely to be very great. If a flexible global 'concert of powers' can manage the heavy task of averting that disaster for anything like the same span of years as its European predecessor, the international community might have sufficient time to devise solutions for the many other problems threatening the future of humanity, such as global warming, world poverty, and terrorism.

ENDNOTES

[1] Population figures are based on UN demographers' 'medium scenario' forecasts for 2005. See *World Population in 2300, Proceedings of the United Nations Expert Meeting on World Population in 2300*, United Nations Headquarters, New York, 2004, available at <http://www.un.org/esa/population/publications/longrange2/longrange2.htm>, accessed 24 October 2007.

[2] The term acquired its current usage from an article by Charles Krauthammer entitled 'The Unipolar Moment' in a special issue of *Foreign Affairs* entitled 'America and the World 1990/91', *Foreign Affairs*, vol. 70, no. 1, 1990–91, pp. 23–33.

[3] For a deeper analysis, see the author's 'The Twilight of the Unipolar World' in *The American Interest*, vol. 1, no. 2, Winter 2005.

[4] See *Securing, Stabilizing and Rebuilding Iraq: GAO Audit Approach and Findings*, US Government Accountability Office Report, No. GAO-07-385T, 18 January 2007, available at <http://www.gao.gov/new.items/d07385t.pdf>, accessed 8 November 2007.

[5] See the 23 March 2006 issue of *London Review of Books* for a detailed but controversial account of the process of decisionmaking in Washington DC during this period. The authors were Professors John Mearsheimer and Stephen Walt, both eminent and conservative US analysts.

[6] *The Joint Communiqué of the Moscow Meeting of the Council of Heads of Government of SCO Member States*, Shanghai Cooperation Organization, 2005, available at <http://www.sectsco.org/html/00648.html>, accessed 24 October 2007.

[7] 'Uzbekistan casts out America', *Strategic Comments*, International Institute for Strategic Studies, vol. 11, issue no. 6, August 2005, available at <http://www.iiss.org/publications/strategic-comments/past-issues/volume-11---2005/volume-11-issue-6/uzbekistan-casts-out-america>, accessed 24 October 2007.

[8] Robert S. Ross, 'Diplomacy and Bipolarity in East Asia', in (eds) Tharza Varkey Paul, James Wirtz, Michel Fortmann, *Balance of Power: Theory and Practice in the 21st Century*, Stanford University Press, CA, 2004, p. 285.

[9] Robert Zoellick resigned as Deputy Secretary of State in June 2006, but not apparently over this speech. He had been heavily involved in the Darfur negotiations and seems to have been disappointed in their outcome. *The China Daily* of 21 June 2006 praised his contribution to US-China relations at his departure, which seems to confirm the assumption that Beijing welcomed the signal in his speech a year earlier.

[10] Frank Whitman, 'Black Construction Gets Guam Global Hawk Contract', *Pacific Magazine*, 6 May 2007, available at <http://www.pacificmagazine.net/news/2007/05/06/black-construction-gets-guam-global-hawk-contract>, accessed 24 October 2007.

[11] See Robert D. Blackwill, 'The India Imperative' in *The National Interest*, no. 80, Summer 2005, pp. 9–17.

[12] Doug Bandow, 'Seoul Searching', *The National Interest*, no. 81, Fall 2005, p. 116.

[13] Bandow, 'Seoul Searching', *The National Interest*, no. 81, Fall 2005, p. 107.

[14] Hans Binnendijk, 'Modernising NATO: A new strategic basis for US forces in Europe', *International Herald Tribune*, 28 February 2003, available at <http://www.iht.com/articles/2003/02/28/t-hans_ed3_.php>, accessed 24 October 2007. For current figures, see International Institute for Strategic Studies (London), *The Military Balance 2007*, Routledge, Taylor & Francis, Essex, January 2007, pp. 28-41.

[15] See Laurence Korb and Peter Ogden, 'Winning Congressional Support for the Global Partnership with India' in *The American Interest*, vol. 1, no. 2, Winter 2005, pp. 18–29.

[16] US Department of Defense, 'Defense Department Statement on India Relationship', 2 March 2006, available at <http://www.defenselink.mil/releases/release.aspx?releaseid=9347>, accessed 24 October 2007. See also Chidanand Rajghatta, 'Now, US offers F-16, F-18 jets to India', *Times of India*, 4 March 2006, available at <http://timesofindia.indiatimes.com/articleshow/1437763.cms>, accessed 24 October 2007.

[17] Eisuke Sakakibara, 'Watch China and India: Adapt to a changing world economy', *International Herald Tribune*, 5 February 2003, available at <http://www.iht.com/articles/2003/02/05/edsak_ed3_.php>, accessed 24 October 2007. See also Angus Maddison, *The World Economy: Volume 1: A Millennial Perspective*, Development Centre Studies, Organisation for Economic Cooperation and Development, Paris, 2001, p. 127.

[18] See also (eds) Ross Garnaut and Ligang Song, *The Turning Point in China's Economic Development*, Asia Pacific Press, The Australian National University, Canberra, 2006.

Chapter 3

Restoring Utility to Armed Force in the 21st Century

Robert O'Neill

The first aim of this chapter is to offer some perspectives on how the nature of armed conflict has changed since the end of the Cold War and how it might look over the next few decades. The sources for this section are largely my own professional experience and studies over some 40 years. The second aim is to discuss the qualities that armed forces will need in order to operate successfully in these new types of conflict. The sources here are my friends who have recently served or are still serving in the US and British armed forces in Iraq and Afghanistan, plus my own experience in Vietnam 40 years ago.

The Nature of Armed Conflict in the 21st Century

The advent of new enemies

During the past decade or so a new type of enemy has challenged Western values and influence. Unsurprisingly, the United States has chosen to confront these enemies vigorously and there is general agreement that the West is now in a global war with challengers known as 'terrorists'—although that term relates to only a small part of their agenda.

One of the most startling features of the Bush Administration's use of armed force over the past five years has been the stark contrast between cost and effectiveness. Colossal amounts of money are being spent—up to US$10 billion per month (including US8.6 billion for Iraq and US$1.4 billion for Operation *Enduring Freedom*)[1] —and huge volumes of rubble and ruins have been generated in Iraq, Afghanistan and Lebanon. Much more importantly, the lives of tens of thousands of Iraqi civilians have been lost and those of hundreds of thousands of others severely blighted. A number of improvements have been made to civil infrastructure in Iraq, but these are outweighed by the damage and insecurity which have resulted from Coalition operations and the subsequent insurgency. Afghanistan remains insecure and its infrastructure badly damaged, while Lebanon took such a pounding in July and August 2006 that it will take some time to be rehabilitated economically, socially and politically. Many more people in the Middle East, running into the tens of millions, have had their fears and prejudices about Western discriminatory attitudes towards Muslims and Arabs, their religion, culture, institutions and societies, reinforced by these events. They are not all going to bear their pain stoically and seek reconciliation. Some are already striking back and we can expect more to store their grievances, their feelings of having suffered injustice and of having been treated like bit-characters in computer war games. They will support those they view as their oppressed fellows. Some will join those who propose exacting vengeance on the authors of their sufferings and those of their friends.

The West has some interesting tests coming up in the next decade or two. We had better get our armed forces and the policies which govern their development, equipment, training and use into better shape. We need to establish control over a situation which looks to be growing steadily worse. If we fail to do so soon, we may slide into a slowly deteriorating security situation with the most serious consequences. Politically, the trends are already quite worrying. One has only to look occasionally at international polls of public opinion and the way in which the trends have been moving over the past few years to comprehend how much worse the situation can become from the perspective of those who are most heavily involved in the application of armed force today. The United States has few allies in Iraq of any real military utility. It has a real problem in ensuring that this number does not decline further and that public opinion in other democracies does become more critical of US policies, especially in supporting intervention in those parts of the world where severe threats might arise. We require a political and military reversal. Moreover, as far as the use of military force is concerned, in future we need to be much cleverer and more successful in its application than we have been for the past several years.

Thinking about the worst threat

I believe that the most severe threat confronting the United States and its allies today is nuclear terrorism. We must be alert to the dangers of nuclear weapons proliferating into the hands of those who abhor the West. Two leading anti-Western states—Iran and North Korea—already have flourishing nuclear weapons programs. Soon they may both be able to pass nuclear warheads into the hands of terrorist agents for delivery against sensitive Western targets. Iran and North Korea will seek to increase their indirect influence among their neighbours and on the global scene simply by their ownership of nuclear weapons. They might even accept the risks involved with blackmailing other governments which are not in a position to retaliate directly. In the worst case, they can make direct use of nuclear weapons in their own names against people that they despise, irrespective of the consequences. There also remains a proliferation risk from other nuclear powers and, indeed, even from other friendly states that happen to have nuclear weapons. They do not all have perfectly inviolable security systems to protect their warheads or fissile material from corrupt sale or outright theft. Nor may all such states be perfectly stable politically or always inclined to avoid confrontation with the West.

Clearly, we have to think seriously about meeting the prospective challenges arising from these kinds of nuclear threats. Our experience during the Cold War taught us that it is best to deal with them by a combination of deterrence and arms control. Yet not all the actors in this expanded cast of characters may prove deterrable, nor may they be amenable to restraint by arms control—particularly should the West appear to be cavalier in its own attitudes towards arms control and its obligations. Nuclear weapons may have had a positive utility in restraining the use of force during the Cold War, but they are now much more of a threat to the leading Western states, particularly the United States of America, than to any one else, especially the people most likely to use them. We should do all we can to avoid further proliferation, and to put into effect a stronger international anti-proliferation regime.

The initiative taken in July 2006 by US President George W. Bush and Russian President Vladimir Putin to establish the Global Initiative to Combat Nuclear Terrorism was very appropriate and timely.[2] It is sad perhaps that more could not have been done earlier because the proliferation problem has worsened markedly since the end of the Cold War, but at least the dangers are being recognised and addressed at the highest levels. I wonder if both leaders really understand that their own national policies will need to be re-shaped and restrained if this Initiative is to prove worth the paper that it is written on.

By way of defences, we particularly need the types of improved security systems that are currently in place at major Western sea and airports, but we require them in greater depth. The model provided by the shipping container inspection arrangements that came into force in hub ports around the world following the 11 September 2001 attacks in the United States is a good starting point, but there are many gaps in the system which must be filled.[3] While anti-missile defences will be important if they can be made cost effective, the likeliest delivery vehicle for a nuclear warhead will be the shipping container or the truck rather than the intercontinental missile. That danger still demands attention. Moreover, we must not forget that Iran and North Korea may still have to be addressed by force if either allows their nuclear weapons to become a direct danger to the United States, its allies and friends.

Wars of protest and vengeance

The second major threat to the United States and its allies and partners is exemplified by the conflicts now taking place in the Middle East. As the nature of international order has changed, so, unsurprisingly, has the nature of war. Regrettably, war in general did not disappear with the Cold War: it simply became more complex and very different in form to what the major powers had been preparing for over the past several decades. The conduct of hostilities has become more complex and more a matter of the intellect, and the means of warfare increasingly technological. These developments offer opportunities to small numbers of determined people, especially if they are prepared to give their lives in order to damage Western interests. They also play to a number of Western strengths, especially in the field of technology (although we should be careful not to get trapped into following too technological an approach).

It seems increasingly unlikely that this century will see the forces of major powers being used directly against each other in a manner similar to the two world wars of the twentieth century. The painful lessons of experience from those wars still seem clearly in the minds of current national leaders. What is abundantly clear from recent experience is that hostilities will occur mainly between the West (led by the United States) and dissident forces (sometimes in the form of a state such as North Korea and Iran, and sometimes in the shape of sub-state elements such as al Qaeda and other shadowy groups of irregular fighters).

The two key issues are how long these confrontations will continue; and the best means by which the West can emerge as the arbiter of a new, more peaceful era?

On the first of these, there is a wide consensus that these conflicts will not be settled in a brief period. We are probably in for a generation of hostilities of varying intensity, assuming that our methods are effective. The formula advocated by the Bush Administration for achieving a cheap, rapid and stable peace (namely political transformation into a democracy) is very hard to apply. Democracy requires deep and solid foundations. Giving it a stable structure in Iraq and Afghanistan is proving formidably difficult. Clearly we need to better understand the process of conversion of dissident states and groups into ones with whom we can coexist peacefully. This process will prove slow and, in some cases, even unfeasible.

Even if it is possible, is it reasonable to assume that the resulting democracies will always see eye to eye sufficiently to avoid war? The Palestinians may continue to elect Hamas or governments like it, particularly if Israeli pressures remain strong. The Lebanese may continue to elect Hezbollah candidates to their parliament who will stake a claim to participation in their government. In August 2005 the Iranians elected Mahmoud Ahmadinejad as their President partly on the basis of his defiance of Western policies in general, including Western demands for Iran to cease its advance towards the development of nuclear weapons. Our troubles with all of these peoples and their leaders may persist even if their political systems evolve into a form of democracy.

We therefore need to approach the questions of reform of our military forces very seriously and on a long-term basis given that we are dealing with major, long-term dangers. The efforts we make to meet them should correspond to the natures of these dangers.

The Qualities That Armed Forces Will Need

The training and development of effective forces for the 21st century

Turning to the second of the two aims for this chapter, namely the best way for the West to prevail in this confrontation, I shall confine myself largely to addressing military means. However, let me say that meeting the challenges of the confronters is much more than a military matter. We need to be properly Clausewitzian in our approach to this problem. Without the right political, cultural, social and economic policies in place, military means will prove futile. Political leaders, civil servants, diplomats and business people therefore need to be continually thinking about better ways to reduce the dangers that we all face by taking countervailing action in their own sectors, especially where these can lead to the elimination of the real grievances which dissident people often have in their dealings with the West.

Size, strain and a long-term burden

Turning now to the shaping of military forces for addressing the wars of protest and revenge, we have to face the fact that Western ground forces have become too small for the tasks ahead of them. The US Army and United States Marine Corps (USMC) are very thinly stretched to cover their responsibilities in Iraq and Afghanistan. The possibilities of further US commitments in the Middle East—especially to contain or influence Iran; and in Northeast Asia to deal with North Korea—raise the spectre of a return of 'the draft' in the United States. Before crossing that Rubicon, everything must be done to increase the deployable strength of the voluntarily enlisted forces, and this means better conditions of service and post-war benefits. A more obviously successful war would also be a strong recruiting agent.

America's allies will be just as loath to introduce conscription in order to provide expeditionary forces to assist those of the United States. These allies also have to be concerned about declining public support for US policies abroad, especially where these involve war. The prospect exists that a large number of potential US allies may choose either not to assist their alliance leader or to limit their assistance to a token form. This factor in turn will feed internal divisions within the United States which have been growing in recent years. It could become increasingly difficult for the United States to provide the essential Western leadership in this conflict should an even higher proportion of the military burden fall on the American people.

At present, and in the near future, the US Government is going to require more military resources to commit in troubled areas with possibly fewer allies contributing effective forces. This crunch could well coincide with a period in which public opinion in the United States will be more critical of Presidential policies of foreign intervention. Turning back to the early 1970s, when a similar set of factors finally bit into Richard Nixon's policy in Vietnam, he had to relent and withdraw from the conflict. He was fortunately able to do so without dire consequences for the American position in the world, because Vietnam and its neighbours (Laos and Cambodia) were indeed marginal to American interests. Should US President George W. Bush, or more likely his successor, face the same set of forces both in the United States itself and among its natural friends and allies, the situation will be much more serious than in 1975.

The Middle East should not now be left to become a sanctuary for insurgents and international terrorists. They would then be able to generate the capacity to become a threat of major proportions to the United States, including the acquisition and possibly the use of nuclear weapons. They would have a large home base for making bombs and rockets. They would not be short of funds or manpower. The dissidents would acquire a significant direct influence on the supply of oil and gas to world markets and hence a powerful lever on the economies of most countries. If the insurgents were allowed to succeed in turning Iraq into such chaos that the United States had to withdraw, their success would probably have a major impact on the growth of radicalism among Islamic peoples—both in the Middle East and further abroad. But unless they are dealt with much more effectively than the insurgents have been in Iraq to date, the global security situation for the United States and its closest friends will deteriorate seriously. A great deal depends therefore on improving the quality and effectiveness of US and allied forces in dealing with insurgencies in critical parts of the world.

Operational methods

Let me now return to the nature and training of appropriate military forces for meeting these challenges. There is a spirited debate underway within the armed forces of most countries that have had to conduct operations against hostile terrorists, insurgents, and government-led forces over the past several years. There are very few military personnel who deny the need for extensive change and reform. They do exist of course, but more generally the debate is between radical reformers and those who believe that the system is more constrained than the radicals accept or who are not sufficiently perceptive to see the requirements for change. As is to be expected, the debate is at its most visible within the US Army and USMC. I would like to draw attention to the draft *US Army Field Manual 3-24*, issued by Lieutenant Generals David Petraeus, US Army, and James Amos, USMC.[4] The doctrines enunciated in this draft are very much in the right direction and are based on hard lessons learned in Iraq, as well as on experience from Vietnam. I would also like to pay tribute to the work of Lieutenant Colonel John Nagl, especially for his book *Counterinsurgency Lessons from Malaya and Vietnam: Learning to Eat Soup with a Knife*,[5] and his recent article 'A better war in Iraq',[6] and to the publications of Dr Carter Malkasian of the Center for Naval Analyses, who has spent three tours in Iraq with the USMC.[7] The US armed forces are not the only ones caught up in the debate. These thoughts are relevant also to America's allies and most are grappling with their implications. I think it fair to say that the British and Australian Armies are higher up the learning curve than most.

The *first requirement* is to equip the military better to relate closely with the people they are trying to help. Given that the long-term aim of the campaigns in Iraq and Afghanistan is to establish secure, stable, democratic states, the personnel of the intervening forces have to engage in a great deal of close interaction (at the level of soldier to soldier, soldier to policeman and soldier to civilian) of the most subtle and multifaceted kind. Successful intervention in a major war of insurgency and counterinsurgency requires the cultural barriers between interveners and those they are trying to help—especially those of language, religion, social mores, knowledge of history, geography and the local economy—to be eroded substantially as obstacles to the development of trust, mutual confidence and straightforward human regard and friendship.

Before soldiers can be committed to the task of assisting local people and parties to reshape their societies, they need to know a lot about the people they are trying to assist. They must be able to understand them and their institutions, respect them, communicate with them and win their trust and respect in return. Not every soldier needs to be a foreign linguist, but quite a number have to be. Every patrol going out on a mission where it might come into contact with the local community needs an interpreter, and it will be very helpful if most officers and senior non-commissioned officers acquire at least the capacity to enter into an informal exchange with the indigenous populace. All personnel should know some history of the people being assisted, their way of life, culture, religion and special attributes such as attitudes towards other groups and parties within their own country. Intervening soldiers need to be able to spend some spare time with local people socially without making spectacles of themselves. They need to be able to offer local people practical assistance towards reaching their own objectives and to compensate for whatever disadvantages the foreign military presence inevitably brings in its wake, from road congestion and dust through to occupation of precious land.

If the interveners cannot successfully achieve this degree of contact, they leave no contest for the local insurgents who will achieve their own close contact by default if not by merit. It is of little use to pick up and transport to an operational theatre young Westerners whose only contact with the local people is off the end of a weapon or from inside a vehicle while the locals are outside on foot. Similarly, once duty is over soldiers should not always return to 'Computerville' and attach themselves to their personal laptops and email, which simply shut them off from the people they are meant to be helping. They must have some social contact with the locals if they are to have a chance of winning their support and cooperation. They must therefore have the necessary knowledge for starting a mutually supportive relationship and the linguistic and social skills necessary for maintaining it.

The *second requirement* is excellent intelligence. We have a tendency in Western armed forces to become too dependent upon the information which comes down the chain of command. It is copious. It is often technologically derived, a strength with which the enemy has difficulty competing. But, it is often irrelevant by the time that operational officers see it because it is out of date. In this kind of war, there is no substitute for local intelligence. Units at battalion and company level need to be able to collect information on their local setting, the people in it, likely targets of enemy action and what the enemy is doing by way of reconnaissance and planning. Intelligence officers need to be able to give their commanders a reasonably accurate forecast of what the enemy intends to do over the next week or two. They will not be able to do this without building local intelligence networks, and then cultivating, extending and protecting them.

A *third requirement* is the development of a very discriminating approach to the enemy. Given all the factors at work against an intervening force, they cannot afford to be wasting precious time and effort by chasing the most obvious, but not the most important, parts of the enemy's forces. A common mistake in the Vietnam War was to focus on the enemy main force battalions and regiments while paying less attention to the well-concealed local Viet Cong cadre personnel, who slipped in and out of villages and organised their own supply of intelligence, resources and people while spreading the news from the Viet Cong perspective and attending as far as possible to the local inhabitants' needs. One village cadre man was generally worth 10 in the main force in terms of effectiveness in the political struggle. In Iraq and Afghanistan, there has also been a tendency to focus on meeting force with force while infiltrators do real damage beneath the surface.

A *fourth requirement* is civilian skills. Troops fighting an insurgency need more than just their military skills. Some need to know how to get an electrical generator running, how to purify water supplies, or even how to maintain houses, schools and hospitals. The local people caught in an operational area will have needs, some of which will be due simply to poverty or the ineffectiveness of the governmental system that they have been living under, but their key facilities are also likely to suffer battle damage. The intervening force needs to be able to help rehabilitate those villages and towns that are not extensively damaged, thereby maintaining its own base of support among the local inhabitants.

This fourth requirement helps to create awareness of a need for a *fifth requirement*: to be reluctant to use fire power. It is all too easy to kill and wound people and create lasting enmity and disapproval among the people whose support is most necessary for the success of the operation. All ranks need to be taught the consequences for local families who lose a member or two, or the potential for wounds to have literally crippling results which last for the lifetimes of those suffering them. Unless troops are highly disciplined, there is a natural tendency when under fire to over-react. Our instincts are to hit back hard and fast. They have to be held strongly in check. The watchword for counterinsurgency is restraint—the use of minimal force. Under-reaction is better than over-reaction. These thoughts apply to indigenous property as much as to local people. The buildings are not ours, troops sometimes feel, so what does it matter? Drive the tank through a house or shop and even flatten a mosque if there might be enemy within. A little of this kind of behaviour goes a very long way in terms of alienating the local population, not least because these amenities are precious, even life-saving to them, and often cannot be replaced easily or satisfactorily.

Sixth, it is essential to develop a light touch even when carrying out suppressive operations against a well-armed, determined enemy. A cordon and search is better than an air attack. Some consideration needs to be given to the feeding and accommodation of local people in areas of operations where their normal lives have been disrupted. Operations into villages and towns are often a good opportunity to offer some medical or dental treatment to the locals. Roads and bridges are necessary for access to markets and the supply of essential civilian goods. A foreign intervening force which does not pay proper attention to this side of the war will soon be irrevocably on the wrong side of local public opinion. A light approach often requires more soldiers and police than a heavy-footed one. Forces need to be designed with this requirement in mind rather than having a lean personnel structure heavily reliant on technology for surveillance, warning, detection and destruction. These are too indiscriminate for effective counterinsurgency operations. It is often better if soldiers can move on foot rather than all being in vehicles. Operations should be carried out by closely linked small teams rather than by massed forces.

Seventh, it has to be kept in mind that the ultimate aim in this kind of operation is to be able to go home and leave the former theatre of conflict peacefully in the hands of a local government supported by capable police and military forces. The intervening force has to raise the local forces to a level of proficiency and motivation whereby they can assume the main burden of keeping the peace and implementing the policy of their government. This is a difficult, demanding and usually very protracted process for both sides. Unless it is tackled from the outset, and given a continuing high priority, it is easy to build a situation which may seem promising and stable, but which instead collapses as soon as the intervening force has started its withdrawal.

Eighth, it is not only a matter of training the local military and police forces. Intervening soldiers need to be able to work well with their foreign allies and partners, and they also have to know how to cooperate with other local government agencies and international non-governmental organisations. In all of these relationships there will be opportunities to learn from others as well as to impart lessons and give practical help. This all requires knowledge of other agencies and forces and frequent contact with them.

Ninth, account must be taken of the fact that outcomes in war can be influenced by perceptions and information. In counterinsurgency, where individual and group opinions are major determining elements in the success or failure for each side, particular attention has to be paid to building and maintaining support by public explanation and analysis of what is occurring in the theatre of operations. Communication techniques have to be developed by intervening forces, both forward to the local people among whom they are working and rearwards to their own governments and media representatives. Responsibility for effective communications has to be delegated widely and therefore a large number of Service personnel, including most officers, need training in effective public communication—both directly through their own words and indirectly by intelligent use of the media. In a protracted war, the battles for public opinion both in the theatre of operations and within the polities of the intervening powers are much more influential than in a shorter conflict.

Tenth, and finally, the politicians (who will be the ultimate commanders of the respective armed forces involved in these conflicts) will also need some special training and development—both through their own experience and learning from that of others. With few exceptions, the West does not suffer from weak leadership at present. It does however suffer from inexperienced and often gullible leaders who neither understand the limitations of their own armed forces nor know when they are being sold an unrealistically optimistic bill of goods by their ministerial colleagues and their military and civilian advisers. The example of the Bush Administration's conduct of Operation *Iraqi Freedom* in 2003 should be recalled frequently as a classically inept way in which to launch and conduct a major military operation. Sadly, it will provide professors of the history of war with a spectacular case study for generations to come. Fortunately that was merely the beginning. What is most important in wars is how they end. We are on notice: lift the standard of our game or we will be bogged down while political will is sapped by dissent at home and weakness around the world. We should have a much better security outlook than is presently the case. Much will depend on how well we absorb and apply the lessons that are spelled out by draft *US Army Field Manual 3-24*, and other forward thinkers such as Colonel Nagl and Dr Malkasian, as we reshape and train our armed forces in future.

ENDNOTES

[1] Amy Belasco, *The Cost of Iraq, Afghanistan, and Other Global War on Terror Operations Since 9/11, CRS Report for Congress*, Congressional Research Service, 14 March 2007, Summary page, available at <http://www.fas.org/sgp/crs/natsec/RL33110.pdf>, accessed 24 October 2007.

[2] White House, *Fact Sheet: Global Initiative to Combat Nuclear Terrorism*, 15 July 2006, available at <http://www.whitehouse.gov/news/releases/2006/07/print/20060715-3.html>, accessed 24 October 2007.

[3] White House, *Fact Sheet: Global Initiative to Combat Nuclear Terrorism*, 15 July 2006. For further details on container security, see 'CSI: Container Security Initiative', US Customs and Border Protection, US Department of Homeland Security, available at <http://www.cbp.gov/xp/cgov/border_security/international_activities/csi/>, accessed 24 October 2007.

[4] David H. Petraeus and James F. Amos, FM 3-24, MCWP 3-33.5, *Counterinsurgency*, Department of the Army and Department of the Navy, Washington DC, December 2006, available at <http://www.fas.org/irp/doddir/army/fm3-24.pdf>, accessed 24 October 2007.

[5] John A. Nagl, *Counterinsurgency Lessons from Malaya and Vietnam: Learning to Eat Soup with a Knife*, Praeger Publishers, Westport, CT, 30 October 2002.

[6] John A. Nagl, 'A better war in Iraq: Learning counterinsurgency and making up for lost time', *Armed Forces Journal*, August 2006, pp. 22–28, available at <http://www.armedforcesjournal.com/2006/08/1931298/>, accessed 24 October 2007.

[7] See, for example, Carter Malkasian, 'Signaling Resolve, Democratization, and the First Battle of Fallujah', *Journal of Strategic Studies*, vol. 29, no. 3, June 2006, pp. 432–52; and Carter Malkasian, 'The Role of Perceptions and Political Reform in Counterinsurgency: The Case of Western Iraq, 2004–05', *Small Wars and Insurgencies*, vol. 17, no. 3, September 2006, pp. 367–94.

Chapter 4
The Rise of China: History as Policy

Wang Gungwu

The topic of this chapter is 'the rise of China' from the perspective of 'history as policy' and, as an historian, I am tempted to tell you of the many rises (and falls) of China over the past three millennia. I will, however, resist that temptation. Taking the long view, this China is not rising from its lowest ever position in its history; nor has it risen to anywhere near its highest position when it was perhaps the richest country in the world. Yet, the speed of the recent rise is unprecedented and China cannot turn to its history for help where its economic development is concerned.

How does one measure a 'rise' of this nature? We have seen dramatic figures that show how the Chinese economy grew by an average of about 10 per cent annually for the past 27 years. When compared with the peak periods of development of Germany and Japan, first in the nineteenth century and then again since the end of the Second World War, such a growth rate is not the highest. All the same, the figures are exceptional for a centrally planned economy transiting towards a market economy. It is this astonishing feature that first attracted attention. Today, the world has gone beyond that to acknowledge that China is marching towards becoming a major economic power. Moreover, given its vast land and population, plus its ability to produce and mobilise skilled manpower quickly, there are expectations that China will continue to grow at high rates for decades to come. The major questions are whether the leaders are ready to initiate political reforms that could trigger even greater changes in Chinese social and cultural life, and whether their failure to do so would sharply reverse the growth rates.

China has now taken its place as a nation in a world of nations. At the heart of this current rise are the experiences of several transformations from an imperial civilisation. China experienced centuries as an emperor-state before evolving into a republican party-state set up by revolutions; and this party-state has the job of shaping a modern nation-state. By this latest transformation, it not only has its own history to fall back on but also the histories of many other nations. The more China opens up to the world, the more world history will influence its policies. In this chapter, I shall focus on three examples—one from China's own history, one from outside previous Chinese experience, and one that illustrates China's creative merging of several histories to serve its current purpose.

The Lessons of History: Imperial China's Continental Focus

China was a continental empire that rose midway up the Yellow River and from the edge of the steppes of Central Asia. Over 2000 years, the empire moved eastwards—including down the other major river, the Yangtze—until its centres were located at the delta regions of both river systems. Although it did eventually build a naval force that boasted the strongest fleet in the world by the fifteenth century, the empire never deviated from its continental commitment. The simple fact was that its really dangerous enemies had always come overland (from the north and west) and certainly never by sea. As a result, the interplay of overland and maritime concerns has always been unbalanced and most Chinese rulers never took naval power seriously. Thus, despite the several defeats by maritime powers in the nineteenth century, it took the Chinese half a century to pay any attention to rebuilding its navy. Even then, they were so helpless at sea for most of the twentieth century that naval capabilities had no role in determining the decisive victory of the Communist Party in 1949.

Here history plays a dual role. It is a burdensome reality that determines the mindset for long periods of time and history, but it could also be interpreted selectively and utilised to induce policy changes. The latter aspect taught Chinese leaders to pay closer attention to the sea while the former continues to inhibit thinking about how best to use maritime power in the most effective way. The story of the debates about the development of the Chinese Navy is too long to relate here. Suffice to say that continental strategies still dominate thinking and place constraints on China's ideas about power projection. Such strategies have stopped China from embarking on the kind of global commitment that the model of British maritime power presented. The Chinese are prepared to leave it to the United States to emulate that. Instead, they have concentrated on land-based nuclear and missile weaponry that would enable them to defend themselves against all kinds of aggression. As for naval force, it is enough to limit that to what would be essential to prevent Taiwan from being used by forces hostile to China's interests. In short, here China's own history has been both a constraint and a reality check and, as far as I can comprehend, the Chinese have examined their historical experiences to good effect.

The Lessons of History: How Other Empires Rose and Fell

My second example arises from lessons learnt from other people's histories, especially those of modern national empires. Chinese leaders have been studying the emergence of the nation-states in Western Europe for a long time now, and noted how many of them were established when earlier empires disintegrated (the classic case of the Netherlands in the seventeenth century has been compared with the United States as the first new nation created out of the British empire). Of particular relevance to China was that some nation-states had expanded to create their own national empires by the nineteenth century. The success of the Dutch, the British and the French set the standards of modern imperial success, and later nation-states (like Germany) so admired them that they set out to build their own national empires.

In Asia, closely emulating both the German and British empires, the Japanese followed suit. The Chinese are well aware that the later entrants to imperial rivalry and the contest for territory were more urgently aggressive than those that existed before them. However, they also note how others are today using the Germany and Japan analogies to speculate about China's nationalist future, and they have been prepared to counter such analogies by policies and actions that would render such comparisons unjustified. Some recent examples are China's self-conscious use of phrases like 'peaceful rise', 'peaceful development', and 'social harmony' as ultimate national goals. One might also include the new Confucius Institute program that emulates the British Council, Alliance Française and Goethe Institute, which are symbols of post-imperial efforts to dilute traditional notions of power projection.

That is one side of the coin. The other side derives from the history of new and smaller nation-states being created out of failed and declining empires, something that larger nation-states and successful empires had encouraged. The best examples were the Austro-Hungarian and Ottoman empires that many Chinese leaders carefully studied. Some of the new entities ended by becoming colonies of other empires—notably those of Britain, France and Russia. Yet there were also examples of the old imperial cores themselves becoming residual states, like that of Austria and, even more strikingly, that of modern Turkey. Decades later, this was repeated with the defeat of Germany and Japan, followed afterwards by Britain, France, Netherlands, Portugal and, after 1990, Soviet Russia. In each case, an empire more or less retreated back to the original nation-state.

China saw early in the twentieth century that this same fate could befall imperial China if empires like Russia, Japan and Britain each had their way. Japan went the furthest by detaching Taiwan and Manchuria and trying to control several Chinese provinces as parts of the Japanese empire. Russia helped to establish an independent Mongolia and failed in Xinjiang, but British India seemed only half-hearted about recognising Tibet as a distinct polity. China was fortunate. By pursuing their own, often competing interests, the Great Powers ultimately accepted Chinese sovereignty over territories defined by Qing imperial borders. The end of the Second World War confirmed those borders when Taiwan and Manchuria were returned to China. In that way, China was an unusual example where the nation-state-to-be was more or less the previous empire—the Manchu empire becoming the Chinese nation, one might say.

China's rise today is tied to its ability to make this emperor-state equal to China the nation-state. Most members of the United Nations that recognise the People's Republic of China have accepted this, but debates about Taiwan, Tibet and the Uighur cause in Xinjiang remain. Such discord reflects shifting views about the security of post-Second World War boundaries. Of course, some of these views were by-products of the Cold War that used all varieties of nationalisms and localisms against international communism. But the threats to Chinese ideas of its national borders remain. Soviet interventions in Hungary and Czechoslovakia had troubled Mao Zedong, and the so-called Brezhnev doctrine was fiercely rejected at the time. More recently, China is not alone in watching the dismemberment of Yugoslavia and the invasion of Iraq with apprehension. An age that threatens regime change, when the supposed sanctity of a country's sovereignty can no longer be taken for granted, calls for close attention to the lessons of other peoples' histories. The Chinese know that these lessons could apply to China itself. If such threats persist, it could feed into the nationalist agenda of those who place China's unification and survival above other goals. That would be a severe test of what the Chinese might have learnt about the need to contain heightened calls for robust nationalism in a suspicious neighbourhood, and to do it before that became too difficult for the leaders to control.

The Lessons of History: Preserving the Empire in the Modern Era

I turn now to my third example where China's own history and the histories of others seem to converge. I refer to perceptions of what the term 'status quo' might mean. The Chinese have learnt how the term was used against them when China is compared with Otto von Bismarck's Germany as a non-status quo power (Japan since the Meiji was also described in a similar way). What does that mean for China? In Chinese history, the idea of status quo can be seen in the famous opening lines of *Romance of the Three Kingdoms* (a thirteenth–fourteenth century classical Chinese text attributed to Luo Guanzhong), which states that periods of division must end with unification, and periods of unity must end in division. To most Chinese, division and reunification invariably alternated. One learnt to live with that rhythm of change in political entities as a norm. In that context, the idea of sovereignty as a permanent condition that could be guaranteed by international law was new and something they came to value as a useful way to defend China's national rights. Can the two ideas be reconciled?

When China was described by the United States as a non-status quo power where Taiwan was concerned, its leaders were unsure what to do or say. Their protestations that the Taiwan issue was an internal matter—an extension of a civil war—went unheeded. A confrontation over Taiwan that pits US guarantees and national credibility against China's integrity and national honour would be very dangerous indeed. The American and European moral high ground raised the historical analogy of 'non-status quo' power—a rising China could be like Germany and Japan. The Chinese have since been concerned enough to pay special attention to the international system operating today to underline their commitment to the status quo. They have made great efforts to show consistency in supporting existing positions across the board. They also wish to affirm that they are content with such a state of affairs, where most nations recognise the People's Republic of China as the only China and that there is no nation called Taiwan. That way, they can argue that anyone who seeks to change this situation would be the 'non-status quo' power and not China. Moreover, the Anti-Secession Act shows that China is prepared to go to war to preserve the status quo. According to the pendulum formula that division followed by unification is the inevitable norm, the Chinese can still contemplate the time when China's unification is generally accepted.

There are many uses of history. I have selected some examples to suggest that, while the Chinese do not believe that history repeats itself, they have always been keen to use historical analogies in their policy analyses, irrespective of how far back in time they elect to go to draw those lessons. This is not necessarily backward-looking. Chinese practice shows that their 'timeless' approach, which sought the most helpful and relevant examples to support their current cause or guide their choice of policy, has been used with care, and often with practised skill. Whether they decided their policies first and then found historical examples to strengthen their case, or whether they searched the records to look for lessons that would be most appropriate for deciding on policy is not always obvious. That all rulers and their officials resorted to the use of history, however, is abundantly clear. Such dependence on analogies from the past often led Chinese elites to act conservatively. This could prove dangerous if it meant that they worked exclusively within their own historical boxes instead of being encouraged to think outside them. There is ample evidence that modern leaders have learnt, sometimes painfully, to adapt quickly to changing circumstances and to use historical analogies more creatively. When they succeed in doing so, it confirms that the practice of closely linking history and policy has served them well.

Chapter 5

Whither the United States and Unipolarity?

Ron Huisken

In terms of weight and influence, or power, America can be said to have sustained a strong, positive trajectory for well over a century.

Washington has presided over the world's largest economy since around 1900. The US share of the world economy ranged from 38 per cent in 1900 to 22 per cent in 1980, rising again to around 25 per cent at the present time. Indeed, for many of the last 100 years, the US economy has been at least twice as big as any other in the world. Today, the second-ranked economy, that of Japan, is about one-third the size of the United States. Moreover, the US economy has always been characterised by muscle and tone as much as by sheer mass, growing as much through gains in productivity as through increases in the quantity of capital and labour.[1] Moreover, the United States has repeatedly demonstrated the capacity to translate this economic weight into decisive military power: for example, by developing its navy from unranked in the 1880s to second-ranked by 1907, awesomely so following the attack on Pearl Harbor in 1941, and more or less continuously following the onset of the Cold War.

America's stature, and the broadly positive regard for it across the world, grew continuously alongside its hard power. To illustrate, in his *The Economic Consequences of the Peace*, a ruthless dissection of the Treaty of Versailles that followed the end of the First World War, John Maynard Keynes observed of America's economic aid in the immediate postwar period, that 'never was a nobler work of disinterested goodwill carried through with more tenacity and sincerity and skill, and with less thanks either asked or given'.[2]

Similarly, at the end of the Second World War, Washington's behaviour continued to defy the lessons of history, to display a light touch that belied its preponderance. It was a colossus with huge military forces, a monopoly in nuclear weapons and an economy that, unlike every other belligerent, was literally bursting at the seams. The United States now resolved to have a bigger hand in rebuilding Europe than it had considered desirable in 1918. The idealism of the United Nations, the far-sighted largess of the Marshall Plan, the early and not particularly popular resolve to make Germany and Japan key stakeholders in the new international system, and the willingness, under NATO, to assume very demanding security obligations to Western Europe even as it continued to demobilise its wartime forces, were all decisively important but gave rise to no anxieties about disproportionate power.

Washington seemed always to manage to be both unmistakably the dominant power and to convey the impression that it had no instincts to take command and to actually exploit fully the power it possessed. Combining power and popularity was Washington's distinctive trick. The United States came to be admired, respected and considered indispensable. Its dominance was occasionally resented, but it was not feared and certainly never inspired countervailing coalitions.

It has always been important to Americans to stand apart from the pack of major powers of the present and the recent past. They had defined themselves in contrast to these powers and bristled at suggestions that the United States had become simply another manifestation of the imperial powers of the past. As America's strategic weight grew, and its presence around the world became more ubiquitous, the characterisations that it was an empire in all but name became harder to counter. It was harder still after 1945 but, as Niall Ferguson has written, the intellectual dilemma was rationalised by contending that the United States might be postured like an imperial power but that the threat from the Soviet Union, an entity that was even more unmistakably imperial in structure and intent, allowed no alternative.[3]

Washington continued to build its reputation through the tumultuous years of the Cold War, despite Vietnam and the tag that it was the pace-setter in the nuclear arms race. Thus, at the end of the Cold War in 1991, when the United States again stood starkly exposed as the highest form of predator the world had ever seen, its 41st, and perhaps most understated, president in 50 years could observe unremarkably that 'they (the rest of the world) trust us to do what is right'.

When the Soviet Union abruptly conceded defeat in the Cold War, America was nonplussed. Georgi Arbatov, an advisor to Mikhail Gorbachev, was being more than usually perceptive when he told Americans in a letter to the *New York Times* in 1987 that the Soviet Union's final unfriendly act would be to deprive the United States of an enemy. But George H.W. Bush, pursuant to his frank acknowledgement that he was not attracted to the 'vision thing', had no discernable appetite to think grandly about what the United States could do with its 'unipolar moment' in the post-Cold War world. Instead, he focused closely on unravelling the central front of the Cold War and reversing Iraq's invasion of Kuwait.

Similarly, President Bill Clinton's focus was the economy and domestic renewal. In the foreign policy arena, the umbrella objective became 'democratic enlargement', but there was no drive to craft a proactive policy architecture to deliver such an outcome. Broadly speaking, the first two American Presidents of the post-Cold War era managed to sustain the knack of making America's disproportionate power accepted as benign and reassuring, characteristics that added immeasurably to its huge stock of hard and soft power.

Walter Lippmann may have put his finger on America's ability to be ominously powerful while not being regarded as an ominous power when he observed, in 1926, that 'our imperialism is more or less unconscious' and that the United States was an 'empire in denial'.[4] Yet conveying the impression of indifference to pre-eminence of imperial proportions was neither accident nor artifice. It had everything to do with America's system of governance, the powerful attachment to checks and balances on authority at all levels. America's founding fathers operated from a remarkably honest and realistic self-assessment. They recognised that Americans, themselves included, would be as prone as leadership groups anywhere and at any point in history to gather as much power as they could get and ultimately expose the union to the abuse of that power. They therefore resolved to design a system of governance that would guard against this basic human trait and ensure that America's history would remain distinct from that observed in all other states. The way America went about its business internally provided the strongest possible reassurance that this awesome power would always remain pointed roughly in the direction of the ideals of life, liberty and the pursuit of happiness as enshrined in its *Declaration of Independence*.

Still, even within an administration that sought, with the support of public opinion, a relatively low profile internationally, events conspired continuously to frustrate that preference. There were several dimensions to this phenomenon, all linked to the fact that the United States now stood exposed as never before in its history as the colossus on the world stage. On the one hand, ever more of the world's troubles and dilemmas found their way to Washington's door, not least the raft of ethnic hatreds that resurfaced after the Cold War. On the other hand, America became ever more exclusively the target of choice of rogue states and terrorists. And finally, even an administration committed to keeping the United States in the company of other states, and to not flaunting its disproportionate weight, began to appreciate that, particularly in the military arena, it did have something approaching absolute power, namely a unilateral capacity to secure a desired military outcome in almost any location and to a point rather high up the scale of conflict.

The Clinton Administration routinely stressed the limits to US capacities and declined being cast as the world's policeman, but it also developed assessments and policy settings little removed from those which we see today. In a Cable News Network television forum in May 1994, Clinton isolated Iraq, Iran and

North Korea as the key threats on the WMD front, stressed that the United States 'will not hesitate to act alone if necessary', and spoke more positively of 'working in partnership with other nations' (in effect, 'coalitions of the willing') than doing so through the United Nations.[5] In an address to a joint sitting of the Australian Parliament in November 1996, he spoke of a 'nexus of new threats—terrorists, rogue states, international criminals, drug traffickers' and of 'taking the fight to the terrorists and drug traffickers' from a standpoint of 'zero tolerance'.[6] By his State of the Union address in January 1998, this nexus of new threats had become an 'unholy axis'.[7]

In sum, the Clinton Administration saw a progressively sharper focus on irregular threats at the margin of the international system as the most immediate challenges to the order that Washington presided over. At the same time, while seeking relief from the broad security obligations it had carried through the Cold War, the administration declined to decrease Pentagon funding beyond the 25–30 per cent cut through about 1995 put in place by its predecessor, with the result that, by the late 1990s, the US defence budget began to approach 50 per cent of world military expenditure. Perhaps most importantly, the Clinton Administration presided over the longest sustained boom in US history, so that even a relatively huge outlay on defence became, at less than 3.5 per cent of GDP, quite inoffensive in economic and, more particularly, political terms.

The Neoconservative Thesis

If President George H.W. Bush was uncomfortable with the 'vision thing', preoccupied with tidying up after the Cold War and with Iraq, and disposed (out of fiscal responsibility) to retaining 'no more than the forces we need', and President Bill Clinton similarly disposed to leading from within the community of states, a radically different response to the end of the Cold War had been developed in the Pentagon in 1989–92. The key players were Richard Cheney, Paul Wolfowitz, Lewis Libby, Zalmay Khalilzad and, initially at least, Colin Powell. It began as a tactical response to the clamour from Congress and the general public for a major 'peace dividend' (of the order of 50 per cent of the Pentagon budget), but developed into a grand design for a new global order under US command based, pre-eminently, on unassailable US military superiority. A first cut in 1990 offered the President a fairly traditional package of arguments—America's international obligations, hedging against a revival of Soviet power, the challenge of containing the spread of WMD and other regional dangers like dictators and terrorism—to counter the pressure for a simplistic 50 per cent peace dividend. President George H.W. Bush endorsed the package and used it (on the very night, 2 August 1990, that Iraq invaded Kuwait) to propose cuts in active duty military personnel and military expenditure of 25 per cent and 30 per cent respectively over five years. But the President and his White House advisors revealed a mindset on America's role and the military power needed to perform that role (no more than necessary) that the policy elite in the Pentagon began to regard as ignorant of the lessons of history and of the dimensions of the opportunity that history had presented to the United States.

With Iraq defanged in February 1991 following the 1990–91 Persian Gulf War and the dissolution of the Soviet Union in December that same year, the clamour for deep cuts at the Pentagon resurfaced and the then US Secretary of Defense Richard Cheney directed a new effort to devise a coherent strategy to thwart this pressure. This further work was also carried out entirely within the Pentagon—there is no indication that, at the time or since, it was subject to the usual whole-of-government review—and involved no small element of insubordination given the letter and spirit of the President's *National Security Strategy* statement of August 1991. This document called for 'deliberate reductions to no more than the forces we need to defend our interests and meet our global responsibilities'.[8] This may explain the leaking of a draft of the Pentagon strategy to the *New York Times* in March 1992, and the President's forceful disavowal of it.

An important inspiration for the Pentagon strategy was the view that the Reagan Administration, in aligning US foreign and security policy with America's values and ideals, had recorded spectacular accomplishments, hastening the end of the Cold War and vastly increasing America's influence worldwide in both strategic and ideological terms. This assessment of the Ronald Reagan years underpinned the neoconservative thesis that America's rise to primacy had suppressed the instability and conflict that was endemic to both Europe and Asia prior to 1945. It seemed to follow that, if the United States vacated this position or sought to share it with others, the probable outcome would be a revival of the accident-prone 'balance of power' system that existed through the first decades of the twentieth century.

Despite his President's disapproval, Cheney privately praised his team for discovering a 'new rationale' to define America's role in the world. Somewhat more surprising is that Cheney managed to release a revised and softened version of this strategy as an official document from the Secretary of Defense just days before Bill Clinton was inaugurated as President in January 1993, placing it on the public record but ensuring its almost complete obscurity.[9]

The Cheney strategy rehearsed the neoconservative thesis that 'it is not in our interests or those of other democracies to return to earlier periods in which multiple military powers balanced against one another in what passed for security structures while regional, or even global peace hung in the balance', but avoided the explicit proposition in earlier drafts that the United States should establish and maintain a military superiority so stark and overwhelming that no other states would even consider seeking to compete. Regionally, Cheney's document proposed that the US objective should be to preclude regional threats and challenges or hostile non-democratic powers from dominating regions of importance to the United States. Such a posture, it asserted, 'is not simply within our means: it is critical to our future security'. Rather presciently, Cheney argued that the US interest in future security challenges may seem less apparent, making public support problematic. To address this problem, the strategy called for the capacity to respond decisively to regional crises, 'to win quickly and with minimum casualties'.

The Pentagon strategy remained buried until September 2000 when the conservative think tank Project for a New American Century revived its main premise as a possible blueprint for US security policy under a Republican president. When the team that had crafted the strategy reassembled under President George W. Bush, together with the like-minded Donald Rumsfeld, it was to become clear that their attachment to it was undiminished. Whether President Bush was fully briefed on the strategy, and endorsed it, is uncertain. It is clear however that no whiff of the doctrine surfaced in the election campaign. To the contrary, the election strategy responded to public sentiments favouring fewer rather than increased obligations and responsibilities abroad. Thus, in an oft-quoted remark, Bush argued in the second presidential debate on 11 October 2000 that a more 'humble' America would attract more respect.[10]

For the foreign and security policy leadership group under President George H.W. Bush, the United States under President Bill Clinton had dithered its way through the first decade of the post-Cold War era but, remarkably and fortunately, had emerged even better positioned, especially in economic terms, to implement its vision. And, as luck would have it, the United States had in its new president an individual with a near-perfect blend of personality traits to allow this vision to be endorsed as policy with absolute conviction. George W. Bush was poorly versed in international affairs and did not pretend to be eager to correct this gap in his experience. Indeed, recruiting the team of seasoned veterans, mostly from his father's administration, was characterised as a deliberate move to counter nervousness on this score. At the same time, the President was possessed—in part at least, many believe, because of his deep faith as a born-again Christian—of quite extraordinary qualities of self-confidence and a deep conviction that great things would be asked of him.

Even though the Bush campaign team had conspicuously avoided seeking a mandate for this new vision of the global role for the United States, it was taken forward at every opportunity provided by the relatively normal circumstances of the first half of 2001. The primacy of military power was particularly evident. Three weeks after his inauguration, Bush gave Defense Secretary Rumsfeld a mandate to embrace unreservedly the 'revolution in military affairs' and to transform the US armed forces to take the fullest advantage of these accumulated possibilities. In that context, the President made the sweeping declaration that 'the best way to keep the peace is to redefine war on our terms'.[11] In May 2001, having already declared that the United States would not ratify the nuclear test ban treaty, the President launched the expected move to abrogate the Anti-Ballistic Missile Treaty. The message to Russia here, and in the associated position that the United States would no longer 'negotiate' nuclear arms reductions but rather determine its requirements unilaterally, was that the United States would cast Russia off as even a symbolic co-manager of the central nuclear balance. The *Quadrennial Defense Review*, released on 1 October 2001 but completed prior to 11 September 2001, similarly had the Pentagon viewing the world as an undifferentiated battlespace and setting out its initial thinking on how the United States could bring decisive force to bear anywhere at very short notice. Of particular note was a scarcely-disguised focus on China, not least through the identification of a new region, the East Asia Littoral (the area from south of Japan, though Australia and into the Bay of Bengal) where the United States needed to develop its capacities to shape developments and conduct military operations. Alongside these prominent signals, Washington's somewhat contemptuous disavowal of the Kyoto Protocol, and its insistence on insulating US armed forces from the reach of the new International Criminal Court, strengthened further the impression that the United States was stepping away from the community of states, positioning itself to shape and manage the international order while divesting itself of constraints on how it could perform this function.

Normalcy, of course, came to an abrupt end on the morning of 11 September 2001. This utterly devastating yet devastatingly simple terrorist strike momentarily felled the most powerful state in the world. In the months and years that followed, senior administration figures would often respond to criticisms of or requests for explanations on policy developments with the simple contention that '11 September 2001 changed everything'. While there is a great deal of truth in this contention, there was at least one constant of importance to this analysis. The neoconservative grand strategy was not set aside until such time as this unfamiliar threat had been dealt with. To the contrary, the grand strategy was hitched to the new 'war on terror', a combination that was to befuddle political and strategic judgements and cause the United States to stumble badly on both fronts. At the time, however, this hitching probably looked irresistible to the skilled operators at the top of the Bush Administration. The terrorist attacks on 11 September 2001 had transformed the political landscape, essentially erasing the domestic political considerations that had mandated some caution in unveiling the new strategy.

By the end of 2001, the Bush Administration was pursuing two major security strategies: the 'war on terror', with its doctrine of pre-emption and the 'axis of evil' as its primary targets, and the grand strategy for a new global order founded on declared and accepted US pre-eminence. The latter strategy of course was still undisclosed. The world at large had certainly noted, and been concerned about, the newly imperious tone and style of US behaviour, but it had not yet traced the dots back to the Pentagon strategy. President Bush lifted the veil in mid-2002. In a West Point speech on 1 June 2002 he said:

> As we defend the peace, we also have an historic opportunity to preserve the peace. We have our best chance since the rise of the nation-state in the seventeenth century to build a world where the great powers compete in peace instead of prepare for war. The history of the last century, in particular, was dominated by a series of destructive national rivalries that left battlefields and graveyards across the earth. Germany fought France, the axis fought the allies, and then the East fought the West, in proxy wars and tense standoffs, against a backdrop of nuclear Armageddon.
>
> Competition between great nations is inevitable, but armed conflict is not. More and more, civilized nations find themselves on the same side—united by common dangers of terrorist violence and chaos. America has, and intends to keep, military strengths beyond challenge, thereby making the destabilizing arms races of other eras pointless, and limiting rivalries to trade and other pursuits of peace.[12]

This was a declaration of empire, an assertion that the United States was taking command. It assembled the starkest formulations of the key propositions advanced in the several iterations of the strategy crafted a decade earlier. The fact that it was in some substantial measure merely codifying reality was beside the point. Most of the world felt that it had not declared a vacancy and instinctively resisted the role which the United States seemed to be claiming for itself; not to mention being so summarily relegated to the second division. Resentment and concern about the new thinking in Washington, which had emerged prior to 11 September 2001 and then been swept aside in the aftermath of the terrorist attacks, now resurfaced as the Bush Administration insisted that its assessment of the terrorist phenomenon as an existential threat and its prescriptions for dealing with it, including regime change in Iraq, could not be contested. By March 2002, barely six months after the terrorist attacks, the most extraordinary 'coalition of the willing' that had assembled spontaneously around Washington was barely visible.

America's unique aura—those intangible qualities of respect, admiration and trust that added so immeasurably to its hard power, and which had been so painfully but magnificently accumulated over the preceding century—had been punctured.

America's dilemma was a real one. It was too powerful to easily blend in with the other powers. The neoconservative prescription was hardly the babbling of madmen, and was not without merit. Its most conspicuous flaw, perhaps, is that it sought to discredit and replace a system of global governance, namely the 'balance of power' system that had functioned after a fashion for several centuries up to 1945—that had been overtaken and was no longer a realistic alternative. In the world of the 1990s—with its nuclear weapons, resurgent interdependence from the priority attached to free trade since 1945, transformed by the information and communications revolutions, anticipating further sweeping transformation through the phenomenon of globalisation, and with most of the former practitioners of 'balance of power' politics wrapped up in the European Union—the neoconservative thesis might have been challenged as a process that arrived first at the preferred solution and then contrived to formulate the problem to make the package as compelling as possible.[13]

Tragically, however, the Bush Administration was clueless on the marketing of its proposed solution to this dilemma, let alone re-shaping its solution into a marketable product. Indeed, a rather strong case can be made that the authors of the solution saw marketing as a sign of weakness, a possible signal to others that the United States lacked the resolve to impose its vision. The President, it would appear, relished the newly black and white world of a United States at 'war' and was quite simply mesmerised by his authority as commander-in-chief.[14] He was not attracted to subtlety and nuance and took ownership of this second strategy, including the manner in which it should be presented, as readily as he had the global 'war on terror'.

Iraq became the issue that wobbled between the two security strategies in play in Washington in 2001–2003, a state of affairs that contributed very materially to the disastrous lead-up to the invasion (the dissipation of the post-11 September 2001 'coalition of the willing' and then the deep fissures within the Western alliance) and to the even more disastrous aftermath.

Regime change in Iraq had much more to do with the Pentagon strategy than with the 'war on terror'. It was seen as a move that would erase what was seen as a black mark on America's *curriculum vitae* as a power that finished what it started, while providing an enduring illustration of the fact that the United States had both the capacity and the will to impose its vision for international order in the future. Early in 2004, President Bush told Bob Woodward that he had been willing to be interviewed at length for the book *Plan of Attack*, because the book would have historic significance. That significance, in the President's view, lay in the fact that the military campaign against Iraq demonstrated that 'America has changed how you fight and win war, and therefore made it easier to keep the peace in the long run'.[15]

Although the case for action against Iraq was broad—the administration developed a veritable laundry list of reasons why it would be in the US interest—it lacked a concrete link to the attacks on 11 September 2001 and to the political window of opportunity for decisive action that the attacks had opened. Regime change in Iraq therefore had to be positioned as a priority in the 'war on terror'. When expectations and hopes that proof of Iraqi involvement in the attacks and/or of some form of strategic association with al Qaeda had to be abandoned, the administration selected WMD as the remaining rationale that was sufficiently focused and compelling to bring Congress and the public on side. As we now know, confirming this rationale proved surprisingly difficult, but Iraq simply had to have a demonstrable WMD program to serve the administration's purposes. The administration therefore found itself slipping into the manipulation and hyping of the intelligence at its disposal only to have the most obvious explanation for the difficulty confirmed after the invasion: Iraq had not possessed WMD for some time, and was not poised to re-acquire them.[16]

The same imperative, using Iraq to herald America's grand strategy, was also important in shaping how the United States conducted the invasion. Doing so with an extraordinary economy of force was critical to the strategic message and this objective was pursued with little regard for the advantages of having an overwhelming military presence for the purposes of occupation and stabilisation.

Thirdly, but related to this point, the window of opportunity to deal with Iraq was deemed to be so precious that the administration elected to minimise the risk that thinking through or planning for possible worst-case developments might reach the public or Congress. This literally meant undertaking hardly any work on the aftermath of the defeat of the Iraqi armed forces.[17] The result was that, after capturing Baghdad, US commanders in Iraq (with no guidance and a confused chain of command back to Washington) stood aside for what seemed like an eternity, dissipating the momentum of their military campaign. This left Iraqis wondering who, if anyone, had replaced Saddam Hussein, and gave those disposed to resist the occupation through insurgent operations a glimmer of hope.

Finally, as the potential enormity of their miscalculations began to sink in, penetrating and destroying the emergent insurgency became a matter of the utmost importance—essentially a matter of doing whatever it took to quell the threat. As the key lay in acquiring actionable intelligence on insurgents, this contributed rather directly, in my view, to the excesses at Abu Ghraib prison. This, together with the inevitably relentless stream of accidents and miscalculations involving Iraqi civilians when a lean top-end combat force is tasked to lighten its touch and engage in counterinsurgency operations, saw the United States lose all the moral high ground.

Iraq has been a catastrophe for the United States. It has in all likelihood intensified and prolonged the era of virulent terrorism; it has foreshortened America's 'unipolar moment'; it has made the United States more of an observer than a player in the wider geopolitical transformations underway; it may have introduced a new inclination toward isolationism within the American public which will narrow the foreign and security policy options for future administrations; and, by generating perceptions of disorder at the top of the international tree, it may have fuelled recklessness and brinkmanship on the part of a number of lesser players.

Looking back, it is hard to escape the conclusion that the abrupt transformation in the style of US engagement with the world—a transformation toward imperious, unilateral leadership—was decisive in triggering a reaction of profound disappointment among so many allies and friends, both old and new. This disappointment matured into a concern that the United States had slipped its moorings, that even its system of governance, so profoundly reassuring for so long, could be subverted and allow a clique in the executive branch to pursue an ideological vision that, although having broad roots in strands of American thinking, had been constructed wholly within the Pentagon and was skewed by an inordinate faith in the utility of military power.

If there was a decisive moment when America's allies and friends sensed that Washington had decided in favour of command rather than leadership, it probably came in the immediate aftermath of the 11 September 2001 attacks. At that moment, essentially the entire world set aside the concerns that had accumulated over the preceding eight months and assembled spontaneously around Washington to jointly confront the new menace of mass casualty terrorism. It was a stunning signal of solidarity, a reflection of the huge stock of respect and goodwill that the United States had accumulated over more than a century, and clear evidence that its centrality to international order and stability was universally appreciated. The Bush Administration, however, seemed scarcely to notice and insisted on an even clearer acknowledgement that the United States was in command. It issued an undifferentiated test to the world community at large—'you are either with us or you are with the terrorists'—and bristled at any quibbling about the strategy, tactics and priorities that it had decided to pursue in response. From late November 2001, perhaps even earlier in diplomatic circles, this included the decision that regime change in Iraq was a priority of the highest order; so high in fact that it pushed out full consolidation of deposing the Taliban regime in Afghanistan and finding Osama bin Laden.

Notwithstanding the tragedy of 11 September 2001, disappointment with the United States spread swiftly. Opinion polls across the world recorded sharp declines in positive attitudes toward the United States. Even governments that determined that they had powerful *realpolitik* reasons to stay with Washington confronted public sentiments to the contrary. And, although there was a great deal of activity to develop international cooperation and collaboration on the menace of terrorism, its effectiveness was diminished by these undercurrents of disappointment with and resentment towards US behaviour, and by the Bush Administration's ever more exclusive focus on Iraq. As Iraq degenerated over the course of 2002 into the issue of determining who was in charge and how that authority would be exercised, the split between America and a number of its strong allies and friends grew. The result, predictably, was an unhappy one. The United States demonstrated that it could act, but also that it had, for the first time, lost the capacity to attract followers.

The frontal challenge to stability and order that attacks like 11 September 2001 so clearly represented was now reinforced by resentment and disunity among the world's leading states, compounding perceptions of a 'world out of balance'—a condition that gave encouragement to jihadist groups, and probably also to actors like Iran and North Korea who perceived in this disunity at the top opportunities to challenge the interests of these powers in comparative safety.[18] More recently, the accelerating erosion of the Bush Administration's conservative support base has added a further dimension of uncertainty: with more than two years to run, what direction might this administration take in these circumstances, and what does it suggest about the inclinations of the next administration?

Looking Ahead

This chapter has argued that the explanation for the invasion of Iraq can be found in an extraordinary fusion of circumstances: the attacks on 11 September 2001; the power and conviction of a clique of officials with a grand vision for an era of American dominance; the personality of President George W. Bush; the conservative ascendancy within the United States, accompanied by rising religiosity; and the achievement of astonishing virtuosity in usable military power. These circumstances combined to allow the US system of checks and balances to be briefly overwhelmed, and for an action to proceed that, because it was viewed as a 'home run' on several fronts, was not critically second-guessed on any of them. The invasion of Iraq was at once an angry giant lashing out in shock at the impudence of the attacks on 11 September 2001 and supremely confident that it could now impose its grand vision more quickly and decisively than 'normal' circumstances might have allowed.

In the eyes of the world and in the eyes of a strong majority of its own citizens, the United States now stands diminished, its legitimacy as the world's pre-eminent state questioned more seriously than ever before. This legacy of the current Iraq War will not soon be erased and historians are very likely to characterise the 43rd president and his administration as the most damaging in the history of the republic.

Looking ahead to the more immediate future, I am inclined to be more optimistic than the views set out in this chapter might suggest. The reasons for this optimism are twofold. First, a deeply-ingrained capacity for the United States to self-correct and (eventually) align itself with basic norms and principles ranks amongst its greatest political strengths. The United States has a singular capacity to renew itself, to step away from a course of action and take a new path with scarcely a trace of baggage from, or embarrassment about, its past policies. This process could be said to be underway. In his second inaugural address and the State of the Union speech in January 2005, President Bush recast the goal of an end to tyranny in the world as an ideal. He said plainly that making America fully secure once more would be the work of 'generations'. And he acknowledged that this task was beyond the gift of the Pentagon alone. Similarly, the administration has become more cognisant of the value of partnerships and consensus, especially as regards Iran and North Korea, and the US State Department under Condoleezza Rice has been permitted to exercise its traditional skills in these arenas. While encouraging, these pointers could still be more in the nature of pragmatic adjustments to a transforming domestic political scene than evidence of a propensity to re-visit earlier policy settings and consider the need for significant recalibration. I would not expect this administration to be attracted to such a recalibration. Nor, perhaps, could it be credible if it tried. The sad and simple fact is that its legacy is wholly inseparable from Iraq, and it has no choice but to press on and hope for something resembling an honourable outcome.

The second reason for optimism is that, even in its diminished and chastened state, America's shoes are way too big to be filled by any other state or, indeed, any imaginable grouping of states. As the prevailing turmoil so strongly suggests, a United States that is confident, engaged and leading remains indispensable to the necessary modicum of order and stability in world affairs. Nor will this state of affairs become questionable for some time. Depending on your projection, and on the exchange rate used, the United States will remain the single largest economic entity in the world for at least another 20 years. Its capacity to bring overwhelming force to bear anywhere in the world, precisely and relentlessly, is likely to remain unmatched for even longer. The point becomes more compelling if one asks when another country might arise with a package of attributes competitive with that offered by the United States: economic strength; military prowess; technological vibrancy; an admired political system; a very marketable set of basic values and beliefs; an appealing culture; a magnificent tradition of leadership and so on. That prospect, it seems to me, lies well into the indefinite future. This suggests that most governments will be only too ready to respond positively to overtures from the United States for a new compact on the governance of world affairs.

The Bush Administration miscued tragically and dissipated a probably unique opportunity to have unipolarity both accepted as a reality and endorsed as an acceptable construct for global governance over the foreseeable future. As Coral

Bell has argued so persuasively (including in this volume), the United States should and, indeed, may now begin to look toward arrangements with the flavour of a 'concert of powers'. A stepping-stone in this direction could be something that a Chinese leader might be tempted to describe as 'unipolarity with democratic characteristics'. The primary vehicle for any new accommodation will surely have to be a joint resolve and a shared agenda to stop the spread of, and gradually wind back, the phenomenon of extremism.

This process will be neither easy nor certain. We cannot return to the *status quo ante*. Equally, however, given the US pronounced and comprehensive edge in strategic weight, no imaginable new construct for relations between the major powers in the decades immediately ahead will be unrecognisably different from the arrangements that have evolved since the end of the Cold War. Despite the belated but resounding step back toward the centre at the mid-term elections in November 2006, the impulses that have driven the United States during the past six years will not vanish in January 2009 when the Bush Administration completes its term. A further complication may be that certain other powers, notably China and (perhaps) Russia and India, probably have a rather different view today as compared to 2000 on how the world should work and of their proper role in the process. We might also consider whether we have applied unreasonable standards to the United States. We may have expected too much 'good international citizenship' from this extraordinary country, and will have to learn to cope with less as its degree of dominance of the international system stops growing and eventually starts to lessen. Whether there will be enough statesmanship in the relevant capitals to forge or to manoeuvre gradually towards a new *modus operandi* is an open question. In my view, over the short to medium term the odds appear reasonably favourable.

ENDNOTES

[1] These statistics are taken from Angus Maddison, *The World Economy: Volume 2: Historical Statistics*, Development Centre Studies, Organisation for Economic Cooperation and Development, Paris, 2003.

[2] John Maynard Keynes, *The Economic Consequences of the Peace*, Penguin Books, London, 1988 edition, p. 273.

[3] Niall Ferguson, *Colossus: The Rise and Fall of the American Empire*, Penguin Books, New York, 2004, p. 83.

[4] Cited in Ferguson, *Colossus: The Rise and Fall of the American Empire*, p. 62.

[5] See United States Information Service, 'Clinton: US Foreign Policy Must Be Willing to Risk Error', *Backgrounder*, 9 May 1994.

[6] William Jefferson Clinton, 'Address by the President of the United States of America', House of Representatives, Australia, *Debates*, 20 November 1996, pp. 7167–72.

[7] See William Jefferson Clinton, 'State of the Union Address by the President', 27 January 1998, available at <http://www.lib.umich.edu/govdocs/text/statun98.txt>, accessed 8 November 2007.

[8] US Executive Office of the President, *National Security Strategy of the United States*, August 1991, available at <http://www.fas.org/man/docs/918015-nss.htm>, accessed 24 October 2007.

[9] See Department of Defense, *Defense Strategy for the 1990s: The Regional Defense Strategy*, Washington DC, January 1993, available at <http://www.informationclearinghouse.info/pdf/naarpr_Defense.pdf>, accessed 8 November 2007.

[10] See the transcript of the Second Gore–Bush Presidential Debate, 11 October 2000, on the Commission on Presidential Debates website, available at <http://www.debates.org/pages/trans2000b.html>, accessed 24 October 2007.

[11] 'Remarks by the President to the Troops and Personnel', Norfolk Naval Air Station, Norfolk, Virginia, 13 February 2001, available at <http://www.whitehouse.gov/news/releases/20010213-1.html>, accessed 24 October 2007.

[12] 'President Bush Delivers Graduation Speech at West Point', New York, 1 June 2002, available at <http://www.whitehouse.gov/news/releases/2002/06/20020601-3.html>, accessed 24 October 2007.

[13] For an insightful analysis of these and related issues, see Robert Jervis, 'The Remaking of a Unipolar World', *Washington Quarterly*, vol. 29, no. 3, Summer 2006, available at <http://www.columbia.edu/cu/siwps/publication_files/WQ1_JERVIS.pdf>, accessed 8 November 2007, pp. 7-19.

[14] Bob Woodward reports an illuminating observation that President George W. Bush volunteered during an interview: 'I'm the commander—see, I don't need to explain—I don't need to explain why I say things. That's the interesting thing about being the President. Maybe somebody needs to explain to me why they say something, but I don't feel like I owe anybody an explanation.' See Bob Woodward, *Bush at War*, Simon & Schuster, New York, 2002, pp. 145–46.

[15] Bob Woodward, *Plan of Attack*, Simon & Schuster, New York, 2004, p. 425.

[16] For two fuller analyses of this issue, that come to rather different conclusions, see Lawrence Freedman, 'War In Iraq: Selling the Threat', *Survival*, vol. 6, issue 2, Summer 2004, pp. 7–49; and Ron Huisken, *We Don't Want the Smoking Gun to be a Mushroom Cloud: Intelligence on Iraq's WMD*, SDSC Working Paper, no. 390, Strategic and Defence Studies Centre, The Australian National University, Canberra, June 2004.

[17] A particularly good account of this astonishing process can be found in George Packer, *The Assassins' Gate: America in Iraq*, Faber and Faber, London, 2006, especially pp. 100–48.

[18] This phrase is taken from the title of a book by Coral Bell which examines the outlook for, and possible alternatives to, unipolarity. See Coral Bell, *A World Out of Balance: American Ascendancy and International Politics in the twenty-first Century*, Longueville Books and *The Diplomat*, Woollahra, NSW, 2004.

Regional Issues

Chapter 6

The 'Arc of Instability': The History of an Idea

Graeme Dobell

It is extremely important to us as Australians that we appreciate that we cannot afford to have failing states in our region. The so-called arc of instability, which basically goes from East Timor through to the south-west Pacific states, means not only that Australia does have a responsibility to prevent humanitarian disaster and assist with humanitarian and disaster relief but also that we cannot allow any of these countries to become havens for transnational crime or indeed havens for terrorism ... Australia has a responsibility in protecting our own interests and values to support the defence and protection of the interests and values of these countries in our region.

Brendan Nelson
Defence Minister[1]

The reason why we need a bigger Australian Army is self evident. This country faces on-going and in my opinion increasing instances of destabilised and failing states in our own region. I believe in the next 10 to 20 years Australia will face a number of situations the equivalent of or potentially more challenging than the Solomon Islands and East Timor.

John Howard,
Prime Minister[2]

Not enough jobs is leading to poverty, unhappiness, and it results in crime, violence and instability. In the Pacific, this could lead to a lost generation of young people.

Alexander Downer
Foreign Affairs Minister[3]

What's sometimes called the 'arc of instability' may well become the 'arc of chaos'. We've seen in the Solomon Islands and elsewhere evidence of what happens when young people do not have opportunities, don't have a sense of hope for their own future.

Bob Sercombe
Opposition spokesman for
Pacific Island Affairs[4]

The arc of instability to our north a decade ago was an academic notion. Now it is a security policy reality. From the Solomon Islands across Melanesia to East Timor. And within this arc of instability, Australia's strategic and economic influence relative to other external powers is declining.

Kevin Rudd
Opposition Foreign Affairs spokesman[5]

My father has the rare distinction of having taken part in opposed landings at both the eastern and western ends of the 'arc of instability'.[6] Lance Corporal Bob Dobell of 2/3 Pioneer Battalion went ashore as part of the 9th Division landings in Lae and Finschhafen, at the eastern end of the arc, and at Tarakan in the west.

I date the Australian thinking that produces a phrase like 'the arc' from the Second World War experience of that geography. Prior to that war, Australia could look around its shores using European or Western eyes. Looking beyond its shores, Australia could see neighbours run by Britain, Germany, France, Portugal, the Netherlands and the United States. From the moment Singapore fell, that European understanding was doomed, and Australia had to think about the arc in new ways.

This brings us to the first issue: how best to define the 'arc of instability'. The easy answer is that the phrase was starting to be used in Australia at the end of the last decade, as the 1997–98 Asian financial crisis led to the fall of Suharto in 1998 and then the conflagration in East Timor in 1999. Certainly, by 1999, the phrase 'arc of instability' was being used widely in the strategic community.

The conceptual basis for the 'arc of instability', though, is to be found in more than 60 years of defence thinking. The arc is the latest product of an intellectual process that stretches back to Australia's moment of truth in the twentieth century—the national trauma and existential struggle involved in the fall of Singapore, the attacks on Darwin (the Japanese sent as many planes as they did to Pearl Harbor), the battle of the Coral Sea and the fight for New Guinea.

As Coral Bell has observed, that patch of history has 'haunted Australian strategic inquiry ever since.'[7] Certainly, it explains much about both sides of Australian politics and the remarkable history of consensus—apart from Vietnam—over Australia's role in the region. It helps explain why the Australian Labor Party has some different military reflexes compared to the Social Democrat parties of Europe or New Zealand Labour. It was John Curtin—advocate of a negotiated people's peace and anti-conscription campaigner in the First World War—who forced Labor in the Second World War to accept that militia forces should be deployed in the Southwest Pacific to defend Australia: 'The defence of Australia is not confined to its territorial limits. Provided adequate forces are available, it can best be secured by denying to the enemy the outer screen of islands from which attack can be launched on the mainland.'[8] For John Curtin, the arc was the outer screen of islands.

Using that 60 year timeline, though, the actual definition of the geography we are describing seems to shift and fade a bit—somewhat like the old joke about the Economics Exam: the questions stayed exactly the same for decades, but the correct answers kept changing. It would be interesting for a psychologist to consider why the hard-edged strategic realists suddenly become extremely polite and somewhat vague when talking about our surrounding geography.

We have an extensive range of euphemisms. The 'region' is a handy standby, as is the 'Southwest Pacific'. The Australian military likes to use the 'inner arc'. Sir Arthur Tange often referred to the 'archipelagic environment'. There is, of course, the sea-air gap—you have sea and air, but to have a gap there must be something on the other side. Chief of the Australian Army Lieutenant General Peter Leahy therefore prefers the idea of a sea-air bridge in what he calls the littoral environment. There is the area of 'direct military interest'. In his 1986 *Review of Australia's Defence Capabilities*, Paul Dibb did name Indonesia, but his key sentence was more polite: 'Because of its proximity, the archipelago to our north is the area from or through which a military threat to Australia could most easily be posed.'[9]

For the purposes of this discussion, let me offer you a definition of the 'arc of instability' based on that Dibb Review, which marked its twentieth anniversary in March 2006. Dibb defined the area of direct military interest—where Australia would seek to exert independent military power. On its east-west axis, it stretched 4000 nautical miles from the Cocos Islands in the Indian Ocean to New Zealand and the islands of the Southwest Pacific in the east. On the other north-south axis, the area started in the Southern Ocean and stretched 3000 nautical miles to encompass the 'archipelago and island chain in the north'. This represented about 10 per cent of the earth's surface.[10]

In defining this geography, Dibb drew on a rich lode of Defence Department thinking from the previous two decades. Look, for instance, at the *Strategic Basis* document adopted by the Australian Cabinet in November 1964, with its discussion of the need to hold Southeast Asia against communist expansion, to deal with Indonesia's 'aggressive policy', the need for Australia to be able to supply military forces in Malaysia, South Vietnam and Thailand, and to deal with the danger of covert Indonesian activity against PNG.[11]

Consider the Defence Department's 1971 paper on the *Environment of Future Australian Military Operations*. It stated that the focus of Australian operations beyond the mainland would be the maritime and archipelagic environment stretching from Sumatra and the Malay Peninsula through Indonesia and New Guinea to the islands of the Southwest Pacific. Contingency planning should cover the possibility of conflict with Indonesia or of maritime power attacking through Indonesia.[12]

Paul Dibb was thus speaking to two sides of the same strategic coin when in the early 1990s he envisioned Australia trying to create a 'strategic shield of ASEAN countries to our north', and by 1999 seeing the other side—an 'arc of instability' extending from Indonesia to PNG and into the South Pacific.[13] In both usages, Indonesia is central.

When first used, at the end of the 1990s, the 'arc of instability' was a euphemism for Indonesia. As used by our politicians today, the arc has moved or morphed. Now it starts in East Timor and is really a Melanesian arc. Of course, the next point the arc touches as it sweeps east from Timor is Irian Jaya (or West Papua). One of the essential elements to keep in view when thinking about the arc is that Australia has given explicit security guarantees to two unstable countries that border Indonesia—East Timor and PNG. Ultimately, the proper management of the arc needs a favourable or at least stable Australia–Indonesia relationship; that is, I suppose, a statement of the obvious for anyone who looks at how Australia has acted in the arc over these 60 years.

To think properly about the 'arc of instability', we need to divide it in two—the ASEAN and the Melanesian sides. In one half lies the Indonesian archipelago stretching to Singapore and Malaysia (where Australia is committed under the Five Power Defence Arrangements). The growing Australian military and police contacts with the Philippines complete the geographic scope of this ASEAN branch of the arc. The only symmetry between the two halves of the arc is that each has a country that is central to Australian concerns and colours Canberra's dealings with the rest of the region—on the ASEAN side it is Indonesia; on the Melanesian side it is PNG.

In the ASEAN branch of the arc, Australia can only bargain and negotiate for its interests. Part of the problem for Australia, as regards the ASEAN half of the arc, is encapsulated by Henry Kissinger's question about Europe years ago: Whom do I call if I want to talk about Europe's position on defence or foreign policy? Despite years of discussion and a large mound of declarations and agreements, ASEAN has taken only a few steps towards its declared intention of creating a Security Community by 2020. ASEAN reaches its fortieth anniversary in 2007; yet it was only in 2006 that the ASEAN Defence Ministers gathered for their first formal discussion.

ASEAN's security achievement has been to avert the likelihood of conflict between its members—to act as a confidence-building mechanism to reassure members about the intentions of neighbouring states. But the crisis that hit East Timor in 1999 and the repeat version in May 2006 revealed ASEAN's limitations. As Dili toppled over into violence in 2006, East Timor could expect no concerted help from ASEAN. Dili made direct calls for assistance to four countries—Australia, New Zealand, Portugal and one ASEAN member (Malaysia).

The equation is different on the Melanesian side of the arc. Australia has shown its willingness and ability to impose its will—by force, if necessary. In fact, as far back as December 1989, Gareth Evans defined the conditions under which Australia would intervene militarily in the South Pacific. Evans denied the creation of what he called 'an Antipodean Brezhnev Doctrine', but in the manner of such diplomatic denials, he was really hinting at Australia's view of its perceived capabilities.[14] The assertive Australian stance in the arc since 2003 is supported by both sides of Australian politics.

The Melanesian arc starts in East Timor and then takes in Irian Jaya, PNG (with quite probably an independent Bougainville in the next decade, under the terms of the current agreement), Nauru (a bankrupt micro-state with Melanesian-style problems), Solomon Islands, Vanuatu and Fiji. For these purposes, let us exclude New Caledonia from the arc, based on the hope that the glory of France will mean the avalanche of French money keeps being unloaded from each aircraft that lands in Noumea.

In days gone by, New Zealand and Polynesia would sometimes complain about Australia's 'dark' view of the Pacific. The criticism has not been made as much since the Regional Assistance Mission to Solomon Islands (RAMSI), but the central reason for that pessimism still pulses in Canberra. Australia often views the Pacific through the PNG lens. And it can be a dark glass, as evidenced by John Howard's recent remark that he views PNG as 'inherently unstable'.[15]

Australian official language about PNG is becoming as explicit as it can be about the danger of economic and social disintegration, pointing to the need to 'overcome major constraints to stability and growth'. PNG is in danger of losing whatever gains it has made on health and education since independence because Port Moresby is unable to support all the programs in its own budget. Alexander Downer commented that the 'most dramatic decline in PNG' has been in the quality of governance: 'The fundamental weakness of governance undermines investment by government, private sector and development cooperation partners, threatening both prosperity and stability.'[16]

Australia's fears about a breakdown of order in Melanesia and broader concerns about South Pacific stability have driven a significant re-weighting of the aid budget towards governance and law and order. The Australian aid budget for 2004–2005 gave about 33 per cent of the Official Development Assistance to 'governance' projects. This was more than a doubling from 1999–2000 when governance received 15 per cent of the Official Development Assistance.

Australia proclaims a more robust approach to the Pacific based on the belief that previous Howard Government interventions have worked. Yet, when talking to Canberra policymakers, it is striking how this assertiveness is linked to a sense of Australian failure. If the region is in gradual decline, then what does that say about Australia's role as the regional leader?

The language of robust policy and urgent action is driven by the fear of what is going wrong in the Pacific. That dualism erupted when the Secretaries of key Australian departments met in Canberra at the end of 2000 to approve a whole-of-government review of policy on the Pacific. The review had been ordered after the twin shocks of the coups in Fiji and Solomon Islands. The draft report was a status quo document, reflecting the then dominant 'stand ready' view of the Department of Foreign Affairs and Trade (DFAT); that Australia should be content to intelligently manage trouble and avoid responsibility for whatever went wrong in the Pacific. The Secretary of DFAT, Ashton Calvert, was quizzed on how the review could conclude that past Australian policy on the Pacific was correct and should continue as before. One of the other Secretaries put the problem succinctly: 'How can we say our policies are working when Solomon Islands is turning to shit?' That line was immediately trumped by the head of the public service, the then Secretary of the Department of Prime Minister and Cabinet, Max Moore-Wilton, who stated: 'Not just Solomon Islands—our policies in the whole of the South Pacific are going to shit!'

A sense of failure and regional danger, as much as any feeling of Australian power, produced the policy reversal that created the regional intervention in Solomon Islands. Those differing emotions still drive much of Canberra's desperate search for firm ground in the Pacific.

The policy somersaults Australia has performed bring to mind an old line about the United Nations—the tragic paradox of the United Nations is that it became indispensable before it became effective. Equally, Australia has been forced to a new acceptance that it is indispensable in the Pacific. Now it has to find out how to become effective.

Australia has stopped talking about 'failing' or 'failed' states. Such terminology was not welcome in Solomon Islands and infuriated the Prime Minister of PNG, Sir Michael Somare. Instead, Canberra now uses the term 'fragile'. One can get a flavour of the discussion by reading the analytical paper on the Pacific Island Countries published by AusAID in the preparations for the Australian Aid White Paper.

The analytical paper suggested that more than one-third of the Pacific Island Countries are weak or fragile—listing Solomon Islands, Tonga, Kiribati, Vanuatu, Fiji and Nauru.[17] Ron Duncan and James Gilling started their analysis by noting that Australia has both humanitarian and strategic interests in the Pacific. But these interests are put at risk by weak Pacific states where health is deteriorating, and where poverty is on the rise, accompanied by 'rocketing' youth unemployment and rapid urbanisation:

> The key problem for the Pacific Island Countries is that they have not taken control of the factors that will determine their fate. Their political governance is weak. Policies are not credible. Political systems have in-built instability. Public sectors are mostly too large and inefficient, often due to support from aid inflows. There is minimal accountability and high levels of corruption.[18]

That, as my old football coach would say, is 'a beaut backhander-and-a-half'.

The key phrase in the background paper, which finds its way into the recommendations of the White Paper Core Group (*Core Group Recommendations Report for a White Paper on Australia's aid program*), is that 'aid and emigration opportunities are probably all that stand in the way of a more serious breakdown of state legitimacy and capacity in the region'. Consider that proposition: aid and emigration are all that is holding back the 'doomsday scenario'. And then reflect that Melanesia has only aid to stave off this more serious breakdown, because it has no emigration opportunities. The White Paper Core Group recommended two things:

> 1. Skills training for Pacific Islanders so they can migrate to Australia.
>
> 2. Open a 'Pacific window' for unskilled migration, either temporary or permanent.

> We suggest that the Government should consider developing a Pacific unskilled migration window to facilitate migration, especially from Melanesia and the microstates. This would complement the recently announced skills training initiative, [the Pacific Technical College] and help achieve more quickly the same aim of promoting migration from the Pacific Islands. ... Migration would not be a panacea for the Pacific Islands, particularly for the larger Melanesian countries, and it would take some time for its impact to be felt, especially in PNG. However, the need is urgent given rapid population growth in the Pacific and the 'youth bulge' some islands are experiencing. Worldwide, much larger countries than PNG are being sustained on the back of migration, including the Philippines and Nepal. And for microstates such as Nauru,

Kiribati and Tuvalu, it is highly unlikely that these economies will be viable in the absence of migration opportunities.[19]

The Government's Aid White Paper (*White Paper on the Australian Government's Overseas Aid Program*), when it was issued in April 2006, endorsed the first idea: Australia would provide skills training for the Pacific Islanders to help labour mobility and migration. The Core recommendation about a 'Pacific window' for unskilled migration was dismissed using a strange formulation. The word 'unskilled' was not mentioned, more study was promised, but policy would not alter: 'Further analysis and research will be undertaken on the relationship between migration and development, especially in the Pacific. Australia's current policies on migration in this regard will not change.'[20]

A translation of this bureaucratese might be: We know there is a growing problem, but we do not want to change policy, so our response is to keep researching that problem. An old Army line is that if you are not terrified out of your mind, it just shows that you do not fully understand the situation. Well—in Canberra—a lot of people understand the Melanesian facts and are feeling pretty terrified.

The 'arc of instability' is a useful term in Canberra, summing up a range of diplomatic, economic and geopolitical forces. The 'arc of instability' is descriptive rather than explanatory or analytical; it does not seem to have much utility when you are standing in one of the individual states it encompasses. What has changed for the people of Melanesia is the way they run their lives, particularly in the cities, in Port Moresby, Port Vila, Honiara or Suva. The middle class and the administrative and political elite in the Pacific know they have a set of problems that seem to be getting worse. The riots and destruction in Solomon Islands and Tonga in 2006 are tragic signs of the new reality confronting the Pacific. It could be called a 'barbed wire' reality.

The 'Barbed Wire' Reality

Barbed wire around the house and bars on the windows, to keep out the rascals, used to be middle class accessories found mainly in Port Moresby. The joke used to be that when the journalists went across from Port Moresby to Honiara to cover RAMSI, they would comment about how peaceful the Solomon Islands capital was compared to PNG. This is no longer the case.

Standing amid the ashes and ruins of Honiara's Chinatown after the riot in 2006 was to experience a profound sense of failure. RAMSI had failed, Australia had failed, and the region had failed, that such devastation could happen. But Solomons society also failed if it could impose such a trauma on itself. For anyone who has spent any time in the South Pacific, it was a visual and emotional shock to stand in the middle of Chinatown after the riot. The street at the commercial heart of Honiara was rubble and ashes for most of its length. This was not the damage of a natural disaster—this cyclone was destruction visited on Honiara by its own people.

Australians looking at this ruin had to ask questions about the failure of intelligence and security that allowed the mob to run amok. Australia had to contemplate its policy lapses. The portents of failure for the rest of the Islands are more personal, more direct. Other governments throughout the Pacific had to look at the ashes in Solomon Islands—and later in the year in Tonga—and then turn a questioning eye on their own society.

The 'barbed wire' reality is no longer confined to Port Moresby. Personal security is an issue for the middle class elite of Melanesia. The people who run government, who teach or do business, now have to worry about the safety of their homes and the security of their families.

The Pacific still has strong societies and weak states, but the middle class can no longer be as confident in the social and religious conservatism that has underpinned Island stability. I am mainly talking about Melanesia, but the same security consciousness is starting to appear in parts of Polynesia.

Along with the barbed wire and the bars, we have seen the arrival of the 'free shopping day'. A 'free shopping day' is a polite way of describing riot, looting and arson. It happens in a Pacific capital when political planets get out of alignment and law and order breaks down. Such moments of madness occurred in Port Moresby during the Sandline crisis in 1997, in Suva in 2000 during the Parliament hostage crisis, in Honiara in April 2006, and in Nuku'alofa in November 2006. The riots and deaths in Dili in May 2006 followed the same pattern.

The 'free shopping day' in Honiara had elements of smooth organisation. The taxi would pull up outside the burning store; the lads would load in the bags of rice and whatever else they had looted, and then head home to drop off the goods before returning to continue the fun. We saw some of the same methods during the rioting in Suva in 2000. A 'free shopping day' happens when thousands of young men with no jobs and little future are hanging around a Melanesian capital.

Samuel Huntington's 'clash of civilisations' thesis ignored the South Pacific. But one part of Huntington's work should interest the region: his discussion of the political explosion that often accompanies a demographic explosion, with large numbers of unemployed young males acting as a natural source of instability. 'Young people are the protagonists of protest, instability, reform and revolution. Historically, the existence of a large cohort of young people has tended to coincide with such movements.'[21] Huntington points to the impact of youth bulges in key moments of history from the Protestant Reformation to the young recruits to Fascism. His tipping point for when a youth bulge becomes revolutionary is when those aged between 15 and 24 start to exceed 20 per cent of the total population.

Parts of Melanesia are heading towards this youth bulge threshold. PNG and Solomon Islands have 19 per cent of their total population between 15 and 24 years of age. Most Pacific countries have around 17 per cent of youths, as compared with Australia which has 9 per cent.[22]

This youth bulge and lack of jobs are part of the explanation for the violent unrest that is becoming all too familiar in the 'arc of instability'. And quite a few people have taken the next logical step: Polynesia is quiet because its young workers can go overseas, Melanesia faces turmoil because its young workers have no jobs and no hope.

Professor Helen Ware talks persuasively about the 'stunning' shift of people to the cities in Melanesia and the need for emigration to provide a safety valve against urban warlordism:

> Polynesian countries, in contrast to Melanesia, have been protected from civil conflict by high levels of emigration. Similarly, Kiribati and Tuvalu have achieved peace at home by sending many of their young men overseas to work as international seamen.
>
> Civil conflict can be understood as involving both a supply of willing participants in violence and a demand for their services. The Pacific supply is found amongst groups of young men who can be as volatile as heaps of tinder ready to be ignited by a small spark. The demand is a more complex matter. Essentially all that is needed is a small group of leaders who expect to benefit from the conflict to make lighting the fire worthwhile. Often these leaders use the excuse of perceived ethnic and/or inter-island discrimination to motivate the young hotheads.[23]

The *Core Group Recommendations Report for a White Paper on Australia's aid program* grappled with the same set of issues when discussing the problem of 'fragile states' in the South Pacific. The group argued that such states are prone to derailment, with factors ranging from instability and conflict to poor political leadership, weak governance and corruption:

> The Melanesian islands of PNG, Vanuatu, Solomon Islands and Fiji appear to be particularly prone to instability. Analysts point to various factors to explain the high level of instability in Melanesia relative to Polynesia (Samoa, Tonga and Cook Islands). For example, Polynesia's much better access to developed labour markets and greater ethnic homogeneity, and Melanesia's weak governance and conflict over natural resources.[24]

The ANU's Demography and Sociology Program has produced a paper on population pressures in PNG, the Pacific Island Economies and East Timor (Timor

Leste), using some fertility and net migration assumptions. The report points to the youth bulge creating

> increasing numbers of long-term, unemployed and under-employed, and illegally employed youth … the large numbers of under-employed youth have been linked to increasing social problems such as drug use, prostitution, crime, and suicide, and also provide one of the ingredients for social unrest. Hence, they become one of the factors behind the low levels of investment and job creation.[25]

The study makes the familiar point that migration has a significant impact on population growth in countries such as Samoa, Tonga and Cook Islands. By contrast, the net migration figure for Melanesia—PNG, Solomons and Vanuatu—is tiny:

> While there is the reasonable likelihood that Australia and New Zealand will put in place some form of temporary work permits for low-skilled and unskilled labour from these countries, the numbers involved will be small and there will remain limited opportunities for such labour to move on a permanent basis.[26]

PNG, Solomon Islands, Vanuatu, Kiribati and Marshall Islands have relatively high fertility rates and low to very low levels of net migration. The ANU study says that unless the gradual decline in their fertility rates accelerates, they will continue to experience population growth rates in excess of 2 per cent. Extrapolating past fertility trends (i.e. a gradual decline in fertility) and assuming little net migration, Vanuatu's population will almost double from 215 800 in 2004, to 409 500 by 2029. In this scenario, Solomon Islands' population will increase from 461 000 to 806 400. Over the same period, PNG's population is set to expand from 5.7 million to 9.8 million.[27]

Putting population and employment projections together, the report offers some estimates of the excess supply of labour that Melanesia will face in the future. Thus, PNG is projected to move from having a working age population of 3.1 million in 2004 to a working age population of 3.9 million by 2015; only 5.8 per cent of these workers are expected to be in formal sector employment in 2015, giving PNG 3.6 million workers outside formal employment. Solomon Islands goes from a working age population of 209 000 in 2004 to 312 000 by 2015; only 10.4 per cent are projected to be in formal sector employment in 2015, leaving 279 000 Solomon Islands workers outside the formal sector. Vanuatu is projected to go from 94 000 workers to 147 000 by 2015, with only 12 per cent in formal sector employment, leaving 129 000 workers outside the formal sector.

Certainly, many outside the formal sector will remain in the villages. But as the study notes:

Those countries with high fertility rates and low formal sector employment will generate the most excess labour and have the greatest demand for overseas employment. The high projected levels of excess supply of labour for the formal sector indicate the enormous challenge that the PNG and Pacific Island governments have in front of them.[28]

Aside from the explicit conclusion about the need for migration as a Pacific safety valve, the Australian Government has replicated most of this academic work in its own recent publications. Pacific Governments can find most of the detailed evidence they need for a Pacific worker program in the AusAID *Core Group Recommendations Report for a White Paper on Australia's aid program* (December 2005), the *White Paper on the Australian Government's Overseas Aid Program* (April 2006) and AusAID's *Pacific 2020: Challenges and Opportunities for Growth* (May 2006).

Pacific 2020 presented three scenarios for the Pacific: Doomsday, Muddling On, and High Growth. Launching the study, Minister for Foreign Affairs Alexander Downer mused about the bleak future of the Pacific if it could not follow the growth path, and the danger of a lost generation of young people:

> The report tells the simple but disturbing truth that per capita income in some Pacific Island Countries is no higher today than it was 20 years ago. Some countries have done a little better, but overall the region is being left behind. The report talks about 'doomsday' and 'muddling on' scenarios. This is not alarmist. Countries that are doing somewhat better than others are largely doing so because of aid and remittances. And no country has become wealthy that way.[29]

The final sentence about no countries becoming wealthy through aid and remittances is the sort of caveat politicians and bureaucrats insert when they want to avoid the ultimate logic of the evidence they have presented. Australian policy does not allow for the unskilled workers of Melanesia to come in to earn remittances. Thus, the value of remittances must be praised with faint damns.

The 'Arc of Instability' and the Future of the US Alliance

Quagmire, fiasco or folly, Iraq is turning into a defining moment for US strategy and future military policy. The change in US military thinking caused by Iraq will impact on close American allies such as Australia. The shape of the post-Iraq future will become clearer after January 2009 when the United States swears in a new president.

The United States will confront a post-Iraq moment in 2009, with some similarities to the post-Vietnam War era that it entered after 1975. This is where the Vietnam analogy starts to matter for Australia: how will the United States rethink its military obligations and aims under a new president, as it confronts the Iraq scars? Australia had to develop new thoughts about the alliance, defence policy and Australia's region after the Vietnam War. The Iraq effect will be similar. A United States less keen on global missions will, in turn, mean an Australia with a clearer regional focus.

The change in US military thinking after Vietnam was a key element in allowing Australia to turn its mind to defending the continent and the countries of the arc. The effect of Iraq on the United States is likely to have a similar clarifying or simplifying impact on the priority Australia is able to give to the 'arc of instability'.

The two constants—the two poles of Australian strategic thinking in the 60 years since the trauma of the Pacific war—have been the US alliance and what is happening in the countries of the arc. Sometimes these poles attract, sometimes they repel, but always they are fundamental. Thus, you have Peter Edwards writing that the External Affairs Department in the early 1960s sought a policy 'based on Australia's national interests in its immediate region and refined, not defined by alliance considerations'.[30]

The tensions between alliance and region are at the heart of the theological debate that has been raging around Canberra this decade. Call it the argument between the regionalists and the globalists. The debate has been strongly driven by an Australian Army that decided it had been unfairly overshadowed by the RAN and RAAF in the post-Vietnam War settlement (Defence of Australia) and went in search of means to get back to the top table. The Army case is given eloquence and intellectual depth in the work of Michael Evans, who argues that Australia could not allow 'geographical determinism to create a paradox between its strategic theory and practice'. Evans said the 'defence of Australia' orthodoxy of the 1980s and 1990s 'overlooked the truth that geography can only ever be the grammar, not the logic, of strategy'. Ultimately, he said, Australia would always see its destiny in 'the global fate of Western civilisation', not a narrow definition of geographic interest.[31]

In Lieutenant General Peter Leahy's view, Australia had acquired its own 'Vietnam syndrome', restructuring almost exclusively for the defence of the continent, to avoid Asian entanglements. Leahy said this was a profound discontinuity with our traditional approach—'an expeditionary military culture that in turn supports a Grand Strategy built on an alliance with the dominant, liberal democratic force de jour'. In this explanation, the 'Army languished as a second tier force ... deemed to be a mere strategic goalkeeper' that only had to mop up the groups that traversed the sea-air gap. The pernicious effect, Leahy said, was to hollow out units, 'based on assurances from planners that we would have significant lead-time to mobilise like a nineteenth century force'. East Timor had set off the alarm bells and *Defence 2000* marked the start of the turn around.

Now the Army was on the march to the networked, hardened future, from being 'a light leg infantry towards a medium weight force'.[32]

Some of that does not fit the facts. Australia did not suffer a Vietnam War syndrome—if anything the Australian Army prided itself on the military victory achieved by its task force in its limited area of operations.[33] Certainly there was no diplomatic version, because Australia maintained diplomatic relations with Vietnam, unlike the United States, which cut ties for two decades. The shift of the Army to the north of Australia decided on in the 1980s has been part of the reason we have been effective in East Timor. It is quite convenient, I suggest, to blame the planners and not the Army hierarchy for the inability to do basic things in East Timor in 1999 such as moving around water. I see no turning away from Asia in our leadership role in the Cambodia peace settlement, the creation of the Asia-Pacific Economic Cooperation (APEC) group and the ASEAN Regional Forum (ARF), or Paul Keating's conclusion of a security treaty with Jakarta in 1995 (a treaty-creation effort replicated by the Howard Government with the signing of the Agreement on Framework for Security Cooperation between Indonesia and Australia in November 2006).

Beyond these quibbles, though, the Army has won on basic grounds—what gets used gets rewarded, even if you do not accept all the Army's version of grand strategy. Prime Minister John Howard says his government has made a 'fundamental reassertion of the strategic importance of the Army—and indeed of the individual soldier—in Australia's strategic culture'.[34] The two extra battalions are a A$10 billion affirmation of the Army's worth.[35] Now the Army confronts the deep, underlying headache—how to build real depth, or to put it directly, get the people to fill the holes. The cancer that has afflicted the Army is hollowing—leave aside the issue of whether that is a result of poor planning by the civilians or the military.

The Army's supporters, though, make much bigger claims for the meaning and direction of the changes. Brigadier Jim Wallace says we should be aiming to create a light armoured brigade, the equivalent of a US armoured cavalry regiment, 'able to conduct reconnaissance or flank protection for a heavier allied force'. On that vision, the next time the United States sends a division into invade, the Australians should be out guarding the left flank.[36] Greg Sheridan says that 'Howard and Bush have transformed the alliance from a predominantly regional affair to a truly global partnership'.[37]

This is where it gets interesting, because if we really have moved from regional to global missions then the game has changed. I note, though, that even Wallace is cautious about the Army giving all its attention to the infantry-armour capabilities you need on the high-tech battlefield of this global partnership. Wallace says not everything the Army needs to patrol the left flank of a US division will 'automatically translate to the non-discretionary regional security operations on which it will increasingly be employed'.[38] The key word here is *discretionary*. Iraq was discretionary, a war of choice, but the 'arc of instability' will be compulsory.

Prime Minister John Howard offers some support to both the globalists and the regionalists. He says that 'attempts to shoe-horn Australia's national security agenda into a form of geographic determinism are even less relevant than in the past'. Yet geography does not die, because in the same speech Howard noted: 'Clearly Australia's most immediate interests and responsibilities lie in Asia and the Pacific, for reasons of geography but also given the region's growing power and importance.'[39]

While the Prime Minister may decry 'geographic determinism', it is worth restating why geographic discipline has been valuable to Australia, and will be again in the post-Iraq era. This determinism was imposed on Australia by a set of demands and needs:

- US demands on its allies for self-reliance after Vietnam;
- Self-respect—the need to show that Australia could defend its own continent;
- Geography placing a discipline on the wish lists that will always come from the Army, Navy and Air Force; and
- Regional demands on Australia from Southeast Asia and the South Pacific.

I look to the United States to resolve the argument between Australia's globalists and regionalists, by sharply reducing the demands for global missions. Political and policy trauma in the United States will turn Australia back to its region after Iraq, in the same way it did after Vietnam. The point about geographic determinism, after Vietnam, was that it responded to fundamental Australian needs and US demands.

The United States will swear in a new President in January 2009. The unilateralist, neo-conservative vision of the first Bush term has already been buried. The new President will read the last rites and the US military will start considering its options. The Democrats have already decided—'The war in Iraq is over, except for the dying.'[40] The Republicans will not be far behind. Lawrence Kaplan describes the growing anger of US military personnel towards their political leaders for sending them to fight with neither the strategy nor the means to win. He quoted a young Army officer in Iraq: 'We've been left holding the bag—and it is full of garbage.'[41]

The next US President will offer a foreign policy more cautious and realist than has already been forced on the Bush second term. For Australia, that is going to translate into new and even more powerful forms of the Nixon Guam doctrine ('defend yourselves') and the Weinberger doctrine. Caspar Weinberger unveiled this realist prescription, with all its post-Vietnam tones, after the 23 October 1983 bombing of the US barracks in Beirut in which 241 US Service (mainly USMC) personnel died. The Secretary of Defense laid down these tests for sending US combat forces abroad:

- Commit only if vital interests are at stake;
- Commit with all the resources needed to win;
- Go in with clear political and military objectives;
- Be ready to change the commitment if the objectives change;
- Only take on commitments that have the support of the people and the Congress; and
- Send US forces only as a last resort.[42]

Australia needs to examine the sort of changes that the Vietnam War syndrome forced on the United States in the years after 1975, and prepare accordingly. Our fundamental aim will be to preserve the alliance. We avoided any blame after Vietnam, even though we had been one of the prime movers. This time, we can argue that we did not urge, but merely followed. Yet there must be some alliance blowback, even if it is only as part of a general US review of the way it operates internationally. As Owen Harries noted, it is extremely dubious whether 'uncritical, loyal support for a bad, failed America policy' will enhance Australia's standing as an ally: 'A reputation for being dumb but loyal and eager is not one to be sought.'[43]

US grand strategy in Asia will head for the seas at an even faster rate than it did in the years after Vietnam. The United States will aim to continue as the maritime power, while China can be the continental power. Northeast Asia will matter, Southeast Asia will be something to sail through, and the South Pacific will fall off the map for everybody except the US Commander Pacific Fleet.

A former US deputy Secretary of State, Richard Armitage, says America will leave responsibility for the South Pacific to Australia. Armitage, who retired as the number two man in the US State Department in February 2005, handed care of the South Pacific to Canberra with his normal jocular flourish:

> I'll freely admit that no Americans understand the South Pacific. And we leave that to you. Be glad to help you in any way you see fit. But we just don't understand it. Perhaps it's a good thing we don't understand it—we keep our meddlesome hands off it and leave it to you.[44]

A regional mission rather than a global partnership should change the way Australia thinks about some of its big-ticket defence purchases.

Kim Beazley defined one element of such a rethink when, as Opposition Leader, he promised that Labor would cancel the Navy project to buy two amphibious ships, designed to carry the Army to distant conflicts: 'The government's proposed massive amphibious ships are the sort of platform that would be needed to drag an armoured force across the Indian Ocean and lodge on Africa's eastern shores.'[45] Instead, he said, Australia should buy three or four ships half the size, plus some fast catamarans, to run around the region.

The lesson to take from East Timor in 1999 was not how well it ended, but how dangerously it started. Consider for a moment what could have gone wrong as the first Australian ships headed into Dili, if that Indonesian submarine nosing around the fleet had not been pulled back. An Australia-Indonesia version of the *General Belgrano* incident would have sunk more than a submarine.[46]

The key alliance point from East Timor in 1999 was that the United States did not want to act. The deputy Prime Minister, Tim Fischer, said the 'truth' was that Washington 'could not have been weaker in its initial response to Australia's request assistance with East Timor during September 1999'.[47] The first failure says as much about Australia confusion leading up to the crisis as it does about US lack of attention, but it is a failure that holds lessons for the future.

In the end, what the United States provided for East Timor was essential—logistics, transport and Naval assistance—and not the least contribution was the way Washington was able to lean on Jakarta to force Indonesia to accept an international intervention led by Australia. Yet Australian policymakers should always be reminded of two images from the epicentre of the crisis, in the days when failure was still a likely outcome. One image is that of US national security adviser Sandy Berger telling journalists that the United States had no more responsibility for solving East Timor than he did for cleaning the mess his daughter created in her own apartment. The other image is John Howard sitting in a radio studio, almost pleading over the airwaves for American 'boots on the ground' in Timor. That failed call for US troops ignored the Vietnam trauma and the lessons that should have been taken from US refusals to back Australia over Dutch New Guinea or the Confrontation.

If all that history is still considered inconclusive, then perhaps Australia should keep in mind the shock that hit the UK Thatcher Government when it found that the 'special relationship' didn't guarantee US support in the Falklands War. 'It is a frightening thing that our greatest ally is not wholly on our side', British Defence Secretary John Nott observed in the midst of the 1982 conflict.[48] The official British historian of the Falklands campaign Lawrence Freedman concluded that a close alliance and close personal relationships between political leaders are no guarantee of Washington's support in a conflict: 'The policies adopted by the United States are a product of shifting power balances within a particular administration as much as a product of any built-in ideological disposition.'[49] Alliance management will always matter for Australia, no matter how much time and effort Canberra devotes to the 'arc of instability'.

Let me end by shifting from high policy back to Lance Corporal Dobell, in that first landing at Lae. He was taken ashore by US sailors steering US landing craft. That lesson will continue to matter. One other point, going ashore in Lae, my father had on his back the giant two-way radio he had used at El Alamein. Next to him was another soldier carrying the giant batteries. The radio worked a treat in the Western Desert, sending a signal for miles. In the humidity and jungle of New Guinea, that radio was unable to throw a signal 10 yards. The kit you want for global missions is not always the one you want in the 'arc of instability'.

ENDNOTES

[1] Brendan Nelson, *House of Representatives Hansard*, 8 August 2006, p. 13.

[2] John Howard, Press Conference, Defence Department, 24 August 2006. See also 'A Stronger Army: Two More Battalions', Media Release, 24 August 2006, available at <http://www.pm.gov.au/media/Release/2006/media_Release2091.cfm>, accessed 8 November 2007.

[3] Speech by Alexander Downer at launch of Pacific 2020: Challenges and Opportunities for Growth', Sydney, 10 May 2006, available at <http://www.ausaid.gov.au/media/release.cfm?BC=Speech&ID=8653_9801_6672_4399_5645>, accessed 8 November 2007.

[4] Bob Sercombe in interview with Graeme Dobell, ABC Radio Australia Pacific Beat, 21 June 2006.

[5] Kevin Rudd, 'The Mismanagement of Australia's National Security: the death of disarmament as a priority of Australian diplomacy', Address to the Commemoration of the 10th Anniversary of the Canberra Commission, Brisbane, 2 August 2006.

[6] Parts of this chapter also appeared in Graeme Dobell, 'Australia and the Pacific's lost generation', *Quadrant*, March 2007, pp. 9–17. The material is included here with permission.

[7] Coral Bell, *Nation, Region and Context: Studies in Peace and War in Honour of Professor T. B. Millar*, Canberra Papers on Strategy and Defence, CP 112, Strategic and Defence Studies Centre, The Australian National University, Canberra, 1995, p. 51.

[8] John Curtin, *House of Representatives Hansard*, vol. 173, 3 February 1943, p. 265.

[9] Paul Dibb, *Review of Australia's Defence Capabilities*, Report to the Minister for Defence, Australian Government Publishing Service, Canberra, 1986, p. 4.

[10] Dibb, *Review of Australia's Defence Capabilities*, pp. 3–4.

[11] Garry Woodard, *Asian Alternatives: Australia's Vietnam Decision and Lessons on Going to War*, Melbourne University Press, Melbourne, 2004, p. 177.

[12] Peter Edwards, *Arthur Tange: Last of the Mandarins*, Allen & Unwin, NSW, 2006, p. 193.

[13] Graeme Dobell, *Australia Finds Home: The choices and chances of an Asia Pacific Journey*, ABC Books, Sydney, 2000, p. 249.

[14] Gareth Evans, *Ministerial Statement*, December 1989, p. 22.

[15] John Howard, Press Conference, Defence Department, 24 August 2006.

[16] Alexander Downer, 'Australia's International Development Cooperation 2004-2005', Statement by the Minister for Foreign Affairs, Commonwealth of Australia, Canberra, 11 May 2004, available at <http://www.ausaid.gov.au/publications/pdf/budget_2004_2005.pdf>, accessed 8 November 2007, p. 13.

[17] Ron Duncan and James Gilling, Companion Volume to *Core Group Recommendations Report for a White Paper on Australia's aid program*, Chapter 8: Pacific Island Countries, Box 1: View on the fragility of the PICs, AusAID, Canberra, December 2005, p. 8-8, available at <http://www.aciar.gov.au/sites/aciar/files/node/718/companion_report.pdf>, accessed 8 November 2007.

[18] Duncan and Gilling, Companion Volume to *Core Group Recommendations Report for a White Paper on Australia's aid program*, p. 8-5, available at <http://www.aciar.gov.au/sites/aciar/files/node/718/companion_report.pdf>, accessed 8 November 2007.

[19] Ron Duncan, Meryl Williams and Stephen Howes, *Core Group Recommendations Report for a White Paper on Australia's aid program*, AusAID, Canberra, December 2005, available at <http://www.aciar.gov.au/sites/aciar/files/node/718/core_group_report.pdf>, accessed 8 November 2007. p. 69.

[20] Alexander Downer, *Australian Aid: Promoting Growth and Stability, A White Paper on the Australian Government's Overseas Aid Program*, AusAID, Canberra, April 2006, available at <http://www.ausaid.gov.au/publications/pdf/whitepaper.pdf>, accessed 8 November 2007, p. 29.

[21] Samuel P. Huntington, *The Clash of Civilizations and the Remaking of World Order*, Touchstone Books, Simon & Schuster, New York, 1997, p. 117.

[22] Helen Ware, 'Pacific instability and youth bulges: the devil in the demography and the economy', Australian Population Association, 12th Biennial Conference, Canberra, 15–17 September 2004, Canberra, p. 2, available at <http://www.apa.org.au/upload/2004-3E_Ware.pdf>, accessed 8 November 2007.

[23] Ware, 'Pacific instability and youth bulges: the devil in the demography and the economy', p. 1.

[24] Duncan, Williams and Howes, *Core Group Recommendations Report for a White Paper on Australia's aid program*, p. 9.

[25] Heather Booth, Guangyu Zhang, Maheshra Rao, Fakavae Taomia, and Ron Duncan, *Population Pressures in Papua New Guinea, the Pacific Island Economies and Timor Leste*, Working Papers in Demography, no. 102, Demography and Sociology Program, The Australian National University, Canberra, June 2006. p. 1, available at <http://demography.anu.edu.au/Publications/WorkingPapers/102.pdf>, accessed 24 October 2007.

[26] Booth, Zhang, Rao, Taomia and Duncan, *Population Pressures in Papua New Guinea, the Pacific Island Economies and Timor Leste*, p. 7.

[27] Booth, Zhang, Rao, Taomia and Duncan, *Population Pressures in Papua New Guinea, the Pacific Island Economies and Timor Leste*, p. 9.

[28] Booth, Zhang, Rao, Taomia and Duncan, *Population Pressures in Papua New Guinea, the Pacific Island Economies and Timor Leste*, p. 15.

[29] Speech by Alexander Downer at launch of Pacific 2020: Challenges and Opportunities for Growth', Sydney, 10 May 2006, available at <http://www.ausaid.gov.au/media/release.cfm?BC=Speech&ID=8653_9801_6672_4399_5645>, accessed 8 November 2007.

[30] Edwards, *Arthur Tange: Last of the Mandarins*, p. 135.

[31] Michael Evans, 'Island-Consciousness and Australian Strategic Culture', *IPA Review*, vol. 58, no. 2, July 2006, p. 23, available at <http://www.ipa.org.au/files/58-2-EVANS.pdf>, accessed 8 November 2007. For a longer treatment, see his excellent *The Tyranny of Dissonance: Australia's Strategic Culture and Way of War 1901-2005*, Study paper, no. 306, Land Warfare Studies Centre, Canberra, February 2005, available at <http://www.defence.gov.au/Army/LWSC/Publications/SP/SP_306.pdf>, accessed 8 November 2007.

[32] Lieutenant General Peter Leahy, 'The Medium Weight Force: lessons learned and future contributions to coalition operations', *Australian Army Journal*, vol. III, no. 2, pp. 1–8, available at <http://www.defence.gov.au/ARMY/LWSC/Publications/journal/AAJ_Winter06/Leahy_Medium_Weight_Force_revised.pdf>, accessed 8 November 2007. The article is based on a speech by Leahy to the Royal United Services Institute, London, on 8 June 2006.

[33] The official historian of the Army in Vietnam, Ian McNeill, wrote: 'In Vietnam, the task force had no sense of defeat. The final collapse, four years after the task force's withdrawal and at the hands of the North Vietnamese Army, exemplified the tragedy but seemed remote from the experience of the men and their leaders'. Ian McNeill, 'The Australian Army and the Vietnam War', chapter 2 in (eds) Jeff Doyle, Jeffrey Grey & Peter Pierce, *Australia's Vietnam War*, Texas A&M University Press, College Station, Texas, 2002, p. 48.

[34] John Howard, Address to the Australian Strategic Policy Institute's Global Forces 2006 Conference on 'Australia's Security Agenda', Canberra, 26 September 2006, p. 4. The transcript is available at <http://www.pm.gov.au/media/Speech/2006/speech2150.cfm>, accessed 8 November 2007.

[35] The Federal Government announced in August 2006 that the Australian Army would be increased by two extra battalions (an additional 2600 troops). The cost of raising the first battalion was put at A$6 billion over 11 years. The total cost of the two battalions was expected to be about A$10 billion. The first of the extra battalions will be raised in 2007, have core capabilities in place by 2008 and be deployable by 2010. The second extra battalion is supposed to be in place by 2012.

[36] Jim Wallace, former commander of the SAS, 'Stellar year for army but strategic ghosts still linger', *Asia Pacific Defence Reporter Source Book 2003–2004*, p. 29.

[37] Greg Sheridan, *The Partnership: the insider story of the US-Australian alliance under Bush and Howard*, University of NSW Press, Sydney, 2006, p. 13.

[38] Wallace, 'Stellar year for army but strategic ghosts still linger', *Asia Pacific Defence Reporter Source Book 2003–2004*, p. 30.

[39] Howard, Address to the Australian Strategic Policy Institute's Global Forces 2006 Conference on 'Australia's Security Agenda', Canberra, 26 September 2006, p. 2–3. The transcript is available at <http://www.pm.gov.au/media/Speech/2006/speech2150.cfm>, accessed 8 November 2007.

[40] Lawrence Kaplan, 'A military estranged from the architects of war', *Financial Times*, 9 August 2006, p. 9.

[41] Kaplan, 'A military estranged from the architects of war', *Financial Times*, p. 9.

[42] Colin Powell, with Joseph Persico, *A Soldier's Way: An autobiography*, Random House, Sydney, 1995, p. 303.

[43] Owen Harries, 'After Iraq', *Perspectives*, Lowy Institute for International Policy, Sydney, December 2006, p. 7, available at <http://www.lowyinstitute.org/Publication.asp?pid=516>, accessed 8 November 2007.

[44] Richard Armitage, 'Where is the US Going in the World?', Australian Security in the 21st Century Seminar Series, Menzies Research Centre, Canberra, 6 November 2006. For an edited version of the text, see <www.mrcltd.org.au/uploaded_documents/Richard_Armitage_MRC_Speech.doc>, accessed 8 November 2007.

[45] Kim Beazley, 'Beyond Iraq', Address to the Lowy Institute, Sydney, 10 August 2006, available at <http://alp.org.au/media/0806/speloo110.php>, accessed 8 November 2007.

[46] The Argentine Navy cruiser ARA *General Belgrano* was torpedoed and sunk by a nuclear powered submarine during the Falklands War, It was controversial due to disputed claims over the position of the vessel at time of sinking with regard to the maritime exclusion zone around the Falkland Islands. It was all the more significant given that losses from the *General Belgrano* accounted for over half of all Argentine deaths in the war.

[47] Graeme Dobell, *Australia Finds Home: The choices and chances of an Asia Pacific Journey*, ABC Books, Sydney, 2000, p. 265.

[48] Quoted in Lawrence Freedman, 'The Special Relationship, Then and Now', *Foreign Affairs*, vol. 85, no. 3, May/June 2006, p. 67.

[49] Lawrence Freedman, 'The Special Relationship, Then and Now', *Foreign Affairs*, vol. 85, no. 3, May/June 2006, p. 64.

Chapter 7

Jihadism and 'The Battle of Ideas' in Indonesia: Critiquing Australian Counterterrorism

Greg Fealy

> We are engaged in a battle of ideas [with terrorists], a struggle to the death over values.[1]
>
> [The fight against terrorism] is now one of the greatest political challenges of our generation. And I believe our most potent weapons in this struggle are our ideas.[2]
>
> Alexander Downer

The Howard Government has made counterterrorism a cardinal element in its foreign policy. This is evident from the amount of resources—human and financial—which have been devoted to this purpose during the past five years. More than A$8 billion has been committed to the 'war on terror' since late 2001, including about A$400 million in Southeast Asia.[3] Most of this regional expenditure goes to Indonesia, as it is seen as not only having the most severe terrorism problem in the region but as also the Southeast Asian country in which Australian citizens and assets are at the greatest risk of attack from groups such as Jemaah Islamiyah (JI) and the Noordin Mohammed Top network.[4] Counterterrorism assistance takes various forms. The most prominent has been the extensive technical cooperation and training provided by Australian police and intelligence agencies to their Southeast Asian counterparts. This includes assistance with forensic investigations and electronic surveillance, programs to improve terrorism database management, and training in terrorist psychology, ideology and operational methods. There has also been assistance for drafting counterterrorism legislation. In addition to these law enforcement, intelligence and legislative initiatives, the Australian Government has committed substantial sums of money to programs designed to combat terrorist ideas—its 2005 White Paper on regional terrorism (*Australia's National Security: A Defence Update 2005*) made clear that the government regarded 'extremist ideology' as the main driver of terrorism.[5] These programs are diverse and not always placed in an explicitly counterterrorism framework. They include interfaith dialogue conferences, Muslim exchange programs between Australian and Indonesian students, youth leaders and intellectuals, educational assistance programs which are aimed at Islamic schools (such as the Learning Assistance Program for Islamic Schools), and high-level visits to Australia by senior Indonesian Muslim leaders.

These campaigns against terrorist ideology, which the government regards as part of a broader 'battle of ideas', are the focus of this chapter. It will explore the government's perceptions of the 'battle of ideas' and critique the policies deriving from it. I will argue that this aspect of the counterterrorism effort is of questionable benefit, as it is either poorly targeted or fails to address the dynamics of jihadism and the vectors through which it is spread.

The Howard Government and the 'Battle of Ideas'

To gain a better understanding of how the Howard Government defines the 'battle of ideas', it is necessary to examine the statements and publications of key ministers and departments. There are three interlinked themes in this discourse: (1) ideology is the primary driver of terrorism; (2) ideas promoted by terrorists are totalitarian and based on a malign misinterpretation of 'true' Islamic teachings which are tolerant and pluralistic; and (3) Western nations can only defeat terrorism with the assistance of 'moderate Muslims'.

Australian Foreign Minister Alexander Downer has made the most frequent and detailed pronouncements about counterterrorism, and particularly the importance of ideas. In a 2006 speech entitled 'Ideas as Weapons', he said:

> Ordinary Australians ... want to know what is fanning this violent extremism. The answer is: ideas. Even though they are couched in religious terms, the ideas that drive terrorist groups like JI and al Qaeda are political in nature. Their ideas are based on a distorted and selective interpretation of Islam.

On another occasion, he declared:

> The heart of this contest [between moderate and radical Islam] is about the totalitarian mentality of violent extremism. It is about the *values* on which the terrorists base their ideology. ... This ideology can and will be defeated if people of good faith everywhere stand up against it.[6] [emphasis in original]

Downer has been at pains to illustrate the power that ideas can have in motivating global movements. In one speech he compared contemporary terrorism to communism of the last century:

> Soviet Communism began in a back room in London in 1903 with Lenin, a handful of followers and half a dozen pistols. They took an idea and turned it into a plan for political power. That revolutionary regime and its totalitarian ideology was an ideological storm that inflicted

catastrophic results on the world. ... At the beginning of the twenty-first century, terrorism and its extremist ideology is another storm bursting on the world.[7]

Downer pointed to the susceptibility of sections of the Muslim community to radical messages, saying 'as people search for meaning and spiritual fulfilment they can easily be misled by utopian ideas packaged as simple solutions to complex political problems'.[8] He repeatedly asserts the centrality of moderate Muslims to the counterterrorism effort:

> The most successful warriors against the Islamic extremist terrorists will be moderate Muslims.
>
> In the Mosques, in the Islamic schools and more broadly in the Muslim community, it is moderate Muslims who can spread and give life to the great values of peace and tolerance which are at the heart of the beliefs of the overwhelming majority of Muslims.
>
> We must support each other, as people who respect the rights of others, as people who value tolerance. We must support moderate Muslims to ensure that they successfully defeat the divisive message of hate, tyranny and intolerance propagated by the extremists.[9]

Australian Prime Minister John Howard has also spoken regularly, though in more general terms, on the importance of ideology and moderate Muslims to counterterrorism. Fighting terrorism, he says, is

> not only the military battle, but also the battle of ideas. ... We must try and engage and win the confidence of moderate Islamic people. ... Justifying terrorism by a reference to Islam is the common thread of all the terrorist attacks that we've had. Every single one of them has involved some kind of indication or reference point in Islam. Now that is blasphemous, it is a misrepresentation of the Islamic religion. [This] puts obligations on all of us, including in particular moderate Islamic leaders. Because it is their faith that is being blasphemed [sic] and wrongly invoked.[10]

Howard has been especially generous in his praise of 'moderate Muslim leaders' such as Pakistan's President Pervez Musharraf and Indonesia's President Susilo Bambang Yudhoyono. Musharraf is, according to Howard, someone who has played a major role in the fight against terrorism and in leading his country to democracy. Yudhoyono is described even more glowingly as 'one of the most capable moderate Islamic leaders in the world'.[11] Yudhoyono's 'election [in 2004] was a triumph for moderate Islam over the forces of evil and extremism. The terrorists want him to fail. The good, decent moderate Islamic people want him to succeed.'[12] He went on to compliment Pakistan and Indonesia as 'two great Islamic countries, both of whoms [sic] future as pillars and exemplars of moderate Islam is so important to winning the battle of ideas against the extremist elements around the world'.[13]

It is worth noting, in passing, that the language and counterterrorism priorities of the Australian Government are almost identical to that of the Bush Administration, suggesting that the former borrows heavily from the latter. Senior Administration officials refer constantly to the 'battle of ideas' and the need to enlist moderate Muslims in the global 'war on terror'. For example, in 2005 President Bush's National Security Advisor Stephen Hadley declared: 'we must win the battle of ideas' between [the terrorists'] 'grim totalitarian vision' and the free world's 'positive vision of freedom and democracy'. He described this as 'a struggle for the soul of Islam' in which 'Islamic moderates' needed to 'dispute the distorted vision of Islam advanced by terrorists'.[14]

More elaborate expositions on Australian Government counterterrorism thinking and policies are set out in a range of official documents, most particularly in DFAT's *Advancing the National Interest: Australia's Foreign and Trade Policy White Paper* (especially chapter 3),[15] and *Transnational Terrorism: The Threat to Australia* (especially chapter 5),[16] though the analyses of the nature of the 'terrorism problem' and the means of addressing it are, not surprisingly, consistent with the views enunciated by both Downer and Howard.

Critiquing the 'Battle of Ideas'

The Australian Government's discourse, on counterterrorism and the 'battle of ideas', invites several critical observations. The first is that the government's perception of the problem is based on a simplistic, dichotomous typology of Muslims as either 'radical' or 'moderate'. Rarely are definitions offered for either term, though it is often apparent from the use of related adjectives and synonyms how the government views these categories. 'Radical' is most commonly taken to mean 'violent', 'extremist' or 'fundamentalist', but is also often linked to intolerance, theocratic rather than democratic tendencies, and sectarianism; terrorism is located as an extremist sub-category within radicalism. By contrast, 'moderate' is associated to terms such as 'tolerant', 'pluralist' or 'mainstream', and Muslims of this persuasion are seen as democrats and law-abiding. Often, more loaded descriptors are used, such as referring to radical Muslims and terrorists as 'evil', 'medieval' and 'barbarous', or portraying moderates as 'good', 'peace-loving' and 'modern-minded'. Such a discourse revolves around binary opposites, whereby all virtue is ascribed to the 'moderates', and 'radicals' are cast in unrelievedly negative terms. In effect, the 'moderate Muslims' are cast as friends in a common struggle and the 'radical Muslims' are the enemy or at the very least problematic.

In reality, this dichotomy is crudely inadequate to understanding the great complexity within Indonesia's Islamic community (or indeed, any other community). Many Muslims may hold views that are, according to the Indonesian Government's criteria, both radical and moderate. Individual Muslims may be supportive of democracy and modernisation but also favour comprehensive implementation of sharia law and have anti-Semitic or anti-Christian views. For example, one of the most prominent Muslim leaders in Indonesia, Professor Din Syamsuddin, behaves in a way which transcends the radical-moderate division. One part of his public life appears to mark him out as a 'moderate'. He is chairman of the nation's second-largest Islamic organisation, Muhammadiyah, and also deputy chairman of the government-sponsored Indonesian Ulama Council, or Majelis Ulama Indonesia, two positions that would seem to place him squarely in the middle of 'mainstream' Islam. In addition to this, he enjoys a high profile at home and abroad as an advocate of interfaith dialogue. He is co-chair of the World Conference on Religion and Peace, convenor of the World Peace Forum, chairman of the Indonesian Chapter of Religion and Peace and deputy secretary-general of the World Islamic People's Forum.[17] He has also defended Indonesia's religiously neutral state ideology of Pancasila from attack by Islamists who seek to replace it with an explicitly Islamic ideology. On other occasions Din acts like a 'radical'. He has claimed that Indonesian terrorism is a product of Central Intelligence Agency manipulation, and during the US-led bombing of Afghanistan in 2001 he called for jihad against America. He has promoted hardline Islamists to the Indonesian Majelis Ulama Indonesia and backed the Council's controversial 2005 *fatwa* condemning 'pluralism, liberalism and religious secularism' as contrary to Islamic law.[18] At the same time, within Muhammadiyah he has overseen the sidelining of prominent moderate intellectuals and has spoken out in favour of sharia-based local laws, even where these are staunchly resisted by religious minorities. Thus, the range of Din Syamsuddin's thinking and actions are not easily reducible to a single characterisation. Trying to fit him into either a neat 'radical' or 'moderate' category is a Procrustean exercise.[19]

These kinds of complexities can be found across the Indonesian Islamic community. Sometimes they are the product of genuine ambivalence; in other cases they are borne of political calculation.

There is another problem with the radical/moderate characterisation: it encourages narrow thinking on the part of government officials when implementing policies and interacting with Muslims. For example, Indonesian Muslims invited to participate in exchange programs to Australia are carefully vetted to ensure that they have not espoused 'radical views'. Prospective participants who have been publicly critical of the 'war on terror' or advocated strongly Islamist positions are likely to be pushed lower down invitation lists or struck off them entirely. Moreover, some senior Australian officials have adopted a condescending or naively approving tone when meeting Muslims. One senior embassy official in Jakarta was in the habit of visiting mainstream Muslim organisations and commending his interlocutors as 'true Muslims', often to the chagrin of his hosts.

So, using a radical–moderate paradigm as the starting point for counterterrorism policies is inherently flawed as it imposes false boundaries upon Muslim behaviour. A sounder option would be to avoid the use of the term 'radical', as this covers too broad a spectrum of thinking and action within the Muslim community, and focus instead upon those who perpetrate or endorse violence. Thus, Islamists who seek 'sharia-isation' through democratic means or who criticise the 'war on terror' would not necessarily be regarded as 'part of the problem'; the important thing is that they do not use or condone violence.

The second difficulty with the Australian Government's approach is that it promotes the mistaken notion that there is a single 'correct' form of Islam which is inherently peaceable and tolerant. This is in keeping with President Bush's refrain that Islam is a 'religion of peace'. Islam, like other faiths, contains a diversity of teachings, many of which are open to a variety of interpretations. The two central sources of Islamic law—the Qur'an and the example of the Prophet Muhammad (Sunnah)—contain both irenic and bellicose elements. Much depends on Muslim perceptions of their position in the world as to whether tolerant or militant sources of guidance are drawn upon. Muslims who believe themselves to be under attack can find many sections of the Qur'an and Sunnah which sanction aggressive behaviour in such circumstances. By contrast, Muslims who find themselves in a relatively stable and prosperous community are more likely to invoke the pluralistic and quietist sections of scripture.

The third criticism of Australian policies is that they fail to specify the target audience for 'counter-radicalisation' programs and tend to offer undifferentiated programs for both mainstream and jihadist sections of the Islamic community, as if one approach will work for all Muslims (or, indeed, all terrorists). Attempts to involve 'moderate' or 'mainstream' Muslims in counterterrorism efforts appear to assume that terrorists and prospective terrorists are either drawn from mainstream Islam or heedful of moderate *ulema* or Islamic leaders. Both these assumptions are dubious. The available evidence points to most terrorists coming from family, educational or social backgrounds that are already militantly Islamist; very few of the more than 300 terrorists arrested to date have come from non-jihadist or mainstream organisations such as Muhammadiyah or Indonesia's largest Muslim organisation, Nahdlatul Ulama. Moreover, there is abundant evidence suggesting that terrorists and those whom terrorists are seeking to recruit are dismissive of moderate leaders, believing that they are part of Islam's problem. Terrorists accuse moderates of straying from 'true' Islamic teachings and of weakening the faith by being too prepared for compromise on matters that Muslims should rightly hold firm, such as unstintingly implementing sharia and rejecting secularism. The convicted Bali bomber, Imam Samudra, gave some insight into these attitudes when he wrote that mujahideen should only follow Islamic scholars who had direct experience of war:

> How could those ulema who have never fought a jihad or been on the battlefield possibly understand the issues and complexities of jihad? ... When the ulema are increasingly busily submerged in their collections of holy books and the echo of loudspeakers, they no longer care about the despoiling, vilifying and colonisation of Mecca and their holy lands. It was preordained by God that a group of holy war fighters would be born who were truly aware and understood what they had to do.[20]

Hence, the Australian Government's policy to use moderates to influence terrorists seems doomed to failure. Indeed, there is mounting evidence to suggest that the most effective way to wage a 'battle of ideas' among jihadists is to use Islamic scholars who are of similar doctrinal outlook but who reject terrorism in an Indonesian context. Most Indonesian jihadists regard themselves as salafist, a puritanically conservative stream within Islam which seeks to model itself strictly on the example of the first three generations of Muslims. The great majority of salafists are non-violent and pursue their religious and social goals through educational, intellectual and preaching activity. There is, however, a small sub-stream within salafism, usually called jihadi salafism, which regards violence against Islam's enemies as justified. Non-jihadist salafis are strongly critical of terrorism, regarding it as sinful and contrary to the teachings of Islam's founding generations.[21]

A look at the discourse regarding terrorism in Indonesia shows the impact of salafist critiques of jihadi salafism. In 2004, Imam Samudra published his biography and manifesto, *Aku Melawan Teroris* (I Oppose Terrorists), which soon became a best-seller. By 2006, more that 15 000 copies had been sold and the book had been reprinted four times. *Aku Melawan Teroris* gave the first opportunity for many Indonesian Muslims to read a terrorist explaining in detail their thinking and actions, and the author repeatedly justifies his behaviour in terms of salafist principles. Samudra's publication prompted a string of books from critics challenging his interpretations. The first was Nasir Abas's *Membongkar Jama'ah Islamiyah* (Exposing Jemaah Islamiyah).[22] Nasir was a former JI member and head of the organisation's third regional command based in Sulawesi. Although not from a staunch salafist perspective, he accuses Samudra of selective quoting from the Qur'an and of twisting JI's original doctrine. The second 'reply' to Samudra was written by a salafi scholar and former paramilitary leader, Luqman Ba'abduh, *Mereka Adalah Teroris* (They are the Terrorists).[23] The cover is identical to that of Samudra's book and the text offers a closely argued exegetical and jurisprudential rebuttal of *Aku Melawan Teroris* from a salafist viewpoint. (Ba'abduh has also travelled widely through Indonesia, holding public meetings to discredit Samudra's writings.)[24] Another salafist scholar, Abu Hamzah Yusuf At-Atsary, published a shorter tome opposing Samudra entitled *Aku Melawan Teroris: Sebuah Kedustaan Atas Nama Ulama Ahlussunnah* (I Oppose Terrorists: a Fraud in the Name of Sunni Ulema), in which he declares the Bali bomber to be deceiving his co-religionists and of advancing thinking which is un-salafi.[25] The most recent book on this subject, by Muhammadiyah intellectual Abduh Zulfidar Akaha, is critical of Ba'abduh and the attack on Samudra.[26] Not to be outdone, Samudra has, from his cell on death row, written his response to critics, though it has yet to be published.[27] Interestingly, much of his text is taken up with answering salafist criticisms of his original writings.

Thus, it is clear from the foregoing that much of the debate over the legitimacy of terrorism is taking place not in mainstream communities but within fundamentalist and radical Islamic groups. These are the circles from which most terrorists are recruited and if would-be jihadists are to be dissuaded from violent activity, it will be this discourse which is most likely to influence them. Western governments will find it difficult to assist this salafist challenge to terrorism, because most salafist scholars would be averse to receiving Western aid, and would object to many of the views held by salafists. For example, salafists are usually opposed to gender equality, deny Israel's right to exist, are anti-Semitic, and are hostile to the 'Christian West'.

A final criticism of the 'battle of ideas' is that it greatly exaggerates the extent of ideological ferment within the broader Islamic community. Australian politicians frequently talk about the 'battle of ideas' as if large sections of Indonesia's Muslim community were at risk of radicalisation. The reality is that Islamism and jihadism are very much minority phenomena and there is little evidence to support the contention that Indonesia is becoming more radical. In political terms, Islamist parties gained just 16 per cent and 22 per cent at the 1999 and 2004 elections respectively—far below the 43 per cent of the 1955 election. While there are some localities controlled by Islamist parties and currently engaged in 'sharia-isation', these amount to less than 10 per cent of Indonesia's more than 500 provinces and districts. At the national level, attempts to insert sharia clauses into the constitution have been soundly defeated. This suggests that, in terms of mainstream Islam, there is no monumental battle between pluralism and tolerance on the one hand and violent jihad and fundamentalism on the other. There is serious debate over ideological and theological issues related to jihad, but this discourse is taking place within a largely pluralist framework and there is little prospect of the terms of this debate changing dramatically within the short to medium term.

A more important task for Australian counterterrorism than the 'battle of ideas' is to persuade Indonesians of the nature of the terrorism problem within their country. While seemingly most Indonesians now accept that terrorist attacks have been carried out by their fellow countrymen, conspiracy theories regarding the role of foreign intelligence agencies abound and denial of JI's existence in Indonesia remains commonplace. The Australian Government could contribute to a more informed debate in Indonesia by releasing reliable information about terrorists including, where possible, primary source materials gathered by intelligence agencies, and by assisting the Indonesian police to explain terrorist thinking and activities to the public.

Another obstacle for effective counterterrorism is to allay suspicions about Western motives in conducting the 'war on terror'. There are two elements to this. The first is that countries such as Australia and the United States apply different standards when dealing with the Muslim world compared to their own allies and client states. The most often mentioned cases are those of the Israel–Palestine conflict and the treatment of Muslim detainees in Guantanamo Bay's Camp Delta. An indication of the depth of feeling generated by such issues is a recent speech by K. H. Mustofa Bisri, the deputy president (*rais*) of Nahdlatul Ulama. Mustofa, apart from being a noted Islamic scholar, poet and columnist, has also been an eloquent champion of religious tolerance and understanding. And yet, during the Israeli attack on southern Lebanon in 2006, he railed against the role of Western countries, and the United States in particular, in supporting Israel and unleashing emotions that feed terrorism:

> Hatred against Israel and condemnation of its cruelty appear to have failed to stop the US from being arrogant and taking the side of Israel. This can be understood because according to Gus Dur [former Indonesian president and Nahdlatul Ulama chairman, Abdurrahman Wahid], one-third of the leaders in the US are Israelis/Jews. God permits, even if doomsday happens within the next two days, the US will continue to protect Israel even if this means trampling on the principles it has glorified all along such as democracy, human rights et cetera. While supporting Israel, the US is not afraid of losing its face because it has 1000 faces. As the strongest country, which has no match at all levels, the US tends to be arrogant and does not listen to other sides, except those on its side.
>
> The US behaviour—often described as being a double standard—is the cause of all 'indiscriminate' resistance everywhere. It has become the root of terrorism. What can the weak with high motivation do to fight the strongest one? Just like a child abused by parents, the most he/she can do is pelt stones at the roof of the house—an action that will only disadvantage oneself and those not the target of resistance.

In connection with this, we have seen groups that have passion, whose spirit for jihad are [sic] burning, and they want to go to the battle in Lebanon and Palestine. So strong are their passion and spirit that rational considerations are defeated. Even waging jihad requires logical considerations. Look at the jihad waged by Prophet Muhammad SAW [Peace be Upon Him], the great leader and role model for all the faithful!

...

Who would possibly not be angered or outraged by Israel's excessive inhuman actions? But Allah has warned the faithful to uphold truth consistently, justly, and rationally. Outrage and hatred often drag people to inconsistency. That is why Allah has commanded: 'And let not enmity and hatred of others make you avoid justice. Be just, that is nearer to piety'

(Qur'an surah 5 verse 8).[28]

Despite his anger at what he sees as the injustice of Israeli and US actions, and his sympathy for those who oppose it, Mustofa ultimately warns against violent jihad as a reaction.

The second suspicion is that Western countries are using the 'war on terror' as a means of pursuing their strategic, diplomatic and economic interests. One common view within Islamic political circles, for example, is that nations such as Australia have tried to lever Indonesia into supporting the current Iraq War by claiming this as a part of the 'war on terror'.

Conclusion

Australia's counterterrorism efforts have had some impressive achievements. The low-profile but highly successful cooperation between the Australian Federal Police and the Indonesian Police is the most obvious example, but there have also been the significant efforts to improve counterterrorism training and analysis. Other aspects such as assistance to the Islamic education sector are commendable, though unlikely to bring about marked changes in attitude. The 'battle of ideas', by contrast, is one of the more problematic aspects of Australian counterterrorism. It rests upon questionable assumptions about the nature of terrorist recruitment and has tended to be applied in a vague and unsubtle way. While it is clearly desirable to assist moderate Muslim leaders in promoting values of tolerance and pluralism within the Islamic community, there is little chance that such activity will impact on terrorists.

ENDNOTES

[1] Alexander Downer, 'Transnational Terrorism: The Threat to Australia', speech to National Press Club of Australia, Canberra, 15 July 2004, available at <http://www.foreignminister.gov.au/speeches/2004/040715_tt.html>, accessed 24 October 2007, p. 3.

[2] Alexander Downer, 'Ideas as Weapons: Meeting the Ideological Challenge of Extremism', speech to the International Institute of Strategic Studies, London, 15 September 2006, available at <http://www.foreignminister.gov.au/speeches/2006/061215_iiss.html>, accessed 24 October 2007, p. 1.

[3] Alexander Downer, 'Terrorism: Winning the Battle of Ideas', speech to the Sydney Institute, Sydney, 1 November 2006, available at <http://www.foreignminister.gov.au/speeches/2006/061101_terrorism.html>, accessed 24 October 2007, p. 1.

[4] For accounts of these terrorist groups, see Sidney Jones, 'The Changing Nature of Jemaah Islamiyah', *Australian Journal of International Affairs*, vol. 59, no. 2, June 2005, pp. 169–78; and Sally Neighbour, *In the Shadow of Swords: On the Trail of Terrorism from Afghanistan to Australia*, HarperCollins, Sydney, 2004.

[5] Department of Defence, *Australia's National Security: A Defence Update 2005*, Commonwealth of Australia, Canberra, 2005, available at <http://www.defence.gov.au/update2005/defence_update_2005.pdf>, accessed 8 November 2007.

[6] Downer, 'Terrorism: Winning the Battle of Ideas', p. 2.

[7] Downer, 'Ideas as Weapons: Meeting the Ideological Challenge of Extremism', pp. 11–12.

[8] Downer, 'Ideas as Weapons: Meeting the Ideological Challenge of Extremism', p. 7.

[9] Alexander Downer, speech at the Opening of the 'Multifaith Conference for Peace and Harmony', 30 September 2005, Sydney, available at <http://www.foreignminister.gov.au/speeches/2005/050930_multifaith_conference.html>, accessed 24 October 2007.

[10] John Howard in interview with Alan Jones, Radio 2GB, Sydney, 12 September 2006, available at <http://www.pm.gov.au/media/interview/2006/Interview2129.cfm>, accessed 24 October 2007.

[11] John Howard in interview with Gillian O'Shaughnessy, ABC Radio, Perth, 6 April 2006, available at <http://www.pm.gov.au/media/interview/2006/Interview1866.cfm>, accessed 24 October 2007.

[12] John Howard, address to Liberal Party Victorian Division State Council, Melbourne, 2 April 2005, available at <http://www.pm.gov.au/media/speech/2005/speech1293.cfm>, accessed 24 October 2007, p. 3.

[13] John Howard, address at luncheon for the President of the Islamic Republic of Pakistan, His Excellency General Pervez Musharraf, Parliament House, 15 June 2005, available at <http://www.pm.gov.au/media/speech/2005/speech1425.cfm>, accessed 24 October 2007.

[14] Remarks by National Security Advisor Stephen Hadley to the Council on Foreign Relations, 18 October 2005, available at <http://www.whitehouse.gov/news/releases/2005/10/20051018-6.html>, accessed 24 October 2007.

[15] Australian Government, Department of Foreign Affairs and Trade, *Advancing the National Interest: Australia's Foreign and Trade Policy White Paper*, Commonwealth of Australia, 2003, available at <www.dfat.gov.au/ani/chapter_3.html>, accessed 24 October 2007.

[16] Australian Government, Department of Foreign Affairs and Trade, *Transnational Terrorism: The Threat to Australia*, Commonwealth of Australia, 2004, available at <www.dfat.gov.au/publications/terrorism/chapter5.html>, accessed 24 October 2007.

[17] See *Jawa Pos*, 17 August 2006; *The Jakarta Post*, 31 August 2006; and *Republika*, 10 November 2006.

[18] For an English-language translation of the *fatwa*, see (eds) Greg Fealy and Virginia Hooker, *Voices of Islam in Southeast Asia: A Contemporary Sourcebook*, Institute of South East Asian Studies, Singapore, 2006, pp. 461–62.

[19] Publicly, at least, the Australian Government chooses to place Din Syamsuddin in the 'moderate' camp. He has been DFAT 'special visitor' to Australia and meets regularly with Foreign Minister Alexander Downer. In private, though, policymakers are mindful of his Islamist proclivities and are less trusting of Din than his predecessor in the Muhammadiyah chairmanship, Professor Syafii Maarif.

[20] Imam Samudra, *Aku Melawan Teroris*, Jazera, Solo, 2004, translated in Fealy and Hooker, *Voices of Islam in Southeast Asia*, pp. 374–75.

[21] Sidney Jones, of the International Crisis Group, Jakarta, was the first writer to propose the use of salafi ulema to counteract the influence of jihadi salafists. See, *Indonesia Backgrounder: Why Salafism and Terrorism Mostly Don't Mix*, Asia Report, no. 83, 13 September 2004.

[22] Nasir Abas, *Membongkar Jamaah Islamiyah: Pengakuan Mantan Anggota JI*, Grafindo, Jakarta, 2005.

[23] Al Ustadz Luqman bin Muhammad Ba'abduh, *Mereka Adalah Teroris: Bantahan Terhadap 'Aku Melawan Teroris': Bantahan Terhadap Buku Aku Melawan Teroris*, Pustaka Qaulun Sadida, Malang, 2005. Ba'abduh is of Arab descent and is Yemeni educated. He is a former commander of the Laskar Jihad paramilitary forces.

[24] *The Jakarta Post*, 16 January 2006.

[25] Al Ustadz Abu Hamzah Yusuf al-Atsary, et al, *'Aku Melawan Teroris': Sebuah Kedustaan Atas Nama Ulama Ahlussunnah*, Centre for Moderate Muslim, Jakarta, 2005, pp. 12–15.

[26] Abduh Zulfidar Akaha, *Siapa Teroris?, Siapa Khawarij?*, Pustaka al-Kautsar, Jakarta, 2006.

[27] Ustadz Imam Samdura, *Bantahan Terhadap Tulisan Abu Hamza Yusuf al-Atsari*, (forthcoming).

[28] K. H. Mustofa Bisri, 'Israel's Cruelty and Spirit of Jihad', in *Mata Air* bulletin, no. 33, 25 August 2006.

Chapter 8

Security Cooperation in the Asia-Pacific Region

Brendan Taylor

In keeping with the theme of this volume, this chapter examines the evolution and achievements of security cooperation in the Asia-Pacific region, with a view to gauging where it might be headed. 'Security Cooperation' is, of course, a rather broad term that can be applied to a wide range of activities. The analysis undertaken in this chapter will be limited to regional security institutions and other dialogue channels however, given that it is in relation to these processes that the SDSC has typically made its most visible and important contributions to security cooperation in the Asia-Pacific. The chapter is divided into three main sections. It begins by examining the evolution of regional security cooperation in the Asia-Pacific—a process which really only began in earnest during the 1990s. It then considers the successes and shortcomings of regional security cooperation in the Asia-Pacific, including some brief reflections upon the contribution that the SDSC has made toward the furtherance of these endeavours. Finally, the chapter concludes with some observations regarding the main issues and prospects facing regional security cooperation in this part of the world.

Emergence and Evolution of Regional Security Cooperation

Prior to the 1990s, very few channels for regional security dialogue existed in the Asia-Pacific. This was not for want of trying. Several ill-fated efforts were undertaken to establish regional groupings which, over time, provided the basis for a more substantial Asia-Pacific security architecture. These included the Southeast Asia Treaty Organization—an eight member grouping established in 1955 that began to lose members and was finally dissolved in 1977—and both Maphilindo and the Association of Southeast Asia.[1] Likewise, in Northeast Asia, the Asian and Pacific Council—a South Korean initiative established in 1966 and comprising nine member countries—struggled due to the diverging perceptions and interests of its membership, and finally collapsed in 1975.[2] Flowing from this legacy was the more successful sub-regional ASEAN, founded in 1967 and expanded via several avenues, including a major security component—the ASEAN Regional Forum. But even ASEAN's initial collaborative functions were essentially economic, political and cultural; and its latest manifestations—ASEAN-plus-three and the East Asia Summit (EAS)—focus more on these issues than on strategy or geopolitics.

As a consequence, bilateral (namely US-led) cooperation tended to be the primary mode of Asia-Pacific security collaboration throughout the Cold War period. This, of course, stands in stark contrast to the situation today. To be sure, America's Asia-Pacific alliances remain an integral component of the region's security architecture and—notwithstanding the process of 'transformation' which this system of alliances is undergoing to accommodate the dynamics of the post-11 September 2001 strategic environment—some of these relationships (namely the US–Japan and US–Australia alliances) have actually strengthened during the period since the end of the Cold War, contrary to the expectations of conventional theories of alliance politics.[3]

Because the hierarchical aspects of this system are giving way to more fluid processes of intra-alliance consultations, however, new 'minilateral' mechanisms such as the US–Japan–South Korea Trilateral Coordination and Oversight Group and the US–Japan–Australia Trilateral Strategic Dialogue have been formed to address emerging security issues at both the regional and global levels. This 'expansive bilateralism' has been supplemented since the early 1990s by a startling growth in regional institutions, arrangements and structures. According to one recent estimate, over 100 such channels now exist at the official (Track 1) level, including such leading regional security institutions as the ARF, the SCO and the EAS which, despite its largely economic focus, still has the potential to emerge over time as an influential East Asian security mechanism.[4] More ad hoc, but still substantial, multilateral initiatives have also been employed toward specific issues such as the Four-Power Talks and, later, the Six-Party Talks concerning security on the Korean peninsula. The growth in institutions and dialogues at the unofficial (or Track 2) level has been even more profound, with in excess of 200 such channels now estimated to exist.[5] These include the ASEAN Institutes for Strategic and International Studies, which was one of the few facilitators of regional security dialogue prior to the 1990s; the Council for Security Cooperation in the Asia-Pacific (CSCAP), arguably the region's premier second track institution and with whose development the SDSC has been intimately involved; the relatively new Network of East Asian Think Tanks (NEAT), which some analysts regard as a potential (Chinese-led) challenge to more established second track processes such as CSCAP; as well as the annual International Institute for Strategic Studies (IISS) Shangri-la Dialogue, which takes place in Singapore and has essentially become a de facto gathering of regional defence ministers.[6]

Yet, this startling growth in regional security cooperation has been neither steady nor straightforward. The volume of such institutions and activities plummeted in the immediate aftermath of the 1997–98 Asian financial crisis, for instance, and temporarily lost the attention of policymakers in the process. Still, there can be little disputing the fact that regional security cooperation has since recovered well and, moreover, that the general trend in such activity across the decade and a half since the beginning of the 1990s has been upward. So what explains this recent and, indeed, rather dramatic growth in regional security cooperation? I see at least five factors at play.

First, for a number of reasons it is virtually impossible to overstate the catalytic role played by the ending of the Cold War. The collapse of the Soviet Union and its withdrawal from the region subsequently called into question the future of America's strategic presence and level of commitment to the Asia-Pacific. At one level, the establishment of highly consensual security mechanisms such as the ARF was intended to serve the dual purpose of 'tying in' this regional US presence, while at the same time diluting the influence that the sole superpower would be able to exert in the new strategic environment. Added to this, however, it soon became apparent that many of the features of the Cold War had remained intact in the Asia-Pacific and that inter-state conflict remained a very real possibility here. How the region's other major powers—namely China, Japan and India—might react to this intriguing set of developments therefore provided a further source of uncertainty. Hence, as Desmond Ball has observed, 'mechanisms for regionwide dialogue, confidence building, transparency, and cooperation were considered to be essential to the management of this uncertainty'.[7]

The desire to alleviate regional concerns regarding China's rise provided a *second* rationale for the burgeoning in regional security cooperation. One of the primary reasons for establishing the ARF, for instance, was to allow for the greater exposure of decision-makers in Beijing to regional and global norms, with a view to positively influencing the shape of China's foreign and security policy orientation. Since the late 1990s, however, an interesting feature of China's apparent embrace of multilateralism has been the extent to which Beijing has become an increasingly direct contributor to the growth in Asia-Pacific security cooperation through the leading role it has played in the establishment of a number of high-profile regional institutions including the Boao Forum for Asia, the SCO, and the NEAT.

Third, at several levels, economic factors also serve to explain the dramatic increase in regional security cooperation. The 'success' of regional economic cooperative processes, such as the Pacific Basin Economic Council and the Pacific Economic Cooperation Council, generated calls for this positive experience to be replicated in the security sector. Indeed, the institutional make-up of CSCAP—comprising national committees, a steering committee and several working groups—was modelled directly on the Pacific Economic Cooperation

Council process. For at least two reasons—one positive and one negative—the growing economic weight of a number of actors in the region can also be seen to have contributed directly towards the increase in regional security cooperation. The increasing economic (and strategic) weight of Japan and China, for instance, can be seen as a factor which has contributed towards their growing willingness and ability to play more active and stimulatory roles as institutional contributors and even innovators. As India's economic and strategic weight also grows, its desire to play a similar leadership role is likely to increase in kind.

At the same time, however, economic growth has afforded many regional governments the option of increasing national defence expenditure. From the mid-1980s to the mid-1990s, this was a source of much concern as regional arms acquisitions burgeoned at alarming rates on the back of the so-called 'East Asian economic miracle'. Some commentators even went so far as to posit the emergence of a 'new Asian arms race'.[8] As a consequence, the fact that the Asia-Pacific was looking increasingly 'ripe for rivalry' served only to reinforce the urgent need for further security cooperation amongst the countries of this region. The onset of the 1997–98 Asian financial crisis resulted in a temporary slowing of these startling trends in regional arms acquisitions and, as noted previously, took the wind out of Asia-Pacific security cooperation in the process. However, most regional countries have since resumed increasing defence budgets, giving rise to renewed apprehensions that competitive arms processes (if not a regional arms race) are currently re-emerging. As Robert Hartfiel and Brian Job have recently concluded:

> In both Northeast and Southeast Asia, resources are being directed towards externally oriented weapons systems, including submarines, surface ships, fighter aircraft, and missiles of all types. This strongly suggests competitive arms processes that are heavily weighted towards types of weapons that destabilize the military balance. Such a conclusion merits more careful, sober analysis by political decision makers in the region in order to reduce the likelihood of confrontation and conflict.[9]

This finding, while unsettling, could also potentially augur well for regional security cooperation.

Fourth, the continued persistence of traditional security concerns—such as the prospect of a destabilising arms race—has been complicated by the increasing prevalence and potency of a range of non-traditional security challenges including international terrorism, transnational crime, environmental issues and disease-based threats. Moreover, as the continuing North Korean nuclear crisis and plight of a perpetually starving North Korean population demonstrate all too well, there is a growing awareness as to the interdependence between these traditional and non-traditional security agendas—a realisation which has, in turn, fundamentally re-cast the dynamics of regional security cooperation. The

11 September 2001 terrorist attacks against the United States and the onset of the so-called 'war on terror' served as a watershed, giving rise to a flurry of regional dialogue activity addressing a range of terrorism and human security issues. The attendant realisation that terrorism and these other transnational security challenges simply could not be tackled on a solely unilateral or even a bilateral basis has subsequently been reinforced by the Severe Acute Respiratory Syndrome (SARS) crisis of 2003, the Indian Ocean Tsunami of 2004, and the ongoing regional (and, indeed, global) threat posed by H5N1 Avian Influenza (or 'bird flu'). By way of example, even in the case of the US-led system of bilateral alliances—so often preoccupied with more traditional security concerns—there is evidence of a shift of focus (albeit intermittent at this stage) toward non-military security challenges, as demonstrated by the relief effort of late 2004 and 2005 following the 26 December 2004 Indian Ocean Tsunami.

Finally, while still in a nascent phase of its evolution, the desire to realise the potentially powerful idea of an East Asian community has gone some way towards contributing to the growth in regional security cooperation. At the Track 1 level this has been reflected in the creation of a number of high-profile institutions, including the EAS. It is a trend that is also being mirrored at the Track 2 level, as evidenced over recent years in the establishment of the NEAT and its Japanese competitor, the Council on East Asian Community.[10] It ought to be noted, however, that the proliferation of such groupings does not, by itself, necessarily constitute progress toward tangible regional security cooperation. These entities, after all, tend to compete with each other for attention, as much as coordinate. This is a theme that will be re-visited in the concluding section of this chapter.

Successes and Shortcomings

Before reflecting upon some of the successes and shortcomings which have flowed out of this dramatic burgeoning in regional security cooperation, we must acknowledge that this evaluative task is an inevitably subjective one. As Amitav Acharya has observed: 'Despite decades of intense debate, international relations theory provides no agreed and definitive way of assessing what constitutes "success" and "effectiveness" in regional organizations. Understanding the effects of Asian institutions on state behavior and regional order depends very much on the analytical lens used.'[11]

By way of example, many if not most regional players will tend to assess regional security cooperation not in terms of its immediate *outcomes*, but rather as a *process* through which confidence is built, consensus reached and common regional understandings or 'norms' achieved.

This issue of analytical subjectivity notwithstanding, it is, I believe, possible to identify a number of areas where Asia-Pacific security institutions have unequivocally fallen short. As alluded to previously, no regional security institution has been able to respond effectively to the major crises that have erupted in the Asia-Pacific during the past decade and a half—the North Korean nuclear crises of 1993–94 and today; the 1995–96 Taiwan Strait crisis; the 1997–98 Asian financial crisis; the crisis in East Timor of 1999 and again of today; the 2003 SARS crisis or the 2004 Indian Ocean Tsunami. Partly as a result of the consensual style approach to decision-making which has emerged as the preferred *modus operandi* for most if not all of these regional institutions, they have also tended to move rather slowly toward implementing their stated aims and objectives. In the case of the ARF, for instance, it has experienced real difficulties in progressing from the confidence building phase to the preventive diplomacy phase, contributing toward the perception that it is nothing more than a 'talk shop'.[12] Related to this, many regional institutions have struggled to keep pace with and adapt to their changing security surrounds. For example, the fact that APEC does not presently count India—an increasingly significant regional economic power and security actor—among its members seems incomprehensible.

These criticisms notwithstanding—and even if one does not accept the proposition that dialogue and discussion are useful as ends in and of themselves[13]—there are areas where tangible benefits have accrued from the recent growth in Asia-Pacific security cooperation. In my view, first and foremost among these accomplishments has been the engagement (some would say enmeshment) of China in the regional security architecture which has taken place from the mid-1990s onwards. This process has succeeded in significantly dampening regional apprehensions regarding China's rise. At the same time, however, it is interesting to note that while a primary aim of engaging China through Asia-Pacific multilateralism was to 'socialise' it by exposing it to regional and global norms, Beijing has proven rather adept at shaping (or dare I say 'socialising') many of the institutions to which it is a party. In the case of CSCAP, for example, China's deepening involvement has actually allowed it to shape the direction and outlook of this leading Track 2 institution, particularly in relation to the issue of Taiwan.

Second, although Asia-Pacific security institutions haven't been particularly effective in responding directly to regional crises, they have periodically served as useful venues for the discussion of highly sensitive or controversial issues that might otherwise not have been discussed, or as 'circuit-breakers' to stalled diplomatic relationships. The September 1999 APEC Leaders summit, for instance, provided an opportunity for US President Bill Clinton and Chinese President Jiang Zemin to hold their first meeting since the accidental US bombing of the Chinese embassy in Belgrade the previous May. The crisis talks held at this meeting—and particularly a forceful speech delivered at the meeting by the then US President Bill Clinton—also appear to have critically influenced Indonesia's decision to allow a UN force into East Timor.[14] Likewise, the then US Secretary of State, Colin Powell, was able to meet with his North Korean counterpart on the sidelines of the 2004 ARF meeting, which marked the first high-level contact between the United States and North Korea since Madeleine Albright's visit to Pyongyang in 2000. More recently, the Chinese and Japanese foreign ministers were able to hold a productive 20 minute meeting in the toilet in the lead-up to the 2006 ARF, helping to arrest somewhat a deepening rift in Sino-Japanese relations. So, it seems fair to conclude that regional security institutions have served as more than mere 'talks shops' and that they have produced some tangible successes, albeit highly qualified ones and often only at the margins.

Added to this, the very existence and continued evolution of ASEAN can itself be counted as an important success. It is always important to consider counterfactual scenarios in international politics, and to contemplate what type of Southeast Asia might exist today were it not for the existence of ASEAN. It is certainly no small feat that a 'shooting war' amongst its members is today all but unthinkable. As Rodolfo Severino of the Singapore-based Institute of Southeast Asian Studies recently noted:

> The constant interaction and sense of common purpose among the ASEAN members have built mutual confidence and dissipated some of the mutual suspicion that is a legacy of past differences and an outgrowth of current disagreements. ... Partly through the Treaty of Amity and Cooperation in South-east Asia and partly through its own practices, ASEAN has set regional norms for the peaceful relations among states—respect for sovereignty and territorial integrity, the peaceful settlement of disputes, non-interference in the internal affairs of nations, decisions by consensus, equality of status, and so on.[15]

Before moving to conclude with a few observations regarding the main issues and prospects facing security cooperation in the Asia-Pacific, it is worth briefly contemplating some of the contributions that the SDSC has made toward the furtherance of security dialogue in this part of the world.

Given the prominence of bilateral (namely US-led) cooperation as the primary mode of Asia-Pacific security collaboration throughout the Cold War period, it is important to acknowledge the substantial contributions that members of the SDSC have made to better understanding and explaining US alliance relationships in this part of the world. Coral Bell has led the way here through her extensive writings on the US–Australia alliance. Indeed, Bell was present at the signing of the ANZUS Treaty in 1951. Her best known work addressing the US–Australia alliance is *Dependent Ally*, which examines this and also Australia's relationship with the United Kingdom from a historical perspective and which has subsequently been published in three editions.[16] Her more recent Australian Strategic Policy Institute paper, *Living with Giants: Finding Australia's place in a more complex world*, traverses similar analytical terrain, but takes a longer term view as to how Australia might best balance its regional commitments and global alliances in a neighbourhood that will almost inevitably be characterised by an increasingly populous, economically powerful and technologically sophisticated set of societies.[17] Albeit from a completely different perspective, Desmond Ball's path-breaking work on US strategic installations in Australia should also be noted for the impact it has had in terms of markedly expanding the contours of public debate on this subject.[18] Other SDSC members who have made useful intellectual contributions to explaining and better understanding America's Asia-Pacific alliances include Paul Dibb and Ron Huisken.[19]

Since the early 1990s, the contribution of SDSC members to the scholarship and actual practice of multilateral security cooperation in the Asia-Pacific has been equally important and influential. We might like to reflect upon the fact, for instance, that three out of the five Australian representatives on the ARF's register of experts and eminent persons have a very close association with the SDSC—Paul Dibb, Alan Dupont and Hugh White. Paul Dibb has been an active participant in a number of other regional security dialogues, including as Chair of the first security dialogue between China and Australia in 1993 and as Chair of an informal meeting of 18 ARF countries on practical measures for military and security cooperation in 1994. Likewise, in comparison to any other Australian figure, Desmond Ball's contribution to regional second track diplomacy is unparalleled and, for this reason, he is identified by Brian Job as part of an Asia-Pacific Track 2 elite that also includes the likes of Jusef Wanandi, Carolina Hernandez, Ralph Cossa, Paul Evans and the late Noordin Sopie.[20] A number of others, including Ron Huisken and Ross Babbage, have been active participants and contributors to the IISS Shangri-la Dialogue. The SDSC itself has produced an impressive number of monographs and papers addressing regional security cooperation.[21] Last, but not least, it has also been directly involved in the training and education of a number of scholars who have gone on to become leading international authorities on regional security cooperation, including David Capie and Herman Kraft.[22]

Where To From Here?

So where to from here? I'd like to conclude this chapter with a few observations regarding the future of security cooperation in the Asia-Pacific. *First*, while regional security dialogue has now become an established fixture in this part of the world, it seems fair to conclude that its impact is likely to remain relatively limited and largely confined to the margins. Where the most progress is likely to be made is in relation to so-called non-traditional security challenges such as infectious disease, terrorism, transnational crime, energy, and disaster prevention/mitigation. In May 2006, for instance, the inaugural ASEAN Defence Ministers meeting in Kuala Lumpur identified disaster relief cooperation as a priority issue upon which to focus its future work. Likewise, as part of its transition from confidence building to practical cooperation, Barry Desker has recently called upon the ARF to consider developing further collaborative measures addressing non-traditional security challenges, if only to demonstrate its continuing relevance in an increasingly crowded Asia-Pacific security architecture.[23] Addressing these kinds of trans-border challenges, of course, is appealing not only because they are becoming increasingly pressing and potentially affect the region as a whole, but also because they will often tend not to raise the same level of sensitivity (particularly in relation to issues of sovereignty and non-intervention) that more traditional security issues are apt to generate.

Second, one of the factors most likely to stymie the progress of regional security cooperation stems from the fact that the great powers are increasingly viewing Asia-Pacific security institutions as instruments of competitive influence. China led the way and, in some respects, has stolen the march on the rest of the region's major players through its leading role in driving forward such processes as the SCO, the Boao Forum and the NEAT. The quite deliberate exclusion of the United States from the EAS, as well as the open bickering between China and Japan which all but derailed the inaugural gathering of this grouping, can be seen as further evidence of this competitive approach to regional institutions. The United States has been surprisingly slow to respond, but there are signs that it is now doing so through its ongoing efforts to inject a greater security focus into APEC, a new US–ASEAN partnership, as well as a renewed commitment to the ARF (as was reflected by Secretary of State Condoleezza Rice's attendance at the 2006 ARF meeting in the midst of a Middle East crisis). How successful this process of American re-engagement ultimately turns out to be, however, is likely to be heavily conditioned by the reluctance of most Asia-Pacific governments to openly support US-led regional initiatives for fear of antagonising not only China, but also their own domestic constituents.

Third, the growing use of security institutions and activities as instruments of competitive influence is already creating a situation where the nature and scope of their respective agendas are increasingly coinciding—APEC and the EAS being cases in point. This institutional overlap is perhaps also a product of the fact that the sheer volume of security processes in the Asia-Pacific has increased so dramatically over the past decade and a half. As noted previously, however, the fact that this growth has been neither steady nor straightforward does raise the question of whether this upward trend in dialogue activity is going to be sustainable over the longer term. To employ an analogy with which interdependence theorists in international relations would be well acquainted, is there potential for the Asia-Pacific security cooperation to fall victim to an overabundance of transmission belts (at several levels of operation, including inputs from domestic politics that could undermine regional unity) and countervailing norms, leading to the demise (or potentially the demolition) of a number of its existing institutions?[24] In other words, can there be such a thing as too much security interaction among the countries of any given region which yields greater density but insufficient commonality? If so, how much is too much and what are the policy implications of this?

The answer to this important question is, in turn, likely to be heavily conditioned by a number of factors. The 'effectiveness'—both perceived and actual—of regional security institutions and activities is likely to play an increasingly important role in determining whether the upward trend in regional security cooperation can continue and, if not, which processes will ultimately perish or prevail. As noted previously, evaluating the 'success' or otherwise of any regional security organisation is an inevitably subjective exercise. That said, as the number and range of security institutions and activities in the Asia-Pacific become increasingly diverse, it should in theory become easier to rank the performance of those processes by employing such criteria as membership levels, meeting attendance and frequency, as well as funding and resources. More fundamentally, some broad generalisations could be reached as to which forms of security cooperation are making the most impact on core regional security politics—for example highly institutionalised organisations as opposed to smaller, but potentially more nimble processes or alliance and coalition politics as opposed to ad hoc diplomacy in response to the intensification of regional flashpoints (North Korea or Taiwan) or the multiplicity of human security challenges.[25]

Fourth, while this increasingly competitive approach to regional security institutions appears likely to impede meaningful progress towards an East Asian Community—at least for the foreseeable future—it remains important not to completely dismiss this possibility. To be sure, the EAS remains an embryonic institution. At the same time, it is important to recognise that regionalism is a gradual process which takes time to develop and evolve. This reality was clearly not grasped by sceptics of the inaugural ASEAN Summit of February 1976, for instance, who described that gathering as a 'hopeless meeting by hopeless cases'. Moreover, it is important to bear in mind that there are avenues other than the EAS—namely the ASEAN-plus-three process—through which the powerful idea of an East Asian Community could still be advanced.

In the final analysis, the fact that Australia remains, in the words of the American political scientist Samuel Huntington, a 'torn country' that has traditionally tended to face an uphill struggle in its efforts to engage with the Asian region suggests that this latter trend, in particular, is going to require careful monitoring in the years ahead.[26] If history does indeed serve as a reliable guide, then it seems likely that the SDSC will remain at the forefront of this process.

ENDNOTES

[1] John S. Duffield, 'Asia-Pacific Security Institutions in Comparative Perspective', in (eds) G. John Ikenberry and Michael Mastanduno, *International Relations Theory and the Asia-Pacific*, Columbia University Press, New York, 2003, p. 248. See also Charles E. Morrison and Astri Suhrke, *Strategies of Survival: the Foreign Policy Dilemmas of Smaller Asian States*, University of Queensland Press, St Lucia, 1978; and Leszek Buszynski, *SEATO, The Failure of an Alliance Strategy*, Singapore University Press, Singapore, 1983. Maphilindo was the proposed non-political confederation incorporating Malaya, the Philippines and Indonesia.

[2] See C. W. Braddick, 'Japan, Australia and the ASPAC: the rise and fall of an Asia-Pacific cooperative security framework', in (eds) Brad Williams and Andrew Newman, *Japan, Australia and Asia-Pacific Security*, Routledge, London and New York, 2006, pp. 30–46.

[3] See, for example, Stephen M. Walt, *The Origins of Alliances*, Cornell University Press, Ithaca and London, 1987.

[4] See Japan Center for International Exchange, *Towards Community Building in East Asia*, Dialogue and Research Monitor Overview Report, 2005, available at <http://www.jcie.or.jp/drm>, accessed 24 October 2007.

[5] See Desmond Ball, Anthony Milner and Brendan Taylor, 'Track 2 Security Dialogue in the Asia-Pacific: Reflections and Future Directions', *Asian Security*, vol. 2, no. 3, October 2006, pp. 174–88.

[6] Ball, Milner and Taylor, 'Track 2 Security Dialogue in the Asia-Pacific: Reflections and Future Directions', pp. 174–88.

[7] Desmond Ball, 'Security Cooperation in the Asia-Pacific: Official and Unofficial Responses', in Annelies Heijmans, Nicola Simmonds and Hans van de Veen, *Searching for Peace in Asia Pacific*, Lynne Rienner, London, 2004, p. 38.

[8] See, for example, 'Asia's Arms Race', *Economist*, 20 February 1993, p. 19. For a critique of this line of argument, see Desmond Ball, 'Arms and Affluence: Military Acquisitions in the Asia-Pacific Region', *International Security*, vol. 18, no. 3, Winter 1993/94, pp. 78–112.

[9] Robert Hartfiel and Brian L. Job, 'Raising the risks of war: defence spending trends and competitive arms processes in East Asia', *The Pacific Review*, vol. 20, no. 1, March 2007, p. 17.

[10] The Council on East Asian Community was launched in May 2004. Japan's leading 12 think tanks belong to the Council, which also consists of 15 corporate members and 65 individual members comprising a mixture of scholars, journalists and politicians. Representatives from Government Ministries have joined its activities in the capacity of 'counsellors'. The founder and president of this new grouping is Kenichi Ito, President of the Japan Forum on International Relations. The Council on East Asian Community is chaired by former Prime Minister Yasuhiro Nakasone. It is administered through a secretariat based at the Forum and organises a range of second track activities, including a Japan-ASEAN Dialogue, a Japan-China Dialogue and a Japan-Korea Dialogue. For further reading see Taylor, Milner and Ball, 'Track 2 Diplomacy in Asia', pp. 29–30.

[11] Amitav Acharya, 'Regional Institutions and Asian Security Order: Norms, Power, and Prospects for Peaceful Change', in (ed.) Muthiah Alagappa, *Asian Security Order: Instrumental and Normative Features*, Stanford University Press, Stanford, CA, 2003, p. 228.

[12] See, for example, Paul Dibb, 'A New Defence Policy for a New Strategic Era?', in (eds) Clive Williams and Brendan Taylor, *Countering Terror: New Directions Post '911'*, Canberra Papers on Strategy and Defence no. 147, Strategic and Defence Studies Centre, The Australian National University, Canberra, 2003, p. 64.

[13] See, for example, Anthony Milner, *Region, Security and the Return of History*, Institute of Southeast Asian Studies, Singapore, 2003.

[14] Alejandro Reyes, 'Days of Diplomacy: The East Timor Crisis showed APEC's worth—and also its limits', *Asiaweek*, vol. 25, no. 38, 24 September 1999, available at <http://www.asiaweek.com/asiaweek/magazine/99/0924/apec2.html>, accessed 24 October 2007.

[15] Rodolfo C. Severino, 'Asean in need of stronger cohesion', *Straits Times*, 9 December, 2006, available at <http://app.mfa.gov.sg/pr/read_content.asp?View,6027,>, accessed 24 October 2007.

[16] Coral Bell, *Dependent Ally: A Study in Australian Foreign Policy*, 3rd ed, Allen & Unwin, St. Leonards, NSW, 1993.

[17] Coral Bell, *Living With Giants: Finding Australia's Place in a More Complex World*, Australian Strategic Policy Institute, Canberra, 2005.

[18] See, for example, Desmond Ball, *A Suitable Piece of Real Estate: American Installations in Australia*, Hale and Iremonger, Sydney, 1980.

[19] See, for example, (eds) Robert D. Blackwill and Paul Dibb, *America's Asian Alliances*, The MIT Press, Cambridge, MA, 2000; and Ron Huisken, *ANZUS: Life after 50. Alliance Management in the 21st Century*, SDSC Working Paper no. 362, Strategic and Defence Studies Centre, The Australian National University, Canberra, 2001.

[20] Brian L. Job, 'Track 2 Diplomacy: Ideational Contribution to the Evolving Asia Security Order', in (ed.) Muthiah Alagappa, *Asian Security Order: Instrumental and Normative Features*, Stanford University Press, 2003, Stanford, CA, p. 253.

[21] See, for example, Desmond Ball, *The Council for Security Cooperation in the Asia-Pacific: Its Record and Its Prospects*, Canberra Papers on Strategy and Defence no. 139, Strategic and Defence Studies Centre, The Australian National University, Canberra, 2000.

[22] See, for example, David Capie and Paul Evans, *The Asia-Pacific Security Lexicon*, Institute of Southeast Asian Studies, Singapore, 2002; and Herman Joseph S. Kraft, 'The Autonomy Dilemma of Track Two Diplomacy in Southeast Asia', *Security Dialogue*, vol. 31, no. 3, September 2000, pp. 343–56.

[23] Barry Desker, 'Is the ARF obsolete? Three steps to avoid irrelevance', *PacNet*, no. 37A, Pacific Forum CSIS, 27 July 2006, available at <http://www.csis.org/media/csis/pubs/pac0637a.pdf>, accessed 24 October 2007.

[24] This point is raised by John Garofano, 'Power, Institutions and the ASEAN Regional Forum', *Asian Survey*, vol. 52, no. 3, May/June 2002, p. 506. The transmission belt problem has been discussed extensively by Robert Keohane and Joseph S. Nye in *Power and Interdependence*, 2nd ed., Little and Brown, Boston, MA, 2002.

[25] A preliminary study exploring such inter-relationships is (eds) William T. Tow, Ramesh Thakur and In-Taek Hyun, *Asia's Emerging Regional Order*, United Nations University Press, Tokyo, New York and Paris, 2000.

[26] Samuel P. Huntington, 'The Clash of Civilizations', *Foreign Affairs*, vol. 72, no. 3, Summer 1993, p. 42; and Samuel P. Huntington, *The Clash of Civilizations and the Remaking of World Order*, Simon & Schuster, New York, 1995, pp. 151–54.

Australian Strategic and Defence Issues

Chapter 9

The Challenge of Coherence: Strategic Guidance, Capability, and Budgets

Mark Thomson

Strategy is the marshalling of means to achieve ends. In the arena of national defence, the allocation of means to ends occurs at a variety of levels. At the most abstract, a country allocates its limited store of flexibility by forging alliances, committing to treaties and conforming to international norms that it perceives to be in its interest.

More tangible, and of relevance to this chapter, is the matching of means to ends in maintaining and developing an armed force. While some of what follows is generally applicable, the focus will naturally be on the ADF.

The remainder of this chapter is divided into three parts. To begin with, I will argue that—even in principle—maintaining and developing an armed force consistent with identified strategic imperatives is a very complex and difficult task. Then—in keeping with the historical theme of 'History as Policy'—I will survey the last 40 years of Australian defence history and offer some observations about the maintenance and development of the ADF over that period and the influence, or otherwise, of strategic guidance on the shape of the force.[1] Finally, I will turn to the present, and examine how well the Australian Government and its Defence bureaucracy are matching matériel means with strategic ends today, and suggest how greater coherence might be brought to the process of doing so.

The Challenge of Defence Planning

Designing, maintaining and developing the ADF requires three things to be brought together: strategic guidance, military capability, and the budget.

Strategic guidance sets out the approach that Australia will employ to defend itself and protect its interests. Since the 1970s, this package of decisions has been contained in a series of Defence White Papers. These include a series of interrelated decisions about:

- how Australia's alliances, relationships and commitments to international norms will be used to enhance the nation's security;

- the ways in which Australia hopes to influence international affairs to its strategic advantage;
- the military strategy for Australia's defence, including the tasks that the ADF might be called upon to perform and a clear statement of under what circumstances and to what extent Australia will employ armed force and other tools of national power in order to achieve its goals; and
- the broad shape, size and preparedness of the ADF to enable it to achieve that military strategy.

Military capability is the combination of *force structure* and *preparedness* that provides the government with options to use military force. It is important to remember that military capability includes preparedness—that is, the readiness and sustainability to undertake military operations. Capability also includes a time dimension. Current capability is the force-in-being, while future capability is that which is being planned or under development. In Australia, future capability is set out in a Defence Capability Plan that details a decade-long program of equipment acquisition.

The final element, the *budget*, is the amount of taxpayer's dollars that the government is willing to direct towards defence and security.

Having laid out these three aspects—guidance, capability and budget—it is tempting to view the problem in linear terms. First you formulate a strategy, then you submit it to the generals and admirals who advise you what military capabilities are needed to enable that strategy. Finally you send the bill to the Treasurer, who writes a cheque for the amount in full. If only it were that simple.

Despite apparent recent evidence to the contrary, such a linear approach is not likely in practice, nor is it even desirable. Every dollar of defence spending must be balanced against the potential alternative uses for that money; be it health, education or tax-cuts. In practice, this leads to a process where options for strategic guidance, and especially capability and budget, are iterated to produce an affordable package, taking into account the many competing calls on the public purse.

This point is worth dwelling on; various levels of funding can call for diverse strategies and correspondingly different sets of military capability. If the Defence budget where to halve tomorrow, the optimum response would not be to cut the size of every component of the ADF by 50 per cent. Instead, a new defence strategy would be required that made use of a different set of military capabilities that was affordable within the new budget. In this sense, defence planning is not 'scalable'.

If only these factors complicated the planning of an armed force, it would be bad enough, but there are three further complications.

The first complication is that strategic guidance is usually ill-defined. The ambiguity has its roots in several factors. To start with, the tasks which a defence force must accomplish are rarely unique or specific, and are often neither. This is true irrespective of whether planning is conceived around 'threats' or based on meeting 'capability' benchmarks. Furthermore, potential adversaries will seek to complicate our planning in several ways: they will develop multiple military options to use against us; they will conceal the true details of their military capabilities; and they will adapt to the choices we make so as to avoid our strengths and exploit our weaknesses. We can be sure that this will be the case—because it is also the way we operate.

The second complication is that the link between strategic guidance and specific plans for current and future capability is ultimately a matter of judgement. There is no unique military solution to a given task. Back in the late 1990s the US military undertook concurrent studies to determine the best options for delivering 'deep strike'—disruption of enemy command and control and supply lines 100 km behind the forward line of battle. Each Service managed to produce analyses that showed its particular equipment option to be the most effective. This demonstrates that there are indeed many ways to 'skin a cat', but also that operational analysis is to be used with great caution.

The third complication is that, invariably, it is difficult to accurately estimate the relative cost (let alone the relative cost-effectiveness) of alternative capability options ahead of time.

In summary, planning a defence force is difficult as we cannot be sure of the tasks our armed forces will be required to perform. Even if these were clear, we would be uncertain on the best way to proceed, and we are never sure how much things are likely to cost—nor, in fact, do we know with any certainty how much money Treasury may make available. This is a heavy load of uncertainty to feed into an iterative (a mathematician would say non-linear) optimisation process.

Forty Years of Australian Defence Planning

So how has Australian defence planning progressed over the last 40 years, indeed over the life of the SDSC? At the risk of incurring the wrath of professional historians, I have undertaken a quick analysis that samples Australian defence policy and capability (existing and planned) at 10-year snapshots in the years 1966, 1976, 1986, 1996 and 2006. Given the glacial pace at which the force structure evolves, this nonetheless gives a reasonable picture of how things have changed over the past four decades.

The results are set out below by way of a description of each of the years in chronological order in terms of strategic guidance, budget and operational demands. Then follows a discussion of how the capabilities of the ADF evolved over the same period.

1966

In 1966, confrontation with Indonesia had ended, the conflict in Vietnam had commenced, and Australia's military contributions to Malaysia, Singapore and Thailand continued. The Australian Army alone had 6000 personnel deployed operationally (although our commitment to Vietnam was only around 4000 troops, less than half the size it was to grow to in the coming years) and the RAAF had three squadrons deployed to Southeast Asia. Australia was in the midst of its first substantial post-Second World War military build up—so much so that we had to employ trade credits from the United States to soften the impact on our balance of payments of acquisition purchases.

Conscription was gaining traction and the ADF had a permanent strength of 66 774, having grown by 10 500 in a single year (including a net gain of 3000 personnel from volunteer enlistment)—notwithstanding that unemployment stood at just 2 per cent and significant numbers of casualties were occurring in Vietnam.

It was, of course, the height of 'forward defence'; pre-Guam doctrine, and pre-east of Suez. While the defence of Australia, its territory and its interests were the primary goal of defence policy, as the 1966 *Defence Report* said: 'We believe that this can most reliably and responsibly be done by assisting actively the defence efforts of our regional friends and allies.'

The budget stood just on the psychological milestone of A$1 billion (or just under A$8 billion today) representing fully 3.8 per cent of GDP.

1976

A decade later saw a much changed world. The communists had taken control of Vietnam but showed no sign of causing trouble—the last domino had fallen flat, without striking its neighbour. Our regional friends had learnt how to get along with each other, and our allies had largely decamped from Southeast Asia and so had we. We found ourselves with responsibility for our own security in a surprisingly benign environment. Accordingly, the 1976 Defence White Paper, *Australian Defence*, set out the core principles of what we now call the 'defence of Australia' doctrine.

Investment in capital equipment had fallen back to close to pre-Vietnam levels representing less than half the peak of nine years earlier, yet Army had just commenced delivery of 102 new *Leopard* tanks that had been ordered by the Whitlam Government two years earlier.

Conscription had ended, but there were still 68 774 people in the ADF. The defence budget stood at A$2 billion (or just under A$9 billion today) and amounted to 2.3 per cent of GDP.

1986

In 1986 the Dibb Review took the 'defence of Australia' doctrine to its analytic peak, and set the framework for defence priorities for the years that followed. As had been the case for the previous decade, Australia had no major military deployments, and the ADF had settled into a comfortable peacetime routine.

Defence investment had recovered and the force was being re-equipped, including through the purchase of the F/A-18 *Hornet* fighter. In fact, 1986 saw investment reach a post Second World War high of almost A$5 billion per annum in today's terms—a level only just now being approached again.

Consistent with high investment levels, Defence spending had grown to close to A$7 billion (or around A$12 billion in today's terms—a level that was roughly sustained for the next decade). The defence vote accounted for 2.5 per cent of GDP. Personnel numbers had also grown from the decade earlier to 70 048, yet this was below the post-Vietnam War peak of 73 000 reached in 1982.

1996

By 1996 the Cold War was securely in the past and the ADF was largely at home, although it had made a limited (largely naval) contribution to the 1990–91 Persian Gulf War and also provided a modest contribution to relatively benign peacekeeping missions to Somalia, Rwanda and Cambodia. Strategic guidance was in the process of softening the strictures of the 'defence of Australia' doctrine although, from a force structuring perspective, the Australian Army remained tethered to the continent. The year 1996 was also the eve of the Sandline crisis in PNG that gave Australia a taste of how surprisingly unstable our 'arc of instability' could be.

Defence spending stood at A$10 billion, or about where it was a decade earlier in real terms, although it had fallen to only 1.8 per cent of GDP. The absence of spending growth had been made up for, in part at least, by progressive efficiency measures (mainly outsourcing) and cuts to the size of the ADF as a result of the 1991 *Force Structure Review*.

Investment continued at around 75 per cent of the peak reached a decade earlier, but there were looming pressures with a wave of block-obsolescence about to hit. Along with dwindling resources for logistics support, this forced a second wave of efficiency measures the following year under the Defence Reform Program.

The combination of cuts to the force and outsourcing had driven personnel numbers down to 55 574, still well above pre-Vietnam War levels and indeed more so once the impact of outsourcing was taken into account.

2006

A decade later and the wheel seemed to have turned full cycle. In 2006, the ADF was deployed in multiple theatres overseas, a concerted effort was being made to grow the number of personnel in the force, defence spending was on the increase—at 3 per cent per annum—and there were big plans in place to replace (and in some ways expand) the equipment of the ADF. Defence spending today sits at almost A$20 billion per annum or just under 2 per cent of GDP. Nonetheless, it would be wrong to draw too close a comparison between 2006 and 40 years ago. For one thing, Howard's development of the ADF and his deployment of troops overseas, pales in comparison with Menzies' massive military build up and the very significant loss of live suffered in successive Southeast Asian campaigns.

Similarly, it would be wrong to depict the emerging strategy of the Australian Government as simply a variant of 'forward defence'—although there is certainly some sense of that in the echoing rhetoric of 1966 and 2006 with regard to Vietnam and Iraq. Rather, John Howard's strategy (to the extent that it is clear) appears to be more a case of an expanded the 'defence of Australia' doctrine that embraces our immediate region more than before, while doing what is perceived as necessary to bolster the US alliance in the face of greater demand from our principal ally.

Trends

So what can we deduce about the evolution of strategic guidance, capability and budget across the five decades surveyed—what are the drivers of change and do the three components move in some casual unison? Let us begin with spending. The general pattern is clear—there is an underlying long-term rate of increase that is driven by rising intrinsic costs. Superimposed on top of this are peaks and troughs driven by the level of operational activity of the day. Growth is fast in wartime, and slow or static in peacetime. It is important to note that much of the money spent at the peaks of defence spending goes to investment. As a result, it appears that investment for the future is driven by the challenges of the day. No surprise here: people judge that the circumstances they find themselves will persist into the future. It is not hard to find statements to that effect today, such as the risk of conventional war being considered low for the foreseeable future, or that the ADF will remain busy combating terrorism for some time.

Of course, this does not represent incoherence between strategic guidance and budget (I will return to this later). Rather, it simply shows that strategic guidance and investment for the future is readily captured by the events of the day. The exception is the significant boost to investment by the Hawke Government soon after coming to power in the 1980s.

What of capability? Let us first look at preparedness. The readiness of the ADF for near-term deployments rose and fell over the period largely in accord with the perceived likelihood of near-term deployments—just as you would expect. This is not to say that all was perfect. On several occasions the preparedness of the force was not up to the demands that emerged. The Australian Army did not always have what it needed for peacekeeping operations during the 1990s, the RAN was caught short in 1991 getting ready to go to the Persian Gulf, and parts of the RAAF were well below where they needed to be on several occasions in the late 1990s. These events reflect two things: first, a failure of implementation within the ADF because of peacetime malaise and, second, the consequence of deliberate risk management that kept many parts of the ADF at less than full states of readiness.

Where things get interesting is in looking at the second part of capability, namely force structure. Once the changing technology of warfare is taken into account, there is a surprising degree of continuity across the 40 years. Furthermore, where there are changes, they are sometimes difficult to explain in terms of strategic guidance.

Here is how it looks for each Service:

RAN

The number of surface combatants remained largely static over four decades although the mix evolved over time. When more money was available, better equipped vessels were in operation; when money was tight, lesser platforms were employed. At the moment, money is plentiful and the RAN is developing the capability of its surface combatants through upgrades and the purchase of three advanced air warfare destroyers. Overall though, the number of hulls has remained around the same, just as it has for support ships and hydrographic/oceanographic vessels. Similarly, ever since the RAN acquired submarines in the 1960s and patrol boats in 1970s, numbers have been maintained at close to constant levels.

Thus, for the bulk of the RAN, it has been a matter of 'you keep what you've got and, when money permits, expand by adding something more, then keep it'. But there have been some exceptions to this trend. For example, the number of minehunters has fluctuated—it seems we are never sure if we really want them. Having said that, there was at least a clear link between strategic guidance and the acquisition of minehunters in the 1990s.

Of more interest are the demise of the aircraft carrier and the emergence of an amphibious force. It was in the early 1980s that the RAN lost its aircraft carrier. To some extent this represented a tangible shift away from the demands of 'forward defence' (albeit more than a decade after that doctrine had been tossed on the scrap heap). Yet this is far from a complete explanation. In fact, Australia was planning to purchase HMS *Invincible* from the Royal Navy as a replacement until the sale was cancelled by the United Kingdom following the Falkland Islands conflict. It is likely that affordability was as big a factor in deciding to abandon the carrier as any strategic considerations.

The disjuncture between strategic guidance and capability development is most acute in the development of the amphibious force. Over the last two decades, the RAN's surface transport capability has morphed and expanded into an increasingly large amphibious capability based around helicopter carriers. This transformation began back in 1980s and grew steadily—and stealthily—through the 1990s before finally emerging in 2000. Indeed, until *Defence 2000* provided a credible rationale for an amphibious capability such a development was difficult to reconcile with strategic guidance. It is tempting to relate the rise of an expanded amphibious capability with the loss of the carrier—but it is a hard argument to make aside from observing that the latter freed up resources for the former. To some extent, at least, the development of an amphibious capability was the logical response to increasingly foreseeable challenges in the immediate region that strategic guidance was overly slow in acknowledging.

RAAF

Over the past four decades, the RAAF's maritime patrol and transport fleets have remained largely static apart from the addition of four C-17 *Globemaster* aircraft in 2006. In contrast, the number of fighters and bombers has contracted substantially as previously disparate roles have been progressively consolidated onto single platform types. On the surface this appears to be a substantial shift in the balance of the force structure; however it actually just mirrors changes that have occurred in all Western air forces over the same period.

As the technological sophistication and cost of air combat platforms has increased, the number and diversity of platforms has fallen, mitigated in part by force-multiplier capabilities like over-the-horizon radar, air-to-air refuelling tankers and Airborne Early Warning & Control aircraft (all of which the RAAF currently has or is acquiring). Taking these technological trends into account, the relative *capability* inherent in the RAAF's combat air capability has remained largely static.

Army

The story with the Army is simple once changing technology is taken into account. The spectrum of capabilities that make up the Army remains largely static, but its size, condition of its equipment, and its preparedness rises and falls with overall defence spending—hardly surprising given that defence spending correlates with the level of operational activity. This trend encompasses the recent 'Hardened and Networked' Army initiative and the decision to expand the force by two battalions. An important exception is the strategic shift in the Army's disposition northward in the late 1980s and early 1990s (and similarly for two-ocean basing for the RAN that was introduced around the same time).

I do not ascribe to the 'Army as victim' school of thought, which argues that the 'defence of Australia' doctrine caused the Army to be 'run down' or neglected in favour of the other two Services. Under the guidance of the day, the Australian Army (along with the other two 'fitted-for-but-not-with' Services) was equipped on the assumption of warning time being available before a major conflict. In fact, I would argue that the share of resources accorded to the Army under the 'defence of Australia' doctrine far exceeded what was justified had the doctrine been taken to its logical conclusion. For several reasons, a militia force would have been better suited to resisting the occupation of the continent than a standing army.

The tyranny of the balanced force?

The clearest trend to emerge from our 40 year survey is that the level of preparedness and modernisation of the force (and the size of the Army) is driven largely by the operational tempo of the day. Far less clear is the existence of any nexus between strategic guidance and the evolution of the force structure. In fact, once the impact of technology and the changing face of warfare is taken into account, it is surprising how little has changed—notwithstanding that our survey covers three distinct epochs of Australian defence thinking. Aside from the changes to disposition wrought by the 1980s incarnation of the 'defence of Australia', the really significant changes to the force structure—the demise of the aircraft carrier and the rise of the amphibious force—are difficult to ascribe to a changed strategic vision of how to defend the country (or at least one that was articulated at the time).

The result is that the basic defence force conceived and developed by Robert Menzies back in the 1960s under the doctrine of 'forward defence', persisted through the years of 'defence of Australia'. With a couple of extra bells and whistles, it largely remains with us today, and is planned to continue into the foreseeable future. It is as if strategic guidance does not really matter.

There are at least two factors driving this long-term continuity in force structure. First, and perhaps most important, is the underlying continuity in our strategic guidance that derives from our geography. Despite inflated rhetoric, since the Second World War Australia has been a regional maritime power with a boutique army. Although the narrative developed to explain why Australia needs to do so changes, the reality remains inviolate. Yet while this explains much, it seems insufficient to me, and it certainly fails to explain the development of an amphibious capability through the 1990s. Nor, I would argue, does it explain some of the more recent ambitious plans that have emerged.

The second factor is that the Services each have their own priorities—independent of strategic guidance—that they push to the fore. Being conservative by nature, they favour continuity and incremental expansion when money is available. They replace what they have with the latest affordable technology and then move to the next item on the list in order to expand. The result is that nothing much changes: the three Services simply roll on—sharing the bounty in good times and sharing the pain in austere times. In some circles this is seen as a sufficient criterion for building the ADF, because it maintains the so-called 'balanced force'. While many factors, beyond the conception of a 'balanced force', influence the shape of the ADF, it would be naïve to think that this factor has been insignificant.

Australian Defence Planning Today

No doubt Defence would cry foul at the suggestion that such an approach is in operation today. Indeed, they would point to the very detailed and seemingly scientific approach they have to strategic and capability planning. Nonetheless, I assert that, while the bureaucracy surrounding force development is greater now than at any time since the formation of the Department of Defence by Sir Arthur Tange in the early 1970s, the degree of central strategic control is at a low point.

The conditions are ripe for this to occur. To start with, strategic guidance is more ambiguous and opaque than at any time in at least the preceding 30 years. This leaves more than ample room for arguments to be mustered with far fewer constraints than normal. Then there is the fact that defence planning is no longer constrained by a budget bottom line. It is impossible for reliable central planning to occur in Defence when the government is happy to dole out money directly to the Services—as occurred with 'hardening and networking' and the follow-on A$11 billion expansion of the Army initiatives, and similarly with the C-17 *Globemaster* project.

On the surface, this looks good to those who favour stronger defence, and it is fruitless to argue that more capability is not more capability. Yet it is nonetheless undesirable. To start with, such an approach precludes the considered whole-of-force tradeoffs that are necessary when strategically planning an armed force; we don't just want *more* capability, we want the *right* capability delivered as cost-effectively as possible. Worse still, the present ad hoc approach risks committing future taxpayers to costs that may prove unaffordable. In my estimation, there are already significant unfunded demands built into the budget that the promised 3 per cent growth will not address and, unfortunately, as the above survey of the past showed, once the pace of military operations falls so too will the government's willingness to fund Defence.

In the longer term the situation will become even more serious, irrespective of the waxing and waning of perceived threat. For the past 30 years 'the Lucky Country' has been able to retain both a 'balanced force' and a decisive capability edge in the region. This comfortable position will get increasingly harder to sustain as an ageing population erodes our economic growth at the same time as neighbouring economies surge forward. Simply sharing available resources among competing bids by the Services will eventually become a luxury we cannot afford. Hard choices will need to be faced about which military capabilities will deliver the most strategic punch. In fact, given the longevity of military equipment, these are choices we need to be making today.

Three things have to occur before this can happen. First, the Australian Government needs to clarify its strategic guidance, preferably through a new Defence White Paper. Second, Defence has to be given a budget to work within. As long as simply coming back and asking for more is an option, no progress is possible. Third, and most important, discipline and strategic control must be imposed on the capability development process. None of this will be easy to achieve, but it presents the only chance of breaking out of a four-decade cycle of structuring the ADF largely on the basis of replacing what came before.

ENDNOTES

[1] This chapter draws on information contained in Defence *Annual Reports* from 1962 through to 2005. Additional material was drawn from Commonwealth *Yearbooks* for the same period, as well as from (ed.) Ross Gillett, *Australia's Armed Forces*, Nautical Press, Sydney, 1981 and Graeme Andrews, *Fighting Ships of Australia and New Zealand*, Regency House Publishers, Cammeray, NSW, 1973.

Chapter 10

The Higher Command Structure for Joint ADF Operations

David Horner

An effective command structure for ADF operations is one of the most important requirements for the defence of Australia and its interests. Civilian strategic analysts sometimes dismiss their military colleagues' apparent obsession with command. In their view, issues of international relations, strategic and defence policy, force development and budgets are the heart of strategic analysis. But command is fundamental to a military organisation. Put simply, it is the means by which the government's wishes are translated into military outcomes. As the Vice Chief of the Defence Force (VCDF), Vice-Admiral Russ Shalders, put it in 2005, the number one outcome for the ADF, as endorsed by the government, is the conduct of operations.[1]

Command is not just about giving orders and ensuring that they are carried out. It is also about ensuring that the right orders are given—that the plans both reflect government policy and are achievable. There are, of course, two elements to command. The first is the ability of individual commanders to complete their tasks, and this depends on personal qualities, such as technical knowledge, courage, robustness and character. The second element is the command structure. Commanders can only operate within the bounds of their legal authority and within the structures available to them. The command structure includes headquarters, from the strategic to the tactical levels, the communications links between them, and the intelligence systems to inform them. This chapter focuses on the second element—the higher command structure for joint operations—as the most relevant to an enquiry into the broader aspects of defence policy.

The general principles of command are well-known, and most military commanders would agree that unity of command is paramount. Napoleon Bonaparte declared: 'Nothing is so important in war as an undivided command', and Britain's First World War Prime Minister, Lloyd George, said: 'It is not a question of one general being better than another, but of one general being better than two.'[2] Yet, for all these fine sentiments, it has not always been easy to achieve unity of command for joint operations.

The word 'joint' refers to activities, operations and organisations in which elements of more than one Service of the same nation participate. According to the ADF's 'capstone' doctrinal publication, *The Australian Approach to Warfare*, the 'integration of the capabilities of the three Services (Navy, Army and Air Force) in joint operations' is a 'key warfare' concept. The publication continues:

> For Australia, the conduct of joint operations, rather than single-Service operations, is a matter of practical necessity. It is the effective integration of thought and action at all levels of command to achieve the common goal that produces a synergy in the conduct of operations, which is the strength of our joint warfare approach.[3]

The importance of joint operations is a relatively new phenomenon. In earlier times, navies and armies generally conducted their operations separately. When they needed to cooperate, this was normally achieved by a coordinating conference. It was extremely rare for an army officer to command ships or for a naval officer to command army units. It was the advent of aircraft—or more specifically the formation of separate air forces—that provided the impetus for the development of concepts for the command of joint operations. Nowadays, it is difficult to think of major land or maritime operations in which aircraft are not involved. Yet, ironically, it is possible to think of purely air operations, such as strategic bombing campaigns.

While military men have espoused the idea of unity of command, they have been less inclined to accept the idea of an officer of one Service exercising command over the combat forces of another Service. Yet this is what needs to happen if joint command is to be exercised effectively. The modern-day understanding of joint warfare and joint command stems from the Second World War. An early example was when Admiral Louis Mountbatten was appointed Chief of (so-called) Combined Operations in 1941. A more enduring example was when the allies set up joint theatre commands such as the Pacific Oceans Command, the Southwest Pacific Area, and Southeast Asia Command. General Douglas MacArthur, Commander-in-Chief of the Southwest Pacific Area, commanded all naval, land and air forces in his area. But what is the record of the development of joint command in Australia?

Forty years ago, two events occurred that were to have a fundamental effect on the development of the joint command structure for Australian military operations. The first of these was the appointment, on 17 April 1966, of Major General Ken Mackay as Commander Australian Force Vietnam (COMAFV), and the second was the appointment a month later, on 19 May 1966, of Lieutenant General Sir John Wilton as Chairman CSOC. We will return to the importance of these two appointments and how they changed Australian joint command arrangements a little later, but first we need to consider the extent to which Australia had developed joint command arrangements before then.

Before Vietnam

Until 1966, Australian forces had little experience of joint operations. Yet, ironically, if we leave aside Australia's limited contribution to the Boer War after Federation in 1901, Australia's first military operation was actually a joint undertaking. Soon after the outbreak of the First World War in August 1914, the Australian Commonwealth Naval Board directed Rear Admiral Sir George Patey RN, commander of the Australian Fleet, to mount an expedition to seize German New Guinea. A Department of Defence publication has described this expedition as 'the first Australian joint military operation conceived, planned, organised, and executed by Australia with overall political direction leading back to the Government of Australia'.[4] This is not quite correct. In fact, the expedition was undertaken at the urging of the British Government and against the advice of the Australian Chief of Naval Staff, Vice-Admiral Sir William Creswell. In his view the British and Australian naval forces in the Pacific would have been better used to seek out and destroy the powerful German units operating in the western Pacific.[5]

Patey's land force commander, Colonel William Holmes, led the Australian Naval and Military Expeditionary Force, which consisted of two battalions—one a militia battalion and the other composed of naval troops—with little in the way of supporting arms. From the arrival of the fleet near Rabaul to the German surrender, the operation lasted less than six days. It was so swift and uncomplicated, the planning so unsophisticated and the enemy so weak, that it was a campaign in name only. It hardly provides any basis for developing an Australian tradition for joint command and planning at the operational level.

There were no other instances of Australian joint command in the First World War. Rather, Australia's army and navy units fought separately, under British command. After the war, no effort was made to develop joint command arrangements in Australia. In time of war it was expected that the major fleet units would be deployed under Admiralty control. If an enemy tried to attack Australia, the forces defending a major port, such as Sydney, Melbourne or Newcastle, would be commanded separately, although the local commanders would form a committee to coordinate their activities. This idea of a command by committee was taken up in the early years of the Second World War. Nationally, command was exercised by the COSC, assisted by a Central War Room and a Combined Operational Intelligence Centre located at Victoria Barracks, Melbourne. In 1941 area combined headquarters were established at various locations such as Townsville, Melbourne, Fremantle and Darwin to coordinate the defence of those locations.[6]

As in the First World War, Australian forces deployed overseas operated separately under British command. Once Australia faced the threat of invasion in 1942 some joint command arrangements were introduced. For example, the

Commander of Northern Territory Force, a major general, was given authority to command all army, navy and air force units in his area once a land attack had started or was 'clearly imminent'.[7] General Douglas MacArthur, the American general appointed Commander-in-Chief Southwest Pacific Area in April 1942, commanded all the allied forces in his command. But he did not form joint subordinate commands. Thus, when General Sir Thomas Blamey commanded New Guinea Force during the New Guinea offensives in 1943, he needed to coordinate his land operations with those of the commanders of the Allied Naval and Air Forces. Ultimate authority rested with MacArthur. On one notable occasion, the Commander Allied Naval Forces (Vice Admiral Arthur Carpender) refused to allow the Commander New Guinea Force (at that time Lieutenant General Sir Iven Mackay) to reinforce Finschhafen. After a plea from Blamey (who had returned to Australia from New Guinea), MacArthur intervened and ordered the reinforcement.[8] A significant feature of the command structure was that the Australian Chiefs of Staff did not have operational command of their own forces.[9]

The Australian Commander-in-Chief British Commonwealth Occupation Force (BCOF) in Japan between 1946 and 1950 was both a joint and combined commander, but he did not conduct war-like operations. During the Korean War the Commander-in-Chief BCOF became the Commander-in-Chief British Commonwealth Force Korea. He was the Australian national commander as well as being responsible for the administration of the British Commonwealth forces, but he had no operational responsibility whatsoever. The commanders of the RAN ships, the Australian infantry battalions (and later the 28th Commonwealth Brigade) and the RAAF fighter squadron operating in Korea were all responsible to either British or American single-Service superiors.

Back in Australia, during the 1950 and 1960s, there was no joint command structure. The Services had their own command structures leading upwards to their Chiefs of Staff, who in fact were merely the first members of their Service boards. Australian forces in Malaya served under British single-Service commanders. When the Australian Army sent advisers to Vietnam in 1962 and an infantry battalion in 1965, the commander of the Australian Army Force Vietnam reported back to Army Headquarters in Canberra.

Commander Australian Force Vietnam

In March 1966 the Prime Minister, Harold Holt, announced that the battalion group deployed to Vietnam would be expanded to a two-battalion task force. The RAAF commitment to support the task Force was to be increased, and hence the headquarters of the Australian Army Force Vietnam was to become the joint Services headquarters of Australian Force Vietnam. Since the COMAFV was a joint Service commander, he became responsible not to the CGS but to the COSC through its Chairman, Lieutenant General Wilton.

The COMAFV was the Australian national commander with responsibility for the administration of the Australian forces in Vietnam. He had no responsibility for the operational employment of the Australian forces, primarily the Task Force in Phuoc Tuy Province, which came under the command of a US corps commander, but he was consulted on major operational matters, such as the decision in early 1968 to deploy the Task Force into Bien Hoa Province. The COMAFVs were given little political or strategic direction from Canberra and often had to make decisions according to what they thought would have been acceptable in Canberra.[10]

The appointment of COMAFV set a precedent for later ADF operations. The government realised that, for overseas operations, there was great value in appointing a national commander who could ensure that Australian policy was followed. Further, if more than one Service was deployed, there was advantage in having one national joint Service commander deal with allied commanders-in-chief and host governments.

Chairman Chiefs of Staff Committee

The appointment of Lieutenant General Sir John Wilton as Chairman COSC was the most important development at this time.[11] A full-time chairman had first been appointed in 1958, but the incumbent did not gain much influence until Air Marshal Sir Frederick Scherger was appointed in 1961. He was promoted to Air Chief Marshal in 1965, a year before he was succeeded by Wilton. Scherger believed that a single ADF should be formed but, as he said later, 'Vietnam was no time for changing horses in midstream, or even changing the colour of the horses'.[12]

Wilton had no such hesitation. His problem was that he had no command authority over COMAFV. Thus if the COMAFV sought urgent direction from Wilton, he could not give it until he had called the COSC together. In practice, Wilton sometimes gave the necessary direction and sought COSC and ministerial approval later. Writing at about this time, Tom Millar, the first head of the newly-formed SDSC at the ANU, observed:

> Control of actual military operations is effected by the Chiefs of Staff Committee direct to the theatre or operational commander, on the American pattern using the Joint Staff. A joint Service command has been established in Viet Nam and New Guinea, and will clearly be needed in Malaysia while Australian forces remain there. Allocation of resources is made by the Chiefs of Staff, within directives issued by the cabinet or the Minister of Defence and with advice from the relevant intelligence, planning and administrative committees. This means that the Chiefs of Staff have become in effect a joint Commander-in-Chief although in Viet Nam the Australian Task force is operationally under control of the

American Second Field Force, within guidelines laid down by the Australian Chiefs of Staff Committee.[13]

In September 1967, Wilton circulated his proposals for change.[14] His key proposal was the formation of a unified Department of Defence, involving the abolition of the Service departments and ministers. The fighting Services would retain their separate identities to preserve morale and operational efficiency. Wilton's own position should be redesignated Chief of Defence Staff (CDS). Higher direction of the department would be in the hands of a Defence Board of Administration, which would operate in a similar manner to the Service boards. It would be headed by the Minister, and would include the CDS, the Secretary and the Service chiefs. The CDS and the Secretary would exercise joint executive authority. The COSC would be responsible to the Minister for the direction, planning and control of operations, with a joint Service staff to assist it. There should be a joint intelligence organisation, a joint cadet college, a joint staff college, a joint warfare establishment, a joint communications centre and joint medical services. The Service chiefs would remain the professional heads of their Services and would exercise their functions through their own headquarters.

Wilton argued that, as most operations in which Australian forces were likely to be committed would be joint, there should be a 'single clear chain of operational control'. Joint forces, such as Australian Force Vietnam, should report to the COSC, which should have 'statutory authority and some of the powers now vested in the existing statutory Service boards'. Other proposed joint commands, such as Air Defence and Maritime Commands, could report to the COSC through the Chief of the Air Staff and the Chief of Naval Staff respectively. As Wilton put it, the CDS, in 'respect of operations', would be the 'executive agent' of the COSC, issuing instructions to designated joint commands and military establishments and as appropriate to individual Chiefs of Staff. The joint staff and the staffs of the Service chiefs were to be collocated in the same building. It would be another 30 years before this idea was realised.

Wilton was unable to persuade either the Defence Minister, Allen Fairhall, or the Defence Secretary, Sir Edwin Hicks, but he bided his time, and when Sir Henry Bland became Secretary in January 1968 he began implementing changes. By the time Wilton retired in November 1970, with Bland's assistance he had formed a Joint Staff headed by a two-star Director Joint Staff (Rear Admiral Bill Dovers). Wilton chaired a committee that recommended and pushed through the formation of the Joint Intelligence Organisation. He established the Joint Services Staff College; took the first step in forming the Australian Joint Warfare Establishment; and was a prime mover in working towards a tri-Service officer cadet academy (the latter not being approved until after he had retired). He even persuaded the COSC to accept a joint Service badge—the same one that is used today for the ADF, an organisation that at that time had not yet been formed.

Wilton was not the only one agitating for change. Writing in 1969, Millar argued that if Australia were to become involved in 'substantial operations of war', it would require 'a direct command structure'. He wondered whether 'the head of the whole defence organisation should be a professional military man rather than a professional civil servant?' Recognising that this was probably 'not feasible', he thought that 'the senior Service officer at least needs to be given prime operational responsibility, by making him the Chief of the Defence Staff and not simply chairman of a committee'. Defence needed 'a chief and not a chairman. He should be of four-star rank, i.e., general or equivalent. At present the Chairman of the COSC, usually a three-star officer, is at a disadvantage in international military meetings and in dealing with the Chiefs of Staff'.[15] (Wilton had been promoted to general in September 1968; but there was no guarantee that his successor would be promoted.)

In his last year as Chairman, with a new Defence Minister, Malcolm Fraser, and a new Defence Secretary, Sir Arthur Tange, Wilton revived his earlier proposals, but he made no headway. Two years later, after he had retired, he submitted another paper to the Shadow Minister for Defence, Lance Barnard, in which he argued that the COSC should be established as a statutory authority and that its Chairman should be redesignated CDS as a statutory appointment. He would perform his duties 'by virtue of his statutory office rather than as Chairman of the Chiefs of Staff. He should have co-equal status and authority with the Secretary Department of Defence.'[16] Interestingly, the ANU played a minor role in Wilton's approach to Barnard: in mid-1972 Wilton attended a lecture given by Barnard at the university and afterwards explained his concerns to Barnard, who subsequently agreed to meet with Wilton.[17]

Defence Reorganisation

When the Labor Party was elected in December 1972, Barnard became Minister for Defence and immediately directed Tange to undertake a review and to make recommendations leading to the reorganisation of the Defence group of departments. The 'Tange reorganisation', as it was sometimes called, introduced many of the proposals for which Wilton had been agitating for the previous nine years.

The reorganisation of the Defence group of departments was to have a profound effect on Australian command arrangements. The single-Service departments and the Service boards were abolished and one Defence Department was formed with a single Defence Minister. On 9 February 1976, General Sir Francis Hassett, Chairman, COSC, assumed the new appointment of Chief of the Defence Force Staff (CDFS). The CDFS was given command of the Defence Force and the chiefs of each Service were given command (under the CDFS) of their Service. The CDFS could appoint an officer to command a part of the Defence Force consisting of members of more than one Service. The CDFS was the principal military adviser to the Defence Minister and was responsible to him for:

- the conduct of military operations by the Defence Force;
- ensuring the effectiveness of military plans, training and organisation, the effectiveness of the Defence Force in the conduct of joint operations, and the standard of discipline, morale and health of the Forces;
- tendering military advice on the size of the Defence Force and the balance within it in relation to the strategic requirements; and
- ensuring the exercise of command within the Defence Force was within approved policies.

In other words, the CDFS became the top joint Service commander.

The Service chiefs were responsible to the Defence Minister, through the CDFS, for command of their Services, and had the right of direct access to the Minister. They were to plan and conduct single-Service operations and provide forces from their respective Services for assignment to joint operations. The COSC was to provide collective professional advice on military operations, endorse military plans, recommend the allocation of resources and endorse the military aspects of policies concerning joint Service units and installations.

The Secretary to the Defence Department retained his traditional statutory responsibilities as permanent head, and advised the Minister on policy, resources, organisation and finance. With the CDFS, he exercised joint responsibility for the administration of the Defence Force. This was the so-called 'diarchy' of responsibility that has continued through to the present day.

The main weakness flowing from the Defence reorganisation was that the CDFS had completely inadequate staff by which to exercise his command responsibilities. As Sir Arthur Tange often pointed out in later years, under the Defence Act 1903, the CDFS had the authority to exercise command and for some reason failed to put in place the structures to allow him to do so. Some commentators, however, have noted that Tange took no action to encourage the military to develop the necessary joint command structures.

Towards a Joint Command Structure

The new Defence organisation that came into existence between 1974 and 1976 coincided with the development of a new Defence policy, formalised by the release of the Defence White Paper, *Australian Defence*, in November 1976. This policy, often described as 'self reliance within an alliance framework', gave greater attention to preparing forces for the defence of Australia and its near region. As the paper put it:

> In our contemporary circumstances we no longer base our policy on the expectation that Australia's Navy or Army or Air Force will be sent abroad to fight as part of some other nation's force, supported by it. We do not rule out an Australian contribution to operations elsewhere if the requirement arose and we felt that our presence would be effective, and if our forces could be spared from their national tasks. But we believe that any operations are much more likely to be in our own neighbourhood than in some distant or forward theatre, and that our Armed Services would be conducting joint operations together as the Australian Defence Force.[18]

Clearly, the new Defence reorganisation and this new policy required new joint command arrangements, but the CDFS was slow to act. Instead, one initiative came from Robert O'Neill, who had succeeded Millar as Head of the SDSC. In January 1976 he suggested the establishment of three joint operational commands: Continental Defence, Coastal Defence, and perhaps Retaliatory Strike Commands.[19] Apparently, Defence did not even consider this suggestion.

In the *Kangaroo* series of military exercises in the 1970s, various commanders were appointed, but no formal structure was established. During the following decade, Australian forces had no major overseas deployments and the command structures evolved relatively slowly. Indeed, although the ADF had formally come into existence in 1976, it took several years before it was recognised as a new entity.

The Australian Labor Party came to power in March 1983 with a Defence platform stating that it would 'develop an Australian Defence Force functional command structure with a decentralised organisation'. It seemed likely that the new government would be receptive to proposals to improve the joint command structure and, anticipating this, in his 1982 and 1983 exercises, CGS Lieutenant General Phillip Bennett, examined the higher command problems in the Army.[20]

Bennett was appointed CDFS in April 1984, and in September that year he redesignated his staff to form Headquarters Australian Defence Force (HQADF), in order to emphasise his command and administrative functions in relation to the ADF and to underscore his role as the principal military adviser to the government. In October 1984 the government changed the title of CDFS to CDF to reflect more accurately the fact that the CDF commanded the ADF. In 1985 Maritime Headquarters (formerly the Navy's Fleet headquarters) was made responsible to the CDF for joint exercises and operations, but to the Chief of Naval Staff for command of the Fleet. The following year, the Army's Field Force Headquarters and the RAAF's Operational Command Headquarters became joint headquarters with the titles of Land Force and Air Headquarters respectively. Initially these were joint headquarters in name only, but they formally became joint headquarters in 1987. These were fairly conservative changes, reflecting the military's belief that each step needed to be tested before the next one was proposed.

There was considerable opposition to the new command structure. Several retired and serving senior officers feared that the Service chiefs would be eliminated from the chain of command and that the CDF would be able to command operations through his joint commanders without reference to them.[21] Bennett thought that this was a simplistic view of how the chiefs operated. He wrote later that it was 'inconceivable that a CDF would ignore the collective wisdom of his Service Chiefs—or his senior logistics advisers. Every effort would be made by the CDF to present agreed advice to Government, or at the very least, well supported advice, from the Chiefs most involved, and only reached after full consideration of the professional views of all the Service Chiefs.'[22]

General Peter Gration, who succeeded Bennett in 1987, took the changes further when he commissioned Brigadier John Baker to review and recommend changes to the ADF command arrangements. Baker argued that there were three levels of command—strategic, operational and tactical—and these needed to be reflected in the ADF.[23] Following the submission of Baker's report, in March 1988 the government approved the establishment of another joint command, Northern Command, in Darwin. Gration directed the establishment of the position of Commander Joint Forces Australia (CJFA). It was explicitly assigned to the operational level of war. Gration, assisted by HQADF was to concentrate on command at the strategic level. The arrangements were to 'provide, in higher level operations, for an operational level commander, the Commander Joint Forces Australia, to be responsible directly to me, located away from Canberra, and commanding the three Joint Force Commanders'.[24] In September 1988, Gration issued a directive confirming the arrangements with the joint force commanders. The joint commands were now known as Maritime, Land and Air Commands, but in the first instance no-one was appointed CJFA. The Chiefs of Staff were thus removed from the chain of command for operations, much as they had been during the Second World War, although they remained as advisers to the CDF.

1990–91 Persian Gulf War

This was the command structure in place during the Persian Gulf crisis in 1990 and the subsequent war to eject Iraq from Kuwait in the early months of 1991. Gration exercised command at the strategic level with the advice of the augmented COSC. This consisted of the Service chiefs, the VCDF (a position that had been established a few years earlier), the Secretary, and other key civilian and military staff. He was assisted by the HQADF operations staff, headed by the Assistant CDF (Operations) (ACOPS), Rear Admiral Rod Taylor. The Maritime Commander, Rear Admiral Ken Doolan, was responsible for deploying the two RAN task groups to the Persian Gulf. The task groups were commanded at sea by the Commodore Flotillas (COMFLOT), while Doolan remained in overall command of Operation *Damask*.

The Gulf commitment appeared to justify the broad ADF command arrangements that had been introduced during the previous five years. HQADF developed the strategic mission and passed it directly to Maritime Headquarters for its implementation. In view of the speed with which events moved, and their possible sensitivity, this was a much more efficient arrangement than the old system, which would have interposed Navy Office in the chain of command. Navy Office was kept informed throughout. The ability of Maritime Headquarters to command the task group in the Gulf was enhanced by its occupation of its new headquarters building just prior to the deployment, and by the development of the Maritime Intelligence Centre.

The Persian Gulf commitment caused no major change to the command structure, but it signalled an increase in ADF deployments abroad, most of which were mounted and commanded by one of the joint commands. Both the commitments of a signals regiment to Cambodia in 1992–93 and of an infantry battalion group to Somalia in December 1992–May 1993 were mounted and commanded by Land Headquarters. Joint exercises in Australia pointed to the necessity for a commander who could coordinate the operations of the joint environmental commanders. In 1993, Lieutenant General John Sanderson, who had commanded the United Nations force in Cambodia, was appointed CJFA and he did considerable work on the responsibilities and scope of an operational level commander in an Australian setting. But, as CJFA, Sanderson had no command responsibilities.

Commander Australian Theatre

In January 1996, the CDF, General John Baker, announced significant changes to the ADF's command and control arrangements.[25] Baker believed Bennett's initiatives had strengthened the position of CDF, but that he still had insufficient staff to command the ADF adequately. Baker announced that, at the strategic level, the single-Service staffs in Russell Offices would be absorbed as components of HQADF, while the Chiefs of Staff would be redesignated as component commanders to the CDF. The chiefs would change their titles to Chief of Navy, Chief of Army and Chief of Air Force, and their staffs would become Navy, Army and Air Force Headquarters respectively.

At the operational level, there was to be a single joint commander to be known as Commander Australian Theatre (COMAST), who would have a single headquarters (Headquarters Australian Theatre—HQAST) incorporating the existing Maritime, Land and Air Commands as components. The joint staff was to be kept to a minimum size by drawing on the expertise of the components, but would include joint logistics and joint movements staff. A common joint intelligence centre, the Australian Theatre Joint Intelligence Centre, would meet the needs of COMAST and the component commanders.

To enable him to develop operational level doctrine, COMAST was given control of the ADF Warfare Centre at Williamtown. To organise joint exercises he was given the Joint Exercise Planning Staff, previously under the CDF's control in Canberra. Headquarters Special Forces was to move from Canberra and be placed under COMAST for operations. Headquarters Northern Command was to come under COMAST and be developed into a joint headquarters capable of conducting all defensive operations across northern Australia. Two deployable joint force headquarters, one based on the 1st Division headquarters in Brisbane and the other on COMFLOT's staff, would command other joint operations as required. A new headquarters building with the latest information and communications facilities was to be built at a new site, its location to be decided later. This plan, the most sweeping for the ADF since its inception 20 years earlier, was designed to make it into a truly joint force.

In January 1997, Major General James Connolly took up the appointment as COMAST. His headquarters was in a Defence-owned multi-storey building next door to Maritime Headquarters in Potts Point, Sydney. The component commanders—Maritime, Land, Air and Special Operations—continued to work from their own headquarters buildings. Fortunately, Maritime Headquarters was next door to the COMAST building, Special Operations Command was almost next door, Land Headquarters was a couple of kilometres away and only Air Headquarters, at Glenbrook, was more than an hour away.

In some ways the establishment of HQAST facilitated the fundamental changes in Russell Offices that flowed from the report of the *Defence Efficiency Review*, released in April 1997. The formation of a proper operational headquarters made it possible to configure HQADF as a true joint strategic headquarters. The new structure came into existence on 1 July 1997. HQADF was dissolved and replaced by Australian Defence Headquarters headed jointly by the VCDF and the Deputy Secretary (Strategy and Intelligence). It consisted of the three Service headquarters and six staff divisions.

Another key change was the formation of a new joint headquarters and command—Support Command Australia—that was analogous to Australian Theatre Command in that both were at the operational level. The Navy, Army and Air Force Support Commanders became component commanders under the Commander Support Australia. Three years later, the Defence Acquisition Organisation and Support Command were amalgamated to form the Defence

Materiel Organisation. The latter organisation included Joint Logistic Command, responsible for supporting all three Services.

In May 1997 Baker claimed that, with the new command arrangements, 'we are probably at the forefront of military thinking in the world. I would like to claim a lot of responsibility for that.' He admitted that there was 'still a degree of rivalry between the Services and there always will be', but he thought that it had been harnessed for the good of the total organisation.[26]

East Timor—INTERFET

These evolving command arrangements were tested during the deployment of the Australian-led international force to East Timor in 1999. This was not the first time that Australia had led and mounted a joint and combined operation away from Australian shores. In 1994, in Operation *Lagoon*, Australia had led a multinational force to support the Bougainville peace process. But the East Timor operation was on a much larger scale and was more challenging. The headquarters of the International Force East Timor (INTERFET) was based on the Deployable Joint Force Headquarters, and the Commander of INTERFET, Major General Peter Cosgrove, was truly a joint commander.

In exercising strategic command, the CDF, Admiral Chris Barrie, relied on two organisations that were similar to those that had supported Gration in 1991. Instead of Gration's augmented COSC, Barrie had the Strategic Command Group. Within Australian Defence Headquarters, Barrie was supported by Strategic Command Division, headed by Major General Michael Keating. This position was analogous to that of ACOPS during Gration's time.

There was, however, one major difference between command arrangements in 1991 and 1999. In 1991 Rear Admiral Doolan had reported directly to Gration, with Taylor heading Gration's operations staff. In 1999, initially Cosgrove reported to COMAST, Air Vice-Marshal Bob Treloar, in Sydney, who in turn reported to Barrie, with Keating heading Barrie's operations staff. That is, there was one more link in the chain. After a short while, however, and because of the international nature of INTERFET, Barrie changed the chain of command so that Cosgrove reported directly to him.

The institution of this command arrangement raised questions as to whether it was necessary to retain Headquarters Australian Theatre. At least two arguments were presented for retaining it. First, HQAST conducted a huge amount of staff work to maintain the force in East Timor. Second, COMAST commanded several separate operations that were supporting the operation in East Timor, and also conducted or supervised other operations that had nothing to do with East Timor: for example, Australia's commitment to peacekeeping operations. For that reason, despite the INTERFET experience, Barrie decided to retain HQAST. But the experience underlined the fact that Baker had set up

HQAST to conduct operations in 'the Australian theatre' in the context of a defence policy that emphasised the defence of Australia. It was never intended to deploy it overseas. Once a large force was deployed overseas, it was likely that the CDF would require its commander to report to him.

The Bungendore Solution

When General Gration had announced the establishment of the position of Commander Joint Forces Australia in 1988, he had mentioned that the commander needed to be 'located away from Canberra' and, four years later, as he neared the end of his command, Gration went further. He declared that the joint commands needed to be collocated on one site: 'We have not yet fixed on a site, but I think it should be outside Canberra, but not too far—say no more than half an hour by helicopter.'[27] The rationale for locating the headquarters away from Canberra was so that politicians would not interfere at the operational level of command. Over the following years there was much discussion about the eventual site for the collocated headquarters, but eventually, in 2001 the government announced that it was to be near Bungendore, just outside the Australian Capital Territory.[28] There were various reasons for selecting a site near to Canberra, but one was the politicians' desire that it be near enough that they could visit it easily—the very reason why Gration had wanted it to be further away. The project was delayed and in the meantime the shape of the new headquarters was influenced by several more operations.

Operation *Slipper*

In October 2001, following the terrorist attacks on New York and Washington on 11 September 2001, the ADF deployed an Australian national commander to Kuwait, several ships to support the Multinational Interception Force in the Persian Gulf, a special forces task group for operations in Afghanistan, and various types of aircraft to different locations in the region.

Operation *Slipper*, as it was known, was commanded by the COMAST, Rear Admiral Chris Ritchie. The Strategic Command Group met to consider the concept of operations, submitted by Ritchie, and thereafter he was allowed to get on with the operation, although he kept in very close contact with the CDF, Admiral Barrie. Unlike in the INTERFET operation, Australia did not deploy a joint task force headquarters. The Australian national commander for Operation *Slipper*, Brigadier Ken Gillespie, was based in Kuwait where he was collocated with the US Land Component Commander, and only a short flight from the US Maritime and Air Component Commanders. Gillespie did not report to the CDF, but directly to Rear Admiral Ritchie. Both Gillespie and his successor, Brigadier Gary Bornholm, exercised little control over the deployed forces. Rather, the commanders of the deployed maritime, special forces and air elements reported directly to the Australian Theatre component commanders (Maritime, Special

Operations and Air Commanders), while keeping Gillespie informed on operational matters, so that he could, if necessary, veto Australian participation; but otherwise they operated under the operational control of US component commanders.

2003 Iraq War

Command arrangements were slightly different for the 2003 Iraq War. As in the previous deployments, the CDF, General Peter Cosgrove, was assisted by the Strategic Command Group and the staff of Strategic Command Division (later called Strategic Operations Division) under Major General Ken Gillespie. However, because of the very high level of secrecy necessary during the early phase, the initial planning was conducted by Gillespie's staff. The COMAST, Rear Admiral Marc Bonser, was only brought into it somewhat later.

There were similarities with Operation *Slipper*. The Australian national commander, Brigadier Maurie McNarn, was located in Qatar, alongside the headquarters of the US Commander, General Tommy Franks. He reported to the COMAST, Rear Admiral Bonser. As in Operation *Slipper*, he had several task group commanders, in this case four—maritime, maritime patrol aircraft, special forces, and fighters/transport aircraft. These were placed under the operational control of coalition component commanders. They reported on operational matters to McNarn and on technical and administrative matters directly to COMAST.

The major difference between this operation and Operation *Slipper*, however, was that McNarn also reported directly to the Cosgrove, who believed that he needed up-to-date information so that he could report it to the government. Further, in a fast-moving operation, Cosgrove believed that he needed to be able to give orders directly to the commander in the field.

After the successful invasion of Iraq, and the end of Operation *Falconer*, the ADF began a new operation, Operation *Catalyst*. Considerable numbers of ADF units returned to Australia, but the remaining force still contained several different elements, including land and air force elements in Iraq, air force units outside Iraq, and naval units in the Persian Gulf. The command structure changed yet again. This time the ADF formed a joint task force in the Middle East, commanded by a one–star officer, initially Air Commodore Graham Bentley. While the details were extremely complex, in brief, Bentley had operational control of all the Australian components. In turn he reported directly to COMAST. As in Operation *Falconer*, Bentley could speak directly to Cosgrove on matters of strategic and national policy, but these occasions were fewer, and he reported more regularly to COMAST.

The conduct of the Iraq War raised further questions about the efficacy of the higher command arrangements for joint operations. In particular, there were suggestions that, as the planning for the war had been conducted by Strategic Operations Division (at least in the first instance) and as McNarn had reported directly to Cosgrove, there was no need for HQAST. Some of these criticisms were couched in terms of questioning the validity of the concept of the operational level of war, suggesting that it is no longer relevant in modern war, or at least there is no place for an operational level command structure.

This claim misunderstands the nature of the operational level. The operational level is the link between the strategic and the tactical levels, and should not merely be seen in terms of the functions of HQAST. The operational level existed before HQAST was established and does not exist in just one headquarters. The operational level planning for the commitment to the Iraq War was conducted by the Australian planning team at the Headquarters of US Central Command and also at HQAST. The operational command of the Iraq War was conducted by General Franks' US Central Command headquarters level. Brigadier McNarn therefore worked at the operational level headquarters, even if he did not fully command at that level. The restrictions on his exercising his command were caused partly by the coalition nature of the war. When Australia provided the main deployed force, it was as in East Timor in 1999 where Headquarters INTERFET had been an operational level headquarters and the Commander INTERFET an operational level commander. Nonetheless, there were tensions between HQAST and Strategic Operations Division and there was some overlap of work. Undoubtedly, in future operations, the CDF would want to communicate directly with a deployed joint force commander, and he would need timely access to information. Further, in a small defence force it seemed wasteful to maintain a large number of headquarters.

Headquarters Joint Operations Command

Noting these concerns, and aware that planning was underway for the collocated headquarters site near Bungendore, Cosgrove initiated a review of the command arrangements, and in March 2004 the Defence Minister, Senator Robert Hill, announced the establishment of a new Joint Operations Command. The command brought together the former HQAST and the operational functions of Maritime, Land and Air Commands. It incorporated Special Operations and Joint Logistics Commands, and commanded Strategic Operations Division in Canberra, Northern Command in Darwin, the ADF Warfare Centre at Williamtown and the Joint Operational Intelligence Centre in Sydney. The VCDF took on the additional duties of Chief of Joint Operations. The former COMAST became the Deputy Chief of Joint Operations and the former two-star position of Head of Strategic Operations Division was abolished. Until the Bungendore headquarters was constructed, the new Headquarters Joint Operations Command continued to operate using the existing premises and those of its component commanders.

As with previous reorganisations, this was a conservative approach. The new structure recognised that there was overlap between the work of the strategic and operational level staffs, and that the CDF needed the capacity to command a deployed force. But as the time for deciding the shape of the Bungendore headquarters approached, the new CDF, Air Chief Marshal Angus Houston, directed another review of higher command and control arrangements. As a result, in October 2005 Senator Hill announced that the new headquarters was to be modified 'to make it more streamlined and effective in the light of lessons learned from recent successful deployments and swiftly evolving command, control and communications systems and methods'.[29] This low key announcement—which had implications for the tender process for the new buildings—disguised one of the most fundamental changes in joint command arrangements during the past 40 years.

HQAST had been formed with the idea of making a truly joint headquarters, but COMAST had relied heavily on the staffs of the component commanders. The original Headquarters Joint Operations Command had continued the idea of relying on the component commanders. The new Headquarters Joint Operations Command, however, is to be based on abolishing the component commanders. In future, it is to be completely joint. While certain cells within the headquarters will be concerned with specific air, submarine, maritime and special forces operations, in the main ADF operations will be controlled by a joint operations staff. The previous component commanders will revert to their single-Service roles of raise, train and sustain. It is intended that this new structure will begin operation in 2007, well before the Bungendore facility has been constructed. In the first instance, the headquarters staffs will be split between premises at Potts Point in Sydney and Russell Offices and Fairbairn in Canberra. Northern Command in Darwin will be disbanded, and some of its responsibilities will be taken over by the Joint Offshore Protection Command, operating out of Customs House in Canberra. Thus, with the exception of the Joint Offshore Protection Command, there will be only one operational headquarters in Australia, with one operations room—or control centre—namely, Headquarters Joint Operations Command. Current plans envisage the headquarters moving into its new premises near Bungendore in late 2008 and it will take several years for the new arrangements to reach a steady state.

Conclusion

Reflecting on how far the ADF has come since it was formed in 1976, it is noticeable that the changes to the command arrangements have been incremental. As each step was taken, it was possible to discern a further step that might have been taken along the road to a joint command, but which was resisted at that stage. With this latest development, it is hard to see the next step. As far as the actual headquarters is concerned, it is difficult to imagine an even more joint headquarters.

Perhaps the next step is to look at the command structure below the actual headquarters. Already plans are envisaged for a small deployable joint force headquarters to be incorporated into Headquarters Joint Operations Command, ready to be deployed if necessary. Bob Breen has suggested that in future the forces on a short notice for deployment be allocated to a joint Rapid Response Command, answerable to the Chief of Joint Operations.[30] If past experience is a guide, this is unlikely to happen until the planned arrangements have been tested and found to work effectively.

Of necessity, this chapter has been about the apparently esoteric topic of command structures and organisations. But it is a mistake to focus on the bricks and mortar. In reality, command structures are about power relationships. There is a centuries-long belief that only naval officers have the knowledge and understanding to command naval operations, that only army officers can command army operations and that only air force officers can command air operations. The dilemma has been to resolve the problem of who commands joint operations.

Those who have wished to implement new joint command arrangements have always run up against institutional single-Service resistance. There is no doubt that each Service draws its fighting strength from its own ethos and esprit de corps, and this single-Service strength must be maintained. The trick has been to maintain this strength while providing effective joint command.

In my view, the great story of the Australian armed forces during the past 30 years has been the formation and development of the new entity known as the ADF. We now accept it as though it was always there. But without adequate joint command arrangements, it would not exist at all.

ENDNOTES

[1] Vice Admiral Russ Shalders, 'Australian Command of Operations', an address to the United Services Institute, Canberra, 9 March 2005, available at <http://www.defence.gov.au/rusi/state/act%20lectures%20Shalders%2005.htm>, accessed 24 October 2007.

[2] Quoted in Robert Debs Heinl Jr, *Dictionary of Military and Naval Quotations*, United States Naval Institute, Annapolis, MD, 1966, pp. 334.

[3] Department of Defence, Capstone Series ADDP-D-1, *The Australian Approach to Warfare*, Defence Publishing Service, Canberra, 2002, pp. 6-1, 6-2.

[4] Quoted in D. J. Killen, 'The Government's View', in (eds) Robert O'Neill and D. M. Horner, *Australian Defence Policy for the 1980s*, University of Queensland Press, St Lucia, 1982, p. 1.

[5] Stephen D. Webster, 'Vice Admiral Sir William Creswell', in (ed.) D. M. Horner, *The Commanders: Australian Military Leadership in the Twentieth Century*, George Allen & Unwin, Sydney, 1984, p. 51.

[6] Dudley McCarthy, *South-West Pacific Area—First Year: Kokoda to Wau*, Australian War Memorial, Canberra, 1959, p. 9.

[7] McCarthy, *South-West Pacific Area—First Year: Kokoda to Wau*, p. 74.

[8] D. M. Horner, *High Command; Australia and Allied Strategy 1939–1945*, Australian War Memorial and George Allen & Unwin, Canberra and Sydney, 1982, p. 300.

[9] Blamey was Commander-in-Chief of the Army, not CGS. He commanded the Army's operational forces by virtue of his position as Commander Allied Land Forces. The Chief of Naval Staff, Vice Admiral Sir Guy Royle, was appointed Commander Southwest Sea Frontiers, under the Commander Allied Naval Forces, and so had operational command of some of his naval forces.

[10] For a discussion of the COMAFVs, see D. M. Horner, *Australian Higher Command in the Vietnam War*, Canberra Papers on Strategy and Defence, CP 40, Strategic and Defence Studies Centre, The Australian National University, Canberra, 1986.

[11] For a biography of Wilton, see D. M. Horner, *Strategic Command: General Sir John Wilton and Australia's Asian Wars*, Oxford University Press, Melbourne, 2005, p. 262.

[12] Harry Rayner, *Scherger: A biography of Air Chief Marshal Sir Frederick Scherger, KBE, CB, DSO, AFC*, Australian War Memorial, Canberra, 1984, p. 312.

[13] Tom Millar, *Australia's Defence*, 2nd ed., Melbourne University Press, Melbourne, 1969, p. 105.

[14] Wilton to Fairhall, 5 September 1967, Wilton Papers, folder 20, Australia Defence Force Academy Library, Canberra.

[15] Millar, *Australia's Defence*, p. 111.

[16] 'Brief Notes on Australian Defence Organisation', Wilton Papers, folder 19, Australian Defence Force Academy Library, Canberra.

[17] Horner, *Strategic Command*, pp. 363–64.

[18] Department of Defence, *Australian Defence*, White Paper presented to Parliament by the Minister for Defence the Hon. D.J. Killen, MP, November 1976, Australian Government Publishing Service, Canberra, 1976, p. 10.

[19] Robert O'Neill, *Structural changes for a more self-reliant national defence*, Dyason House papers, Australian Institute for International Affairs, January/February 1976. Also published as SDSC Working Paper, no. 3, Strategic and Defence Studies Centre, The Australian National University, Canberra, December 1975.

[20] In preparing for the 1983 *Kangaroo* exercise, General Bennett used D. M. Horner's book *High Command*, published the previous year and based on Horner's PhD thesis, undertaken at the Strategic and Defence Studies Centre between 1978 and 1980.

[21] Air Marshal David Evans, *A Fatal Rivalry: Australia's Defence at Risk*, Macmillan, Melbourne, 1990, pp. 137–39.

[22] Letter, General Sir Phillip Bennett to author, 21 July 2000.

[23] 'Report of the Study into ADF Command Arrangements HQ ADF, March 1988', an abridged version of the report prepared by Brigadier J. S. Baker in November 1987.

[24] General Peter C. Gration, 'The Australian Defence Force, Current Issues and Future Prospects', Strategic and Defence Studies Centre Bicentennial Conference, 6–9 December 1988.

[25] The government had approved the changes on 22 December 1985.

[26] Mark Dapin, 'Top Brass', *Australian Financial Review*, 30 May 1997, pp. 20–9.

[27] General Peter C. Gration, 'The ADF—Today and Tomorrow', CDF Address to the United Services Institute of ACT, 2 December 1992.

[28] Peter Reith, MP, 'Announcement of the New Defence Joint Headquarters', Queanbeyan Council Chambers, 18 July 2001, available at <http://www.minister.defence.gov.au/ReithSpeechtpl.cfm?CurrentId=818>, accessed 8 November 2007.

[29] Robert Hill, 'ADF Headquarters to be Streamlined', media release 166/2005, 5 October 2005, available at <http://www.defence.gov.au/minister/Hilltpl.cfm?CurrentId=5147>, accessed 8 November 2007.

[30] Bob Breen, 'Australian Military Force Projection in the late 1980s and the 1990s: What happened and Why', PhD Thesis, The Australian National University, Canberra, 2006.

Chapter 11

Four Decades of the Defence of Australia: Reflections on Australian Defence Policy over the Past 40 Years

Hugh White

The serious academic study of Australian defence policy can be said to have begun with the publication of a book by the SDSC's founder, Tom Millar, in 1965. The dust jacket of that book, *Australia's Defence*, posed the following question: 'Can Australia Defend Itself?' Millar thus placed the defence of Australia at the centre of his (and the SDSC's) work from the outset. Much of the SDSC's effort over the intervening 40 years, and I would venture to say most of what has been of value in that effort, has been directed toward questions about the defence of the continent. This has also been the case for most of the work by Australian defence policymakers over the same period. In this chapter I want to reflect on that work by exploring how the idea of the 'defence of Australia' has evolved over that time, and especially how its role in policy has changed, from the mid-1960s up to and including the most recent comprehensive statement of defence policy, *Defence 2000: Our Future Defence Force*.

This is no dry academic question. The key question for Australian defence policy today is how we balance priority for the defence of Australia against priority for the defence of wider strategic interests. The starting point for that debate is the policies of the 1970s and 1980s, which placed major emphasis on the defence of the continent. Over the 1990s our policy slowly but steadily evolved to put more weight back on the ability of the ADF to conduct operations beyond the defence of the continent. This evolution is still incomplete. We have not yet worked out the implications of this new emphasis for the way we plan our forces. This is the heart of today's defence-policy challenge. To understand these questions, we need to ensure we understand Australia's motivations. In this chapter therefore, I want to contribute to our current debates by looking back; first at how and why we came to adopt the 'defence of Australia' policies in the 1970s and 1980s, then at the changes in our strategic environment in the 1990s, and finally at the way our strategic policy has evolved in response. All these issues have been quite seriously misunderstood in much of our recent defence debate. Getting them straight will help us to understand the strengths and weaknesses of today's policy, and hence to grasp more clearly where it should go from here.

The 'Defence of Australia' Revolution

It may help to start with a definition. By 'defence of Australia' I mean the idea that the principal function of the ADF, and the core basis for choosing its capabilities, is the defence of the Australian continent from direct military attack, and in particular the ability to do so against any credible level of attack without relying on the combat forces of our allies—the self-reliant 'defence of Australia'. This idea began to evolve at the time of the SDSC's foundation in the mid to late 1960s, and was further developed during the 1970s and 1980s, finding its most complete expressions in the policies of the 1986 Dibb Review and the 1987 *Defence of Australia*. But there was nothing new in the idea that the defence of the continent was one of the key questions for Australian defence policy, or that our defence policy would hinge around choices between a narrow continental view of Australian strategic interests and objectives and a broader view. The Commonwealth's first governments thought that Australia's naval and military forces should be able to defend the continent, at least from limited attacks, and they designed the early Army and Navy accordingly.[1] Still, this emphasis faded after 1914, and the idea of defending Australia did not return to the centre of Australian defence thinking until the collapse of the 'forward defence' posture in the 1960s.

'Forward defence' is often seen as a product of the imperial or global tendency in Australian defence policy, rather than the regional or continental tendency, but in fact it was a response to local security concerns in Asia. Australia faced new and totally unfamiliar regional security challenges after the Second World War. Decolonisation and the real threat of communism made the region suddenly much more complex and rather threatening. 'Forward defence' focused Australia's defence policy on encouraging and supporting the United States and the United Kingdom to stay engaged in our region and to deal with these new local security concerns for us. It made a lot of sense while it lasted, but it did not endure. By the early 1960s it was clear that the United States and the United Kingdom did not share Australia's views on key regional issues like Indonesia, and by the end of the decade both allies had decided, for different reasons, that their strategic postures in our region were unsustainable.

Australia's contemporary conception of 'defence of Australia' emerged as a response to these cracks in 'forward defence'. The demise of 'forward defence' began, much earlier than many people think, in the early 1960s, when the United States would not assure Australia of military support against a disruptive and increasingly well-armed Indonesia. Without declaring a change in policy, the Robert Menzies Government set about transforming the ADF into a force that could defend Australia unaided. It purchased new capabilities, including F-111,

Mirage III, C-130 *Hercules*, and DHC-4 *Caribou* aircraft, UH-1H *Iroquois* 'Huey' helicopters, *Oberon*-class submarines, Guided Missile Destroyers, M-113 Armoured Personnel Carriers, and it also introduced conscription. By 1965 Menzies had, almost by stealth, laid the foundations of a defence force able to protect Australia and its regional interests without relying on allies.

It was as well that he did so, because over the following decade Australia's strategic circumstances underwent a revolution, with both positive and negative aspects. In 1965 Suharto replaced Sukarno as Indonesia's President and the country began to change from a strategic liability into a net asset for Australia. Partly as a result, Southeast Asia as a whole began to emerge from decades of crisis and evolve into a region of peace and development. In the early 1970s the opening to China dispelled for a while one of Australia's major security concerns, and détente promised a safer global strategic balance. All these developments made Australia feel safer. On the other hand, the Vietnam War undermined America's role in our region and prompted, via the Guam Doctrine, a major reduction of America's commitments to Asian allies, including Australia. At the same time, though for different reasons, Britain withdrew strategically from our region too. By the end of the 1960s, the era of 'forward defence' was clearly over. The good news was that our region looked much less threatening than it had for many decades. The bad news was that our allies had made it clear that we would have to deal ourselves with whatever problem might remain.

Well before 1970 it was clear that Australia needed a new defence policy to deal with this new reality. Fortunately, the new challenges stimulated perhaps the most active and informed defence debate we have ever had—in the universities, the press and within government. Coalition Defence Ministers including John Gorton and Malcolm Fraser started airing new ideas in the late 1960s. The debate could not help but echo the founding fathers' debates about imperial versus local defence priorities, but the circumstances were very different, and so were Australia's options. Both the nature of our regional security concerns, and the capacity and willingness of our allies to support us had changed profoundly. In March 1972, the McMahon Government produced a policy discussion paper which confirmed that Australia's strategic policy had to change. It made a blunt assessment: 'Australia would be prudent not to rest its security as directly or as heavily, as in its previous peacetime history, on the military power of a Western ally in Asia.'[2] And it drew the inescapable conclusion: 'Australia requires to have the military means to offset physical threats to its territory and to its maritime and other rights and interests in peacetime, and should there ever be an actual attack, to respond suitably and effectively, preferably in association with others, but, if need be, alone.'[3]

These ideas were conclusively established as the foundations of a new defence policy in *Australian Defence*, the 1976 Defence White Paper, published by the government of Malcolm Fraser. It is a remarkable document. The first chapter explained in a few lines the revolutionary changes of the preceding decade, and concluded: 'The changes mentioned above ... constitute a fundamental transformation of the strategic circumstances that governed Australia's security throughout most of its history.'[4]

A few pages later, under the heading 'Self-Reliance', *Australian Defence* explained the implications of this transformation:

> A primary requirement arising from our findings is for increased self-reliance. In our contemporary circumstances we can no longer base our policy on the expectation that Australia's Navy or Army or Air Force will be sent abroad to fight as part of some other nation's forces and supported by it. We do not rule out an Australian contribution to operations elsewhere, if the requirement arose and we felt that our presence would be effective, and if our forces could be spared from their national tasks. But we believe that any operations are much more likely to be in our own neighbourhood than in some distant or forward theatre, and that our Armed Services would be conducting operations together as the Australian Defence Force.[5]

While Sir Arthur Tange forged the unified Defence organisation needed to implement this vision, the implications of these bold new ideas for the ADF were painstakingly worked out. Progress was slow, and many logjams remained when Kim Beazley became Defence Minister in 1984. To break these, Beazley commissioned Paul Dibb to review Australia's defence capabilities, and then write a new Defence White Paper, *Defence of Australia*, released in 1987. Neither Beazley nor Dibb invented 'defence of Australia': their contribution was to work out how to implement it. They converted the bold new ideas of *Australian Defence* into a robust approach to force planning. Their work was very successful. It won popular support by appealing to a sense of national self-confidence. It reassured our neighbours about our strategic objectives. It provided a clear basis for disciplined decisions about capability priorities. And it stepped around the electorate's deep post-Vietnam War allergy to expeditionary operations.

One measure of this success was the willingness of governments and electorates to fund the policy. Defence spending averaged 2.3 per cent of GDP during the 1980s, compared with an average of 2.1 per cent (of an admittedly larger GDP) during the 1990s.[6] This appears surprisingly high in a period when threats seemed remote and deployments were rare. Perhaps it showed that that public understood there was no alternative to a policy of self-reliance, so we needed to make long-term investments in the necessary capabilities. Certainly the 1980s saw big investments in major capabilities, including the F/A-18 *Hornet* aircraft, *Collins* class submarine, guided missile frigate, ANZAC ship, air-to-air refuelling tankers, and a major expansion of our basing infrastructure in Australia's north and west.

Australians took a while to accept the new policy. Most thought we did not have the weight to look after ourselves—a sentiment Jim Killen alluded to in 1977 when saying we couldn't defend Botany Bay on a sunny Sunday afternoon. But once we got used to it, Australians warmed to the idea that we could defend our own continent without having to call on the help of our allies. When Gareth Evans, soon after taking over as Foreign Minister in 1989, said that Australia's self-reliant defence policy had 'liberated' Australia's foreign policy, he was perhaps indulging in a little of his own characteristic flamboyance.[7] But there was something to his statement. As General John Baker often remarked, taking responsibility for our own defence provided Australians with a new sense of confidence in their engagement with Asia. It also made a subtle but important difference to the way we viewed our alliance with the United States. Self-reliance helped ease the stigma of dependency in the relationship, and made it much easier to construct an account of the alliance which enjoyed broad support across the political spectrum in Australia. We were no longer seen to support the United States in the hope that one day in the future it would come to our defence, but because the alliance directly served specifically Australian strategic interests.[8]

Was 'Defence of Australia' isolationist?

In recent times, however, the 'defence of Australia' doctrine of the 1970s and 1980s has received a bad press. It has been criticised as isolationist and reactive. These criticisms derive primarily from the view that 'defence of Australia' totally precluded Australian military operations beyond the narrow defence of the continent. This is, at least in part, a misunderstanding, and it is important to clear it up. A more accurate view of how 'defence of Australia' balanced continental defence with wider strategic interests, and of the consequent strengths and weaknesses of the policy, will help us understand better how policy on this central question has evolved since then, and where we need to go from here.

The policy revolution that resulted in 'defence of Australia' was not driven by a deep ideological predisposition against military operations beyond Australia's shores. There was an element of that in some of Gough Whitlam's statements,[9] but the idea that really drove the new policy was self-reliance. Australia abandoned 'forward defence' primarily because our allies were no longer strategically committed to our region. Without them, our new defence policy imperative was to maximise Australia's military capacity to protect our security unaided. This is clear from the passages quoted above from the 1972 Discussion Paper and *Australian Defence*. The main message in both papers was that, in future, Australia's forces would need to operate independently of allies. The ADF might need to operate not just in defence of the continent but also 'in operations elsewhere'. The *Review of Australia's Defence Capabilities* (or Dibb Review) and the 1987 *Defence of Australia* took the same view. For example, *Defence of Australia* said:

> A requirement has also been identified for Australia's defence policy to take account both of developments in the South-West Pacific and South-East Asia—our region of primary strategic interest—and to be capable of reacting positively to calls for military support further afield from our allies and friends, should we judge that our interests require it.[10]

This language was not just for show. In private, the government of the day was very focused on a number of scenarios in which Australian forces might be deployed on expeditionary operations—such as the then much-feared contingency of a clash on the Indonesia–PNG border. It vigorously maintained Australia's forward commitments in Asia through the Five Power Defence Arrangements[11] and in other ways, and when crises arose (for example in Fiji and in the Persian Gulf in 1987), it was quick to deploy forces.

So expeditionary deployments were in no sense precluded by the 'defence of Australia' policies of the 1980s. Nonetheless, they did place much less emphasis than previous policies on operations to defend Australian interests beyond the continent, and it is worth asking why. The explanation has several elements. First, these were years in which public support for expeditionary operations suffered a deep nadir, which certainly provided strong incentives to present policy in other terms. It can be hard now to recall just how strongly Vietnam turned Australians against expeditionary operations. As Millar wrote in 1979: 'No political party is interested in deploying the Defence Force overseas.'[12] Some people, such as Robert O'Neill,[13] had the foresight to suggest that this feeling might not endure, but it did last through the 1980s. As late as 1991, fears of 'another Vietnam' shaped public, political and policy responses to Iraq's invasion of Kuwait.

These reservations were backed by a sense—perhaps, in retrospect, rather exaggerated—of our own weakness. Following the withdrawal of the United Kingdom and the United States from the region, it was likely that Australia would have to mount any future regional operations alone. Few Australians at this time thought we had the capacity to do that. And governments were also cautious: *Australian Defence* downplayed Australia's ability to shape our region with military power,[14] and the Dibb Review said: 'There are clear limits to our defence capacity and influence.'[15] These limits were real. When most Australians doubted we could defend the continent, few indeed thought we could do much to stabilise the region.

But perhaps more than any of these factors, the relatively low priority given to offshore operations in the policies of the 1970s and 1980s reflected the unusual strategic circumstances of the time, which did much to shape those policies. At the time, it made sense to focus Australia's defence efforts on the continent rather than on defending wider interests, because in those last two decades of the Cold War our wider strategic environment looked unusually benign. By the mid-1970s, the Cold War was largely over in our part of the world. At the global level, after easing with détente in the 1970s, Cold War tensions intensified again in the early 1980s. The global balance between the United States and the Soviet Union was important to Australia's security,[16] but it did not seem to have much bearing on Australia's own defence. We felt no need to build forces to help fight the Soviet Union (with the possible partial and special exception of submarines), and the United States did not press us to do so. It seemed clear that any Australian military contribution to a global superpower war would be too small and come too late to count. We hosted important US–Australian Joint Facilities instead.

This sense of detachment from the conventional military competition between the superpowers induced a similarly detached view of strategic developments in Northeast Asia. Strategic relations between Asia's major powers seemed permanently frozen by the Cold War into a stable and, for Australia, relatively benign pattern. After the US opening to China, both Japan and China were, in their different ways, aligned with the United States. The Soviet threat guaranteed that the United States would remain strategically engaged in Northeast Asia, which would preserve the resulting strategic balance. So, short of the threat of global war itself, Australia seemed to have nothing to fear from Northeast Asia. *Australian Defence* made this point very starkly when it said: 'No more than the former great powers of Europe can we expect these powers [India, China and Japan] individually to play a large military role in strategic developments directly affecting Australia's security in the foreseeable future.'[17]

The paper went on to dismiss the risk that these 'large external powers' would acquire strategic influence in Australia's nearer region.[18] As a result, the 'defence of Australia' doctrine gave little or no thought to military contingencies in Northeast Asia.

This is why the policies of 1976 and 1987 focused Australia's defence policy on Southeast Asia and the Southwest Pacific—what the 1987 *Defence of Australia* called our 'Region of Primary Strategic Interest'. *Australian Defence* and 1987 *Defence of Australia* clearly emphasised Australia's direct strategic interests in this region. They both explicitly acknowledged that Australia might need to undertake military operations to protect these interests.[19] However, threats to those interests seemed much less likely in these years than at any other time before or since. As we have seen, by the mid-1970s many of our most pressing concerns about Southeast Asia had dissipated, as the region was transformed from an area of crisis to a model of political stability, economic growth and regional cooperation. In the South Pacific, as independence came to PNG and other Southwest Pacific neighbours, Australia's strategic commitments seemed to be shrinking as well. Our newly independent neighbours were expected to be stable. There seemed few circumstances in which Australia would need to intervene in our backyard. And so it proved. The 'defence of Australia' doctrine evolved during a period in which remarkably few demands were made on our defence forces. In these years the ADF was deployed on only a handful of relatively minor and benign peacekeeping operations. Our neighbourhood generally enjoyed peace and prosperity, and the wider strategic balance in Asia did indeed remain fixed in the grip of the late Cold War. In retrospect, it was a fortunate time to overhaul Australia's defence policy.

The policy balance

In these circumstances, it made sense to focus Australia's military capabilities on the defence of the continent. This was a new task for the ADF, and it raised important and complex questions. Yet the old issue remained: how to balance the new priority for continental defence with the enduring need to be able to defend wider interests? What did the demands of military tasks beyond continental defence mean for Australia's capability priorities in the age of 'defence of Australia'? There was a simple answer: the forces we built for the defence of Australia could do all we needed to protect our wider interests, so there was no need to build forces specifically for this purpose. As the 1987 *Defence of Australia* noted: 'Should the Government wish to respond to developments in areas other than our own, the capabilities being developed for our national defence will, subject to national requirements at the time, give a range of practical options.'[20]

This has been one of the core principles of Australian defence policy for several decades, and the question of its future is at the heart of our current policy debate. The idea is simple enough, but it has been more disputed than analysed. To supporters, it has been a kind of self-evident truth, while critics have dismissed it as a sophistic sleight of hand. I can understand the critics' suspicions. It seems almost too good to be true that we can simply dissolve the traditional dilemma at the heart of Australian defence policy by asserting that forces developed solely for the defence of the continent could do everything else as well. Indeed, the critics might fairly say that this has always been more an assertion than a careful conclusion based on detailed argument. So far as I am aware, there was never any attempt to analyse in detail what kind of interests Australia might have beyond the defence of the continent, and what forces we might need to protect them. Moreover, in retrospect, one can see that the constraints imposed on the Australian Army's planning by the 'defence of Australia' discipline were counterproductive, and failed to provide a credible basis for force development. On the other hand, supporters of the 'defence of

Australia' approach can fairly argue that it has been proved true in practice. Over the 30 years since the 1976 Defence White Paper *Australian Defence*, Australian Governments have always been able to send forces sufficient to meet their strategic objectives whenever the need for overseas commitments arose. So the policy worked. That is a significant vindication of the 'defence of Australia' doctrine. The question, or course, is whether it would keep working.

The Post 'Defence of Australia' Revolution

Events are merciless on policy. In the late 1980s, just as we had settled our post-Vietnam defence policy, another series of major changes in Australia's strategic environment were starting to unfold. Even as the 1987 *Defence of Australia* was being published, some of these revolutions were in train. By 1987 Mikhail Gorbachev was already in the Kremlin, market economics had come to China, Indonesia's Suharto was entering his twilight, Fiji's first coup had ended the South Pacific's post-colonial honeymoon, and Osama bin Laden was building an organisation in Afghanistan. These were early portents of long-term developments which would transform Australia's strategic circumstances during the 1990s. Their impact has been comparable to the revolutionary developments of the late 1960s and early 1970s that impelled the 'defence of Australia' doctrine revolution, but their implications are quite different. They would reassert the importance of protecting Australia's broader strategic interests, and require us to reconsider the priority balance between protecting wider interests and defending the continent. How we respond to these changes remains the key issue in Australian defence policy today. So it is worth spending a few paragraphs exploring these developments, before considering how our defence policy has responded to them thus far. We can identify four key trends: (1) new global demands for peacekeeping and stabilisation operations; (2) new uncertainty in the strategic balance between Asia's major powers; (3) increased instability in Australia's nearer region; and (4) the steady erosion of Australia's relative strategic weight and military capabilities compared to our region.

New roles

Following the Cold War we witnessed a sharp change in the ways that governments used armed force around the world. Many different forms of peacekeeping and intervention became more common, and broadly-supported principles of humanitarian intervention started to emerge. Australia, like other countries, was initially cautious about this trend. However, governments around the world faced strong humanitarian and political pressures to get involved, and for Australia alliance considerations also played a role. The result was a startling increase in the number of expeditionary deployments. In the early 1990s, after years of relative inactivity, the ADF was suddenly very busy in remote places. It undertook substantial deployments to Namibia in 1989, Western Sahara in

1991, Cambodia and Somalia in 1992, and Rwanda in 1994, as well as repeated deployments to the Persian Gulf and many smaller operations and commitments near and far.[21] Suddenly, Australia's forces were being deployed globally again.

Nor was this just a global phenomenon. For reasons we will examine shortly, the same trend was also evident in Australia's nearer region. Starting perhaps with the first tentative deployment to the waters around Fiji at the time of the first coup in 1987, Australia found itself during the 1990s increasingly contemplating or undertaking military deployments in our own backyard—in Vanuatu, Bougainville, Irian Jaya and other parts of Indonesia and PNG—to undertake operations as diverse as famine and disaster relief, peace monitoring, evacuation of Australian citizens, and restoring law and order.

Two particular deployments—at either end of the decade—were especially significant for Australia's future strategic choices. The first was the 1990–91 Persian Gulf War, which was not a peacekeeping operation but a full-scale armed conflict—our first since the Vietnam War. The swift and relatively bloodless victory over Iraq restored the credibility of expeditionary operations in support of allies, and it did much to lift the shadow of Vietnam, and restore the credibility of the United Nations. The second really significant operational deployment of the 1990s was INTERFET in East Timor. INTERFET gave Australians a new level of confidence that we could launch and lead substantial overseas operations ourselves, rather than simply joining as a junior coalition partner. It left an increased sense of our power, and our responsibility, in the immediate neighbourhood.

None of these commitments—even, thankfully, East Timor—turned out to be very demanding military operations, but they raised important issues for our defence policy. The Army naturally bore the brunt of many of these operations and some analysts naturally questioned whether that Service should not be reshaped specifically to handle the tasks it was now being asked so often to perform. Partly this was a question about whether our defence forces should be configured for non-military tasks and, on that question, Service chiefs and Ministers were adamant that the ADF should not be downgraded from a warfighting to a peacekeeping force. Yet many of these commitments involved genuine military operations, which thus raised legitimate questions about whether hypothetical 'low-level contingencies' were as important for the Australian Army's future as these demanding new expeditionary deployments. So even before East Timor, the new pattern of operations had raised doubts that the Army's future was limited to preparing to repel raids in northern Australia.

Northeast Asia

While the ADF's many new deployments grabbed the most attention, the final collapse of the Soviet Union was propelling a second and more profound change in Australia's strategic circumstances. The end of the Cold War threw into doubt our comfortable assumptions about strategic dynamics in Northeast Asia and their significance for Australia. The Soviet Union's collapse liberated China's strategic policy from the Soviet threat and opened new strategic opportunities, just as its economic growth was starting to deliver Beijing real increases in strategic and military clout. It became clear that China might one day surpass Japan and even challenge the United States as an economic power, and ex-Soviet military technology assisted China in accelerating the expansion of its air and naval forces. People started to view China as an emerging strategic power with the potential to disrupt the international system in much the same way that Germany had done in late nineteenth century Europe.

The end of the Cold War had dissolved the glue in the US–China relationship, and raised the prospect of increasing strategic competition between them. At the same time, America's own role in Asia was thrown into doubt. Many believed that the United States had neither the reasons nor the resources to sustain its old Cold War posture in Asia now the Soviet Union had vanished, and that America's instinctive isolationism would re-assert itself. When Bill Clinton became President in 1993 with the slogan 'It's the economy, stupid', such fears seemed reasonable. And the US–Japan relationship, also now without the Soviet threat to hold it together, was under strain from differences over trade and strategic burden-sharing. No one could assume that it would last forever. Suddenly the major power balance in Asia, which had seemed so stable, looked very uncertain. By mid-decade, the question being asked was: Would Europe's past be Asia's future?[22]

All this posed a major challenge to the judgements underlying 'defence of Australia' that had more or less completely excluded Northeast Asia from Australia's strategic policy calculations. It quickly became clear that strategic competition between the great powers of Asia could in future—as in the past—intrude into and destabilise Australia's nearer region, and potentially pose threats to Australia itself. Quite suddenly Northeast Asia was restored to the traditional place it held before 1970, namely as a key focus of Australia strategic attention and concern.

Two crises around mid-decade reinforced the change. In 1994, tension over North Korea's nuclear program found Australian policymakers facing the possibility that we might have to send forces to another Korean War. Two years later, when the United States deployed carriers to the waters round Taiwan, Australia had to consider whether we would join the United States to fight China if the crisis flared into combat. In both cases the forces we had been developing for the 'defence of Australia'—especially our air and naval forces—provided a range of military options for government if needed. But the precepts that guided

Australian defence planning during the 1980s were already starting to look badly outdated.

Turbulent Neighbours

The third big change in Australia's strategic situation in the decade after the end of the Cold War was a growing concern over the stability of our nearer neighbourhood. By 1990 it was already evident that Indonesia's future after Suharto remained unclear, and possibly unstable. When he fell after the 1997–98 Asian financial crisis, an era of comparative certainty in Australia's relations with Indonesia seemed to have passed, to be replaced by an uncertain future. And, more broadly, the financial crisis shook our confidence in Southeast Asia as a region of growth and stability, deepened the sense that ASEAN was a 'spent force', and raised doubts about the dynamics of Southeast Asia as a whole. What all this meant for Australia's future defence remained uncertain, but it was clear that the comfortable assumptions about Southeast Asian stability that underpinned the 'defence of Australia' were no longer valid.

Further east, the situation seemed in some ways to be even more of a concern. By the early 1990s it was becoming clear that the newly-independent states of the Southwest Pacific faced systemic problems that threatened their viability. The Bougainville crisis, which dragged on throughout the 1990s, both demonstrated and exacerbated these problems in our largest Pacific neighbour. It deepened Canberra's pessimism about the ability of PNG to manage its own problems and steer towards a stable and sustainable national future, and raised the spectre of further fragmentation. These concerns, and their implications for the ADF, came to a head in the Sandline crisis of 1997, when the possibility arose that the ADF might need to be deployed to Port Moresby to deter or reverse a coup by the PNG Defence Force against the legitimate though incompetent government of Sir Julius Chan. That crisis was averted, but the lesson was plain: there was a high likelihood that the ADF would probably soon be deployed on relatively major independent operations to preserve stability in our immediate neighbourhood.

In the event, of course, that happened not in PNG or elsewhere in the South Pacific, but in East Timor. INTERFET sounded the tocsin for the idea that the Australian Army should be organised, trained and equipped primarily for operations on Australian soil. It became clear that the security of Australia's immediate neighbourhood was going to be an increasing priority for the ADF, especially the Army. What Paul Dibb had labelled in 1998 'the arc of instability' was moving back to a central position in Australian defence concerns.

Losing the Technology Edge

Fourth, over the 1990s the levels of military capability in the Western Pacific increased significantly. In the 1970s and early 1980s it was reasonable for

Australia to assert with some confidence that our forces would retain a decisive advantage in military technology over credible regional adversaries. Over the 1990s this became ever less credible. Critical military technologies such as Beyond Visual Range air-to-air combat had become commonplace by the mid-1990s. It became clear that Australia would need to rethink both the way it developed its forces and the way it planned to use them, if it was to remain strategically competitive in this more demanding military environment. As the economies of our neighbours grew, the long-term trends were going against us, despite the 1997–98 Asian financial crisis. Some confident assumptions about our ability to defend the continent unaided were coming under pressure, and so was the assumption that the forces we developed for that task would provide all the options we needed for more distant contingencies. If we wanted to be able to compete in Asia's more competitive military environment, we would have to plan more carefully for it.

The Evolution of the 'Defence of Australia'

Today's defence debate often assumes that the current official policy—essentially the policy of *Defence 2000*—is in all essentials identical to the 'defence of Australia' policies of the 1987 *Defence of Australia*. This is not so. During the 1990s, in response to the four major trends described above, Australian defence policy underwent significant change, the most important of which was a growing emphasis on operations beyond the defence of the continent. In the following paragraphs, we shall track that process through a few of the more important policy documents of this time.

Australia's strategic planning during the 1990s

In the latter months of 1989—even before the Berlin Wall fell—it became clear to Defence policymakers that Australia's strategic horizons needed to expand. *Australia's Strategic Planning in the 1990s*, approved by Cabinet that month, though not released until 1993, made the point clearly: 'The strategy described in this document goes beyond the defence of the nation against direct attack to include promotion of our security interests.'[23] And a few paragraphs later:

> Our national defence policy has evolved over recent decades. It has come from a position of defence dependence on allies (and consequent involvement in their strategic interests) through concentration on the immediate needs of self defence, to a positive acceptance of both the needs of self-reliance and our need to help shape our regional strategic environment, in which we are a substantial power.[24]

This passage offers a fascinating contrast with the policies of the preceding two decades, and the last phrase—describing Australia as 'a substantial power'—suggests how much Australia's strategic self-confidence had grown over the 1980s. The paper went on to identify many of the regional trends which were to shape strategic policy over the following decade and beyond: instability in PNG and the Southwest Pacific,[25] the post-Suharto transition in Indonesia,[26] Japan's evolving strategic role,[27] and the importance of keeping the United States engaged in Asia.[28] It accurately identified key underlying trends: 'a growing view that the strategic stability of the Asian region should be primarily a matter for the local powers'[29] and the 'increasing military power of some Asian nations'.[30] Interestingly, however, it underestimated China. Writing a few months after the Tiananmen Square incident, and two years before the collapse of the Soviet Union, the paper said that, 'while China is developing strategic influence and reach, its preoccupations will remain internal. Economic growth will slow and China's capacity to provide resources for Defence will be impaired ... the Soviet Union will continue to be its main military concern'.[31]

This interesting lapse notwithstanding, *Australia's Strategic Planning in the 1990s* stands up very well to the scrutiny of hindsight. It followed up the predictions quoted above by quite accurately foreshadowing how Australian defence policy would respond to these regional trends: a move away from a defensive and reactive operational concept to a more proactive one,[32] the need to provide capabilities specifically to support stability in the South Pacific,[33] and, most importantly, the need to take a broader view of our strategic objectives and interests in planning our capabilities. The paper said: 'We have in the past made comfortable judgements that the force-in-being developed for our national defence would provide suitable options for meeting other tasks. But the regional uncertainties noted above suggest that this judgement may be less justified in future.'[34]

So, by 1989, defence policy was already moving away from the idea that forces developed for the defence of Australia would provide all the options we might need to protect Australia's wider interests. How far this was true, and what we might do about it, were to become the key issues in Australian defence policy over the following decade.

Defending Australia 1994

Some of the ideas foreshadowed in 1989 took clearer form in the 1994 Defence White Paper, *Defending Australia*. Emphasis was given to operations beyond the direct defence of Australia:

> Planning for the defence of Australia takes full account of our broader strategic interests. Australia has important interests beyond the direct defence of our own territory, and the ADF will be called upon in the future, as it has in the past, to undertake activities and operations elsewhere in our region, and in other parts of the world in cooperation

with neighbours, allies and international institutions, particularly the United Nations.[35]

After the doubts expressed in 1989, the experience of successful operations since 1989 in Iraq, Somalia, Cambodia, Rwanda and the immediate neighbourhood had restored a measure of confidence that 'forces developed for the defence of Australia give us a sufficient range of options'[36] to undertake such operations. But deeper questions about our future defence needs had emerged. *Defending Australia* bluntly predicted that Australia's technological edge over potential adversaries was under long-term pressure[37] and, in response, hinted that Australia would need to take a more expansive view of the defence of the continent, and adopt a more proactive strategic posture, with increased emphasis on longer-range operations[38]—though still framed in terms of the 'defence of Australia' itself.

More fundamentally, the *Defending Australia* paper took a strikingly gloomy view of Australia's strategic environment. It deviated from earlier policy papers by focusing not on Australia's nearer region—Southeast Asia and the Southwest Pacific—but on the wider Asia Pacific as a whole, and it identified two key trends that would shape that region over coming decades. The first was shifting relationships between the major powers after the Cold War. The United States, it predicted 'will neither seek nor accept primary responsibility for maintaining peace and stability in the region'.[39] As a result, 'the strategic affairs of the region will be increasingly determined by the countries of Asia themselves. ... Much will depend on the policies of the major Asian powers themselves—Japan, China and India—and on their relationships with one another and with other countries in the region'.[40]

The second key strategic trend identified in *Defending Australia* was economic growth, especially in China. By 1994 the central role of China in Australia's strategic future was fully understood:

> Over the next fifteen years, the most important focus of economic growth in Asia will be China. If the patterns of recent years are sustained, China's economy will become the largest in Asia and the second largest in the world within fifteen years. This will affect global power relationships and become a dominant factor in the strategic framework in Asia and the Pacific.[41]

And while noting some hopeful signs, the paper identified a number of trends that 'could produce an unstable and potentially dangerous strategic situation in Asia and the Pacific over the next fifteen years'.[42] The implications were set out quite starkly:

> Previously our defence planning was able to assume a degree of predictability in our strategic circumstances. Now we need to take

account of a more complex and changeable strategic environment. Australia's ability to shape that environment will become more important to our security, and our policies will need to encompass a wider range of possible outcomes than in the more predictable decades of the Cold War.[43]

Australia's Strategic Policy 1997

All of these ideas were picked up and carried forward with much greater clarity and force in *Australia's Strategic Policy* which was published in 1997. This was the first major defence policy statement of the Howard Government. The new government largely accepted its predecessor's policy settings, but John Howard's first Defence Minister, Ian McLachlan, thought that policy still took too narrow a view of Australia's strategic interests and capability needs. He wanted a more forward posture. With his encouragement, the broad statements of the *Defending Australia* were translated into more specific policy.

Australia's Strategic Policy did that in several ways. *First*, it affirmed and amplified the judgements in *Australia's Strategic Planning in the 1990s* and *Defending Australia* about the trajectory of Australia's strategic environment. It spoke explicitly of the 'uncertainties about the direction Indonesia will take when President Suharto eventually leaves office',[44] emphasised the risks posed by endemic weakness among our smaller neighbours,[45] and dealt at length and with surprising frankness about the challenges of China's rise:

> China is already the most important factor for change in the regional security environment. ... China's growing power is an important new factor in Australia's security environment, and it is not yet clear how that power will be accommodated within the regional community. ... It would not be in Australia's interests for China's growing power to result in a diminution of US strategic influence, or to stimulate damaging strategic competition between China and other regional powers. Such competition is not inevitable, but there are some—in China and elsewhere—who are inclined to see it that way.[46]

Second, it went further than either *Australia's Strategic Planning in the 1990s* or *Defending Australia* to explicitly discard the idea that Australia's primary strategic interests were concentrated in a region of primary strategic interest covering Southeast Asia and the Southwest Pacific:

> In the 1970s and 1980s Australia defined its region of primary strategic interest as Southeast Asia and the Southwest Pacific. At that time, strategic events in Asia beyond that closer region affected our security only through their consequences for the global balance, rather than more directly.

That is no longer true. Today, our strategic interests are directly engaged throughout the wider Asia-Pacific region.[47]

Third, Australia's Strategic Policy picked up and amplified the idea first hinted at in *Australia's Strategic Planning in the 1990s*, namely that Australia's force planning should focus more on the kinds of operations we might need to undertake to defend wider interests beyond the defence of the continent, both in the Asia-Pacific and beyond. To underline this new approach, the paper deliberately dropped the iconic phrase 'defence of Australia' and used instead the fresher and more active 'defeating attacks on Australia'. In a major change, 'defeating attacks on Australia' was described, not as the sole primary task of the ADF, but as one of three basic tasks: 'There are three basic tasks which could require the ADF to undertake combat operations: defeating attacks on Australia, defending our regional interests, and supporting our global interests.'[48]

The paper affirmed that DAA (using the Defence Department's abbreviation for 'defeating attacks on Australia') remained the highest priority task and the most important criterion in force planning,[49] but it gave significant and sustained attention to the new task of Defending Regional Interests. The paper referred to the significant possibility that 'we might want to make a direct contribution to the maintenance of broader regional stability, in a future conflict in which Australia's strategic interests were engaged'.[50] By this the drafters meant that we needed the capability to make a meaningful contribution to conflicts involving the major powers of Asia if, as seemed possible, our interests were caught up in conflicts between them—for example over Taiwan. That was a sobering thought, and the paper went on to draw out its implications with some care:

> The strategic interests at stake in the range of situations that could arise in our region are very important to our security. Australia must have the capability to make a substantial military contribution in many different circumstances.
>
> The strength of these interests means we will need to pay close attention to the adequacy of our forces for this task. Rather than assuming that the forces developed for the defence of Australia would be adequate for any regional tasks, we need to demonstrate whether this would be the case.
>
> ...
>
> The capabilities of the ADF will therefore be developed to defeat attacks against Australia, and provide substantial capabilities to defend our regional interests. Priority will be given to the first of these tasks, but decisions will be influenced by the ability of forces to contribute to both tasks.[51]

The eclipse of 'defence of Australia' as the cynosure of our defence planning was plain: 'In the end, our judgement on the priority we give to defeating attacks on Australia will be tested to see how well a force developed on this basis is able to perform other tasks.'[52]

Fourth, *Australia's Strategic Policy* broke new ground by offering a clearer, more systematic and substantive definition of Australia's strategic interests in the Asia-Pacific region than had been set out in an official policy document for some decades, if ever.[53] The need to do this was clear: if the 'defence of Australia's' regional interests was to become an increasingly important task for the ADF, and a growing influence on its force structure, it was important to be able to give a clear and rigorous statement of those interests.

Fifth, the paper gave specific attention to the third of the basic tasks of the ADF—Supporting Global Interests.[54] The way this task was treated in *Australia's Strategic Policy* drew together two elements of Australia's strategic environment: (1) the increasing importance of non-traditional military tasks including peacekeeping and humanitarian operations; and (2) the growing importance of global security interests, including the need to support both the United States and the United Nations in their emerging roles as supporters of stability in the post-Cold War world. By running these two together, the paper did not specifically identify what was soon to become a prime driver of defence policy—the need to undertake, and to take the lead in, stability operations in Australia's immediate neighbourhood. But by identifying Supporting Global Interests as a third basic task for the ADF, the paper did significantly raise the profile both of stability operations and of the significance of global commitments to Australia's broader security—thus moving policy in important ways away from the 1980s paradigm, and clearly foreshadowing important future developments.

Sixth, the paper sounded a sombre warning about the importance of long-term economic trends for Australia's future security. If, as seemed likely, long-term economic growth among our neighbours exceeds that of Australia, our relative economic and hence strategic weight in the region would gradually decline. Australia therefore faced a twin challenge: to meet increasingly demanding strategic circumstances with resources which were dwindling relative to those of potential strategic competitors and adversaries.[55] For several years following the 1997–98 Asian financial crisis this warning seemed a little too gloomy, as Australia's economic growth continued while that of some of our neighbours collapsed. But as the long-term trends have reasserted themselves, the importance of this challenge is again clear.

The answer, according to *Australia's Strategic Policy*, was to focus harder than ever on spending our defence dollars on those capabilities which are most cost-effective in meeting our needs, and to deliver those capabilities as efficiently as possible.[56] The paper made at best a modest start to these tasks: it proposed a simple hierarchy of capability priorities,[57] and highlighted the need for further efficiency improvements in Defence. The paper did not attempt a rigorous financial analysis of capability options and long-term funding needs. All it did was sound an important warning that while current funds if carefully managed could sustain current forces in the short term, long-term cost pressures were going to force some tough choices. It concluded: 'The current budget does not make it possible to contemplate developing major new capabilities in the form of new fighter aircraft or new surface combatants.'[58]

Defence 2000 — Our Future Defence Force

This was the challenge that the Australian Government had to confront when, after the 1998 election and the appointment of John Moore as Defence Minister, it announced the preparation of a new Defence White Paper. In the event *Defence 2000: Our Future Defence Force* was not published until December 2000. As a result, the paper was influenced in important ways by the experience of East Timor in late 1999, although *Defence 2000* was not primarily a response to East Timor. Its aim was to draw together the defence-policy trends that had emerged during the 1990s and articulate some clear answers to the questions they had posed. Only by doing so could we create the kind of rigorous policy which *Australia's Strategic Policy* had signalled was necessary to meet Australia's underlying strategic challenges.

In particular, the government needed clear new policy directions to make a well-informed decision about the long-term future of defence funding. Over the 15 years since 1985, defence funding had broadly held steady in real terms, while costs (especially real per-capita personnel costs) had risen inexorably. Personnel numbers had been cut sharply to compensate, but the scope for further cuts was inevitably dwindling. The government faced a simple choice: to either provide long-term funding increases or scale back capabilities and hence strategic options. In the event, the government decided to commit to a significant long-term increase in defence funding after Australia's National Security Committee had considered at length how Australia's policy should respond to the strategic lessons of the 1990s and the trends of the new century. In many ways these discussions foreshadowed the wider public debates since 2001. During 2000, Ministers considered whether the ADF still needed to prepare to fight conventional wars, or whether it should plan instead to focus on stability and other non-conventional operations. They considered whether 'defence of Australia' needed any longer to be a major policy priority, and whether in the new security environment higher priority should be given to the Australian Army at the expense of the RAN and the RAAF.

The policy framework that was developed to answer these questions drew strongly on the ideas that had been evolving throughout the 1990s, and especially those presented in *Australia's Strategic Policy*. But it went significantly further in many ways. Building on the policy paper, a specific statement of Australia's broader strategic interests and objectives was developed and set out in Chapter 4 of *Defence 2000: Our Future Defence Force*. These interests covered not only the defence of the continent and its direct approaches, but the stability of the immediate neighbourhood, the security of Southeast Asia and the wider Asia-Pacific, and support for global security.[59] They provided the foundation for the statement of strategic tasks for the ADF in Chapter 6 of that paper, which included not only defending Australia but contributing to the security of the immediate neighbourhood, and supporting wider strategic interests.[60] This was a significant elaboration of the 'three basic tasks' set out in *Australia's Strategic Policy*, and took defence policy even further away from the classic 'defence of Australia' construct of an ADF developed simply to defend the continent against direct attacks. *Defence 2000* clearly set out the government's aim to see the ADF evolve into a flexible instrument designed to achieve a wide range of different functions beyond the defence of Australia.

This was reflected most clearly where it mattered most—in *Defence 2000*'s plans for ADF capabilities. *First*, the government decided that in order to ensure the ADF could help defend our interests in the wider Asia-Pacific, air and naval forces had to be able to operate effectively in coalition operations against the region's major powers like China. This was critical to the Australian Government's decision to undertake major long-term enhancements of Australia's air and naval forces. In particular, it underpinned the largest single capability decision in *Defence 2000*—the allocation of major funding for a large number of new fifth-generation combat aircraft.

Second, the *Defence 2000* overturned earlier thinking about the role of the Australian Army. It described the increasing demands of non-traditional military tasks (including stability and humanitarian operations) and concluded:

> The Government believes that this is an important and lasting trend, with significant implications for our Defence Force. Over the next ten years the ADF will continue to undertake a range of operations other than conventional war, both in our own region and beyond. Preparing the ADF for such operations will therefore take a more prominent place in our defence planning than it has in the past.[61]

The implications were spelled out clearly when *Defence 2000* dealt with the future of the Australian Army's capability. The decision was made to increase permanently the number of high-readiness battalions from four to six, and to invest in new capabilities, including larger amphibious ships, to improve significantly the ADF's capacity to deploy and sustain land forces beyond Australia's shores. The rationale was spelled out quite clearly:

In view of the issues raised in earlier chapters of this White Paper, the development of our land forces needs to reflect a new balance between the demands of operations on Australian territory and the demands of deployments offshore, especially in our immediate neighbourhood. While still giving priority to the defence of Australia in our overall strategic and force planning, the development of our land forces will take fuller account of the demands of possible short notice operations in our immediate neighbourhood. For much of the last two decades, land force planning has been dominated by preparations to meet lower level contingencies on Australian territory. This focus will now be broadened to meet wider range of possible contingencies, both on Australia soil and beyond.[62]

We had come a long way from 1976 and 1987.

Next Steps

Yet have we gone far enough? Although *Defence 2000* went some way to respond to the major changes of the 1990s, and focused significantly on tasks for the ADF beyond the defence of the continent, it has been criticised for being still too narrowly concerned with the defence of the continent. There is some basis for that charge, at least as far as declaratory policy is concerned. *Defence 2000: Our Future Defence Force* said that the defence of Australia remained 'the primary priority for the ADF', which 'provides a clear basis for our defence planning'.[63] At several places one can find an uneasy tension between the significant innovations in approach and outlook described in the last section, and affirmations that the defence of the continent remained the core of Australian strategic policy. How do these divergent policy ideas fit together? Does it really make sense, for example, to say that our policy gives overriding priority to the defence of Australia, and then say that the key role of the Army is to support stability in our immediate neighbourhood? Or to state that a key factor shaping our air-combat and strike forces is the need to contribute to coalition operations in the wider region against major powers like China? On the critical question of the balance of priorities between continental defence and the defence of wider interests, *Defence 2000* does seem inconsistent.

As we have seen, *Australian Defence* and the 1987 *Defence of Australia* argued that the capabilities developed for the defence of Australia would provide government with an adequate range of options for other contingencies. But *Australia's Strategic Planning in the 1990s* and *Australia's Strategic Policy* both questioned this approach. They said that the adequacy of our 'defence of Australia' defence force to meet wider needs should be carefully tested as the demands of offshore contingencies grew with changing strategic circumstances. *Defence 2000*'s approach therefore marked a reversion to the earlier doctrine. It claimed, in similar terms to the 1987 *Defence of Australia*, that 'forces built primarily to defend Australia will be able to undertake a range of operations to promote our wider strategic interests',[64] even though it specifically proposed that forces should be developed for strategic tasks beyond the defence of Australia. This tension is not resolved. While setting out the elements of a new, more expansive strategic posture for Australia based on the defence of a set of broad interests, *Defence 2000* still held on to the ideas which had formed the foundation of defence policy for the preceding 25 years, without explaining how the old and the new fit together. The result was a measure of policy 'dissonance' (to use Michael Evans' term).[65]

Such instinctive conservatism is perhaps not all that surprising. This document was after all a product of the Howard Government. Policy centred on the defence of our own territory had worked well for many years, attracting widespread public support and bipartisan political consensus in Australia. It was readily accepted by Australia's neighbours, and offered a clear basis for setting capability priorities. While the strong urge to cling to it is hardly surprising, it is no longer tenable. The key strategic trends of the past 15 years have significantly increased the weight that Australian defence policy needs to give to our wider strategic interests. It is artificial to claim, as *Defence 2000* did, that we still develop forces primarily for the defence of the continent. This artificiality prevents us addressing squarely the real and complex problems of policy that our new strategic circumstances present. To build a credible, effective and sustainable defence policy for the coming decades, we need to rethink the place of 'defence of Australia', and bring Australia's wider strategic interests out from under its shadow. So moving beyond 'defence of Australia' is not just a matter of more credible public presentation. It is important to getting the content of our policy right. Unfortunately the atmosphere of the five years since the terrorist attacks of 11 September 2001 has been unconducive, indeed counterproductive, to this effort. The preoccupation with the 'war on terror', and especially the political imperative to frame defence policy in terms which supported the decision to join the United States in invading Iraq, made it difficult to take a balanced, long-term view of the nature of Australia's wider strategic interests, and of the kinds of forces that could most cost-effectively protect them. This is the task upon which Australian defence policy, and scholars who study that policy, must now focus. It is rather different from, but in a way analogous to, the one Tom Millar posed back in 1965, and to which the SDSC has made such a major contribution. I hope the SDSC can contribute as much to this new task.

ENDNOTES

[1] A wise and witty account of early defence debates which illustrates this point can be found in an essay 'The True Principles of Australia's Defence' by Colonel the Hon. James McCay, written in 1908 and republished in the *Australian Army Journal*, vol. II, no. 2, Autumn 2005, pp. 255–263, available at <http://www.defence.gov.au/Army/LWSC/Publications/journal/AAJ_Autumn05/AAJ_Autumn05_retrospect_26.pdf>, accessed 24 October 2007.

[2] Department of Defence, *Australian Defence Review*, Australian Government Printing Service, Canberra, 1972, p. 11.

[3] Department of Defence, *Australian Defence Review*, p. 5.

[4] Department of Defence, *Australian Defence*, Australian Government Printing Service, Canberra, 1976, p. 2, paragraph 13.

[5] Department of Defence, *Australian Defence*, p. 10, paragraph 6.

[6] Australian Strategic Policy Institute, *ASPI Almanac 2004-2005*, Canberra, September 2004, p. 63.

[7] Gareth Evans, 'Australia's Place in the World: The Dynamics of Foreign Policy Decision-Making', Address by the Minister for Foreign Affairs and Trade to the ANU Strategic and Defence Studies Centre Bicentennial Conference 'Australia and the World: Prologue and Prospects', Canberra, 6 December 1988, available at <http://www.crisisgroup.org/library/documents/speeches_ge/foreign_minister/1988/061288_fm_australiasplace.pdf>, accessed 24 October 2007.

[8] See Kim Beazley, *Thinking Defence: Key Concepts in Australian Defence Planning*, Roy Milne Memorial Lecture, Perth, 6 November 1987.

[9] See for example, J. L. Richardson, 'Australian Strategic and Defence Policy', in (eds) Greenwood and Harper, *Australia in World Affairs*, Cheshire/Australian Institute of International Affairs, Melbourne, 1974, p. 246.

[10] Department of Defence, *The Defence of Australia*, Australian Government Publishing Service, Canberra, 1987, p. 8, paragraph 1.43.

[11] For example, see a speech delivered in Singapore by then Defence Minister Kim Beazley on 19 November 1987, 'Australian Perspectives in Regional Security Issues' published in *Selected Speeches 1985–1989 by the Hon. K. C. Beazley MP Minister for Defence*, Department of Defence, Canberra, 1989, p. 171ff. Beazley said, for example, that 'the security of Southeast Asia is as important to Australia today as it has ever been', and announced a new program of rotational naval deployments to Southeast Asia to underscore Australia's continued strategic engagement there.

[12] Tom Millar, *The Political-Military Relationship in Australia*, SDSC Working Paper, no. 6, Strategic and Defence Studies Centre, The Australian National University, Canberra, 1979, p. 12.

[13] See Robert O'Neill, 'Strategic Concepts and Force Structure', in (eds) Robert O'Neill and D. M. Horner, *Australian Defence Policy for the 1980s*, University of Queensland Press, Brisbane, 1982, pp. 164 and 173. Also see Michael Evans, *The Tyranny of Dissonance: Australia's Strategic Culture and Way of War 1901–2005*, Study paper, no. 306, Land Warfare Studies Centre, Canberra, February 2005, available at <http://www.defence.gov.au/Army/LWSC/Publications/SP/SP_306.pdf>, accessed 8 November 2007.

[14] Department of Defence, *Australian Defence*, p. 11, paragraph 17: 'Insofar as we can directly influence developments shaping our strategic prospects, this will often be by the political rather than the military arm of policy.'

[15] Department of Defence, *Review of Australia's defence capabilities*, Report to the Minister for Defence by Mr Paul Dibb, Australian Government Publishing Service, Canberra, March 1986, p. 42.

[16] See, for example, the interesting formulation in *Defence of Australia*, the 1987 White Paper, p. 3, paragraph 1.13, which says: 'Australia is part of the Western community of nations. Australia therefore supports the ability of the United States to retain an effective strategic balance with the Soviet Union. A redistribution of power in favour of the Soviet Union in the central balance, or an extension of Soviet influence in our region at the expense of the United States, would be a matter of fundamental concern to Australia, and would be contrary to our national interests.'

[17] Department of Defence, *Australian Defence*, p. 5.

[18] Department of Defence, *Australian Defence*, p. 5, paragraphs 24 and 28.

[19] See, for example, the striking formulation in *Australian Defence*, the 1976 Defence White Paper, paragraph 24 on p. 6, which says: 'For practical purposes, the requirements and scope for Australian defence activity are limited essentially to the areas closer to home—areas in which the deployment of military capabilities by a power potentially unfriendly to Australia could permit that power to attack

or harass Australia and its territories, maritime resources zone and near lines of communication. These are our adjacent maritime areas: the South West Pacific countries and territories; Papua New Guinea; Indonesia; and the South East Asian region.'

[20] Department of Defence, *The Defence of Australia*, p. 8, paragraph 1.46. See more generally paragraphs 1.43–1.48, 9.4 and 9.7.

[21] Australian Strategic Policy Institute, *ASPI Almanac 2004-2005*, Canberra, September 2004.

[22] Aaron L. Friedberg, 'Will Europe's Past be Asia's Future', *Survival*, vol. 42, no. 2, Autumn 2000, pp. 147–59.

[23] Department of Defence, *Australia's Strategic Planning in the 1990s*, Canberra, September 1992, p. 2.

[24] Department of Defence, *Australia's Strategic Planning in the 1990s*, p. 3.

[25] Department of Defence, *Australia's Strategic Planning in the 1990s*, pp. 6–8.

[26] Department of Defence, *Australia's Strategic Planning in the 1990s*, p. 9.

[27] Department of Defence, *Australia's Strategic Planning in the 1990s*, p. 15.

[28] Department of Defence, *Australia's Strategic Planning in the 1990s*, p. 13.

[29] Department of Defence, *Australia's Strategic Planning in the 1990s*, p. 19.

[30] Department of Defence, *Australia's Strategic Planning in the 1990s*, p. 21. See also p. 27, paragraphs 5.3 and 5.4.

[31] Department of Defence, *Australia's Strategic Planning in the 1990s*, p. 17. Gareth Evans' statement *Australia's Regional Security* published in December 1989, the month after Cabinet considered *Australia's Strategic Planning in the 1990s*, made a similar judgement about China: *Australia's Regional Security: Ministerial Statement* by Senator The Hon. Gareth Evans, QC, Department of Foreign Affairs and Trade, Canberra, December 1989, paragraph 24, p. 7.

[32] Department of Defence, *Australia's Strategic Planning in the 1990s*, p. 23, especially paragraph 4.11.

[33] Department of Defence, *Australia's Strategic Planning in the 1990s*, p. 26, paragraph 4.21. See also p. 34, paragraphs 5.33 ff, and p. 39, paragraph 5.50.

[34] Department of Defence, *Australia's Strategic Planning in the 1990s*, p. 21, paragraph 4.4.

[35] Department of Defence, *Defending Australia*, Australian Government Publishing Service, Canberra, 1994, p. 15, paragraph 3.11.

[36] Department of Defence, *Defending Australia*, p. 15, paragraph 3.11.

[37] Department of Defence, *Defending Australia*, p. 27, paragraph 4.25.

[38] Department of Defence, *Defending Australia*, pp. 28–9, especially paragraph 4.31.

[39] Department of Defence, *Defending Australia*, p. 8 paragraph 2.6.

[40] Department of Defence, *Defending Australia*, p. 8 paragraph 2.7.

[41] Department of Defence, *Defending Australia*, p. 9 paragraph 2.12.

[42] Department of Defence, *Defending Australia*, p. 8, paragraph 2.8.

[43] Department of Defence, *Defending Australia*, p. 10 paragraph 2.19.

[44] Department of Defence, *Australia's Strategic Policy*, Commonwealth of Australia, Canberra, 1997, p. 12, available at <http://www.minister.defence.gov.au/sr97/SR97.pdf>, accessed 8 November 2007.

[45] Department of Defence, *Australia's Strategic Policy*, p. 13.

[46] Department of Defence, *Australia's Strategic Policy*, p. 14.

[47] Department of Defence, *Australia's Strategic Policy*, pp. 9–10.

[48] Department of Defence, *Australia's Strategic Policy*, p. 29.

[49] Department of Defence, *Australia's Strategic Policy*, p. 36.

[50] Department of Defence, *Australia's Strategic Policy*, p. 32.

[51] Department of Defence, *Australia's Strategic Policy*, p. 36.

[52] Department of Defence, *Australia's Strategic Policy*, p. 36.

[53] Department of Defence, *Australia's Strategic Policy*, p. 8.

[54] Department of Defence, *Australia's Strategic Policy*, pp. 32–3.

[55] Department of Defence, *Australia's Strategic Policy*, p. 5.

[56] Department of Defence, *Australia's Strategic Policy*, p. 5.

[57] Department of Defence, *Australia's Strategic Policy*, Chapter 7.

[58] Department of Defence, *Australia's Strategic Policy*, p. 51.

[59] Department of Defence, *Defence 2000: Our Future Defence Force*, Chapter 4, Commonwealth of Australia, Canberra, 2000, available at <http://www.defence.gov.au/whitepaper/docs/WPAPER.PDF>, accessed 8 November 2007, p. 30.

[60] Department of Defence, *Defence 2000: Our Future Defence Force*, pp. 46–53.

[61] Department of Defence, *Defence 2000: Our Future Defence Force*, p. 10, paragraph 2.8.

[62] Department of Defence, *Defence 2000: Our Future Defence Force*, p. 79, paragraph 8.11.

[63] Department of Defence, *Defence 2000: Our Future Defence Force*, p. 46, paragraph 6.2.

[64] Department of Defence, *Defence 2000: Our Future Defence Force*, p. 46, paragraph 6.2.

[65] See Michael Evans, *The Tyranny of Dissonance: Australia's Strategic Culture and Way of War 1901–2005*, Study paper, no. 306, Land Warfare Studies Centre, Canberra, February 2005, available at <http://www.defence.gov.au/Army/LWSC/Publications/SP/SP_306.pdf>, accessed 8 November 2007.

Index

Abas, Nasir (*see under* Jemaah Islamiyah)
Abu Ghraib prison (*see under* Iraq)
Acharya, Amitav 121
Acheson, Dean 44;
    Acheson White Paper 1949: 38, 39
ADF (*see* Australian Defence Force)
Advancing the National Interest: Australia's Foreign and Trade White Paper (*see under* Department of Foreign Affairs and Trade)
Afghanistan 3, 7, 41, 45, 52, 171;
    bin Laden, Osama in 77, 171;
    Operation *Enduring Freedom* in 35, 49, 53, 55, 56, 109;
    Operation *Slipper* in 156–57;
    Taliban in 77
Agreement on Framework for Security Cooperation between Indonesia and Australia (*see under* treaties)
Ahmadinejad, Mahmoud 52
air warfare destroyer 22–24, 137
aircraft:
    air-to-air refuelling tanker 138;
    Airborne Early Warning & Control 138;
    C-17 *Globemaster III* heavy transport 22, 138, 140;
    C-130 *Hercules* tactical transport 165;
    combat aircraft 14, 23–25(*n*41), 43, 120, 138, 144, 156–57, 181–83;
        F-16 *Fighting Falcon* 43;
        F-35 *Lightning II* joint strike fighter 24;
        F-111 *Aardvark* (US)/*Pig* (Australia) 164;
        F/A-18 *Hornet* 43, 135, 166;
        Mirage III 165;
    DHC-4 *Caribou* tactical transport 165;
    UH-1H *Iroquois* 'Huey' helicopter 165
aircraft carrier 137, 139
Akaha, Abdu Zulfidar 112
al Qaeda 31, 52, 76, 106
Albright, Madeleine 123
Allende, Salvador 36
Amos, James 54
amphibious capability 137–40;
    ships 22–24, 100, 182
Anti-Ballistic Missile Treaty (*see under* treaties)
ANZUS Treaty (*see under* treaties)
APEC (*see* Asia-Pacific Economic Cooperation)
Arbatov, Georgi 68
'arc of instability', concept of 6, 24, 85–89, 91–97, 99, 101–102, 135, 174
ARF (*see under* Association of Southeast Asian Nations)
Armitage, Richard (Rich) 100
Armoured Personnel Carrier (M-113) 165
ASEAN (*see* Association of Southeast Asian Nations)
ASEAN Institutes for Strategic and International Studies (*see under* Association of Southeast Asian Nations)
ASEAN Regional Forum (ARF) (*see under* Association of Southeast Asian Nations)
Ashton, Calvert 90
Asia-Pacific Economic Cooperation (APEC) 98, 122, 125
Asian financial crisis of 1997–98: 3, 86, 119–20, 122, 174–75, 180
Association of Southeast Asia 117
Association of Southeast Asian Nations (ASEAN) 3, 88–89, 117–18, 123-26, 174;
    ASEAN Institutes for Strategic and International Studies 118;
    ASEAN Regional Forum (ARF) 98, 117–19, 122–25
At-atsary, Abu Hamzah Yusuf 112
AusAID 91, 96;
    Pacific 2020: Challenges and Opportunities for Growth 96;
    White Paper Core Group 91;
    Core Group Recommendations Report for a White Paper on Australia's aid program 91, 94, 96;
    White Paper on the Australian Government's Overseas Aid Program 91–92, 96

Australia 1–8, 11–25, 29–33, 35, 38–39, 43, 55, 73, 85–101, 105–114, 118, 123–24, 126, 131–41, 143–60, 163–84;
Bungendore, NSW, new defence facility near, in 156, 158–59;
Cabinet 13, 21–22, 24, 88, 90, 147, 175, 186(*n*31);
cadet college, proposed formation of, in 148;
Canberra, policymaking in 88–89, 90, 92, 97, 100–101, 147, 174;
(*see also* Australian defence policy);
Darwin 86, 145, 152, 158–59;
External Affairs, Department of, in 97;
Federation 11;
Five Year Defence Program 15;
funding by 20–21, 126, 132, 181–82;
Gross Domestic Product (GDP) on defence by 3, 8, 134–36, 166;
(*see also* budget);
Joint Intelligence Organisation 148;
Potts Point, NSW 154, 159;
Strategic Basis of Australian Defence Policy documents for 1964, 1967, 1971, 1973, 1979, 1983: 14, 16, 87;
Treasury 133;
Australia's National Security: A Defence Update 2003: 22
Australia's National Security: A Defence Update 2005: 22, 105
Australia's National Security: A Defence Update 2007: 7–8
Australia's Strategic Planning in the 1990s: 175–76, 178–79, 183
Australia's Strategic Policy, 1997: 20, 178–183
Australian Army 18, 85, 87, 97–98, 103(*n*33), 103(*n*35), 134–35, 137, 139, 146, 170, 172, 174, 181–82;
Army Development Guide 18;
Australian Approach to Warfare 144;
Australian Army Force Vietnam (*see under* wars);
(*see also* Australian Defence Force (ADF))
Australian Commonwealth Naval Board 145

Australian Defence, 1976: 11, 15, 134, 150, 165–69, 171, 183, 185(*n*19)
Australian Defence Force (ADF) 2–4, 6–8, 12, 15–25, 131–32, 134–37, 140–41, 143–45, 147, 149, 151–60, 163–64, 166–67, 170–71, 174, 176, 179–83;
ADF deployment to Western Sahara 171;
ADF Warfare Centre 154, 158;
Australian Theatre Command 154;
Australian Theatre Joint Intelligence Centre 154;
Chief of Defence Staff (CDS) 148–49;
Chief of the Defence Force (CDF) 17–18, 151–59;
    Assistant CDF (Operations) (ACOPS) 153, 155;
    Vice Chief of the Defence Force (VCDF) 143, 152, 154, 158;
Chief of the Defence Force Staff (CDFS) 149–51;
Chiefs of Staff Committee (COSC) 18, 145–50, 152, 155;
Commander Australian Theatre (COMAST) 153–59;
Commander Joint Forces Australia (CJFA) 152–53, 156;
Commodore Flotillas (COMFLOT) 153–54;
'defeating attacks on Australia', doctrine of 179–80;
Joint Exercise Planning Staff 154;
Joint Logistics Command 158;
Joint Offshore Protection Command 159;
Joint Operations Command 158–60;
    Chief of Joint Operations 158, 160;
Joint Services Staff College, concept of and as forerunner to Joint Warfare Establishment 148;
Joint Warfare Establishment, concept and establishment of 148;
Kangaroo military exercises 151, 161(*n*20);
Strategic Command Group 155–57;

Strategic Operations Division 157–58;
  Strategic Command Division, as
    forerunner of 155, 157;
  Support Command Australia 154;
  Supporting Global Interests 180;
  (*see also* Headquarters; wars)
Australian defence policy 1, 5–6, 11–13,
  15–16, 131, 133, 139–40, 163–64,
  170–71, 174–76, 184
Australian Defence Review, 1972: 14, 165
Australian Federal Police 114
Australian National University (ANU) 45,
  94–95, 147, 149;
  Demography and Sociology Program at
    94;
  Strategic and Defence Studies Centre
    (SDSC) at 16, 117–18, 123–24, 126,
    133, 147, 151, 163–64, 184
Austria 46, 63
Austro-Hungarian empire 63
'axis of evil', concept of 73

Ba'abduh, Luqman 111–12, 116(*n*23);
  Mereka Adalah Teroris (They are the
    Terrorists) by 111
Babbage, Ross 16, 26(*n*26), 124
Bachelet, Michelle 36
Baghdad (*see under* Iraq)
Baker, John 152–53, 155–56, 167
'balance of power', concept of 42–44, 71, 75
'balanced force', concept of 139–41
Ball, Desmond 16, 119, 124
Bandow, Doug 40–41
Bangladesh 33
'barbed wire' reality, concept of 92–93
Barnard, Lance 14, 149
Barrie, Chris 155–56
'battle of ideas' (*see under* Indonesia)
Bay of Bengal 73
Beazley, Kim 2, 100, 166, 185(*n*11)
Beijing (*see under* People's Republic of
  China)
Beirut (*see under* Lebanon)
Belgium 46

Bell, Coral 80, 81(*n*18), 87, 123;
  Dependent Ally by 123;
  *Living with Giants: Finding Australia's
    place in a more complex world* by 126;
  'world out of balance', concept of 78,
    81(*n*18)
Belgrade (*see under* Serbia)
Bennett, Phillip 18, 151–53, 161(*n*20)
Bentley, Graham 157
Berger, Sandy 101
Berlin Wall (*see under* Germany)
Bevin, Ernest 44
Beyond Visual Range air-to-air combat 175
Bien Hoa province (*see under* Vietnam)
bin Laden, Osama (*see under* Afghanistan)
'bipolar world', concept of 29, 40;
  (*see also* 'multipolar world'; 'unipolar
    moment'; 'unipolar world')
'bird flu' (*see* H5N1 Avian Influenza)
Bisri, K. H. Mustofa 113
Blackwill, Robert 40
Blamey, Thomas 146, 161(*n*9)
Bland, Henry 148
Boao Forum for Asia 119, 125
Boer War (*see under* wars)
Bolivia 36
Bonaparte, Napoleon 143
Bonser, Marc 157
Borneo 11
Bornholm, Gary 156
Bougainville 89, 155, 172, 174;
  Operation *Lagoon* 155;
  (*see also* Papua New Guinea; Solomon
    Islands)
Boxing Day Tsunami (*see under* Indian
  Ocean)
Brabin-Smith, Richard 26(*n*23)
Brady, Martin 26(*n*23)
Brazil 32, 33, 36
Breen, Bob 160
Brezhnev Doctrine (of Leonid Brezhnev) 64;
  Antipodean Brezhnev Doctrine 89
budget 120, 132;
  Australian aid budget 90;
  Australian defence budget 3, 6, 8, 16,
    20–21, 24, 131–36, 140–41, 143, 181;
  US budget 70

191

Bungendore, NSW (*see under* Australia)
Burma 36
Bush, George H. W., administration of 68, 70, 72
Bush, George W. 36–37, 42, 44, 51, 54, 72, 74–75, 78–79, 81(n14), 98–99, 110;
administration of 5, 31, 37–38, 43, 49, 52, 58, 72–75, 77–80, 99

Cable News Network (CNN) (*see under* media)
Calderón, Felipe 36
Cambodia 20, 54, 98, 135, 153, 172, 177
Canberra (*see under* Australia)
Capie, David 124
Carpender, Admiral Arthur 146
Castro, Fidel 36
Central Intelligence Agency (*see under* United States)
Chan, Sir Julius 174
Chávez, Hugo 36, 37
Chen Shui-bian 38–39
Cheney, Richard (Dick) 70–72
Chile 36
China (*see* People's Republic of China)
Clinton, William (Bill) 68–72, 122, 173
CNN (*see under* media)
Cocos Islands 87
Cold War 2–3, 20, 29, 38, 41–42, 49, 51, 64, 67–72, 80, 118–19, 123, 135, 169–71, 173–74, 177–78, 180
Collins-class submarine (*see under* submarines)
command and control arrangements 7, 16, 133, 153, 159
Commander Australian Force Vietnam (COMAFV) (*see under* wars)
communication 4, 14, 33, 44, 58, 75, 143, 148, 154, 186(n19)
Communism 11, 13, 64, 106, 164
'concert of powers', concept of 40, 42–44, 46, 80
Concert of Powers 4, 43, 45–46
Conscription 53;
in Australia 87, 134–35, 165

continental 62;
defence 7–8, 14, 167, 170, 183;
forces 6, 62, 100, 151;
operations 22, 62;
view 164
Cook Islands 94–95
Coral Sea, battle of the (*see under* wars) 86
'core force', concept of 15–17, 20
Cosgrove, Peter, 155, 157–58
Cossa, Ralph (*see under* 'Track 2')
Council for Security Cooperation in the Asia-Pacific (CSCAP) 118–19, 122
counterinsurgency (*see under* insurgency)
counterterrorism (*see under* terrorism)
Creswell, William 145
Crews, Bill 26(n23)
Cuba 36
Curtin, John 87
Czechoslovakia 64

da Silva, Lula 36
Darwin (*see under* Australia)
Defence Acquisition Organisation 154
Defence Act 1903 150
Defence Capability Plan 20–21, 132
Defence Efficiency Review, 1997: 154
Defence Materiel Organisation 154–55
'defence of Australia', doctrine of 1–3, 6, 11–12, 16–18, 20–23, 87, 97, 134–36, 139, 151, 156, 163–64, 166–71, 173–77, 179–84, 185(n16)
Defence of Australia, 1974: 14
Defence of Australia, 1987: 1, 11, 19, 164, 166, 168–71, 175, 184
Defence of Australia: Fundamental New Aspects (*see under* O'Neill, Robert)
Defence Reform Program 135
Defence Report, 1966: 134
Defence 2000: Our Future Defence Force (*Defence 2000*) 3, 6–7, 12, 20-21, 97, 138, 163, 175, 181–84
Defending Australia, 1994: 20, 176–78
Demography and Sociology Program (*see under* Australian National University (ANU))

Department of Foreign Affairs and Trade (DFAT) 90, 108, 115(*n*19);
Advancing the National Interest: Australia's Foreign and Trade White Paper 108;
Transnational Terrorism: The Threat to Australia 108
Desker, Barry 125
DFAT (*see* Department of Foreign Affairs and Trade)
Dibb, Paul 1–2, 87–88, 124, 174;
Review of Australia's Defence Capabilities, 1986 (Dibb Review) by 1, 11, 17, 19, 87, 135, 164, 166, 168
Dili (*see under* East Timor)
Din Syamsuddin (*see under* Indonesia)
Discussion Paper, 1972: 165, 167
Dobell, Bob 86, 101–102
Dobell, Graeme 6
Doolan, Ken 153, 155
Dovers, Bill 148
Downer, Alexander 85, 89, 96, 105–107, 115 (*n*19)
Duncan, Ron 91
Dupont, Alan 124
Dutch New Guinea (*see under* New Guinea)

East Asia Summit (EAS) 118, 121, 125–26
East Asian Community 121, 126;
    Council on East Asian Community 121, 127(*n*10)
East Timor 3, 21, 24, 85–86, 88–89, 94, 97–98, 101, 122, 155, 158, 172, 174, 181;
    Dili 89, 93, 101;
    (*see also* International Force East Timor)
Edwards, Peter 97
El Alamein, Egypt 102
European Union, 30, 33–34, 41, 45, 75
Evans, Gareth 89, 167, 186(*n*31)
Evans, Michael 97, 184
Evans, Paul (*see under* 'Track 2')
expeditionary:
    capability 1, 7–8, 23;
    forces 6, 11–12, 24, 53, 145;
    military culture 97;
    operations 1, 7, 23, 166, 168, 171, 172

External Affairs, Department of (*see under* Australia)

Fairhall, Allen 148
Falklands War (*see under* wars)
Ferguson, Niall 68
Fiji 89, 91, 94;
    coups in 90, 168, 171–72;
    Suva 92–93
Finschhafen (*see under* Papua New Guinea)
First Gulf War (Persian Gulf War) (*see under* wars)
First World War (*see under* wars)
Fischer, Tim 101
Five Power Defence Arrangements 88, 168
force structure 2–4, 11, 15–18, 20–25, 132–33, 135, 137–39, 180;
    Force Structure Review 1991: 135
'fortress Australia', concept of 11
'forward defence', doctrine of 11, 16, 21, 134, 136, 138–39, 164–65, 167
Four-Power Talks 118
Fox, Vincente 36
France 46, 63, 74, 86, 89
Franks, Tommy 157, 158
Fraser, Malcolm 14, 15, 149, 165–66
Freedman, Lawrence 101

G7 and G8 44–45
Garnaut, Ross 45
General Belgrano incident (*see under* wars)
geography (*see* strategic geography)
George, Lloyd 143
German New Guinea (*see under* New Guinea)
Germany 33, 61, 63, 64, 65, 67, 74, 86, 173;
    Berlin Wall, fall of, in 175
Gillespie, Ken 156–57
Gilling, James 91
Gleneagles meeting, 44–45
Global Initiative to Combat Nuclear Terrorism (*see under* nuclear)
globalisation 4, 29, 33, 75
Gorbachev, Mikhail 68, 171
Gorton, John 165
Gration, Peter 152, 155–56

Gross Domestic Product (GDP) (*see under* Australia; budget)
Guam (*see under* United States)
Guam Doctrine (*see under* Nixon, Richard)
Guantanamo Bay Naval Base, Cuba (*see under* United States)
Gulf (*see* Persian Gulf)
Gulf War (*see under* wars)

H5N1 Avian Influenza 121
Hadley, Stephen 108
Hartfiel, Robert 120
Hamas (*see under* Palestinian Territories)
Harries, Owen 100
Hassett, Francis 149
Hawke, Bob 137
Headquarters 17, 143, 145–46, 148, 151–60;
  Air Headquarters 152, 154;
  Australian Defence Headquarters 154–55;
    Headquarters Australian Defence Force (HDADF), superseded by 17, 151–54;
  Deployable Joint Force Headquarters 154–55, 160;
  Field Force Headquarters 151;
  1st Division Headquarters 154;
  Headquarters Australian Theatre (HQAST) 154–56, 158–59;
  Headquarters Northern Command 154;
  Headquarters Special Forces 154;
  Land Headquarters 153–54;
  Maritime Headquarters 151, 153–54;
  Operational Command Headquarters 151
Hernandez, Carolina (*see under* 'Track 2')
Hicks, Edwin 148
Hill, Robert 22, 158–59
HMS *Invincible* (*see under* United Kingdom)
Holmes, William 145
Holt, Harold 146
Honiara (*see under* Solomon Islands)
Houston, Angus (*see also* Royal Australian Air Force (RAAF)) 159

Howard, John 85, 89, 98–99, 101, 107–108;
  Government of 12, 20, 90, 98, 105–106, 136, 178, 184
Huisken, Ron 124
human security, challenges of 121, 126
humanitarian interests and relief operations 85, 91, 171, 180, 182
Hungary 64
Huntington, Samuel 93, 126
Hussein, Saddam 76

India 4, 32–35, 40, 42–43, 44–45, 63, 80, 119–20, 122, 169, 177
Indian Ocean 87, 100;
  26 December 2004 tsunami in 121–22
Indonesia 3, 5–6, 15, 19, 33, 87–88, 98, 101, 105–107, 109–114, 122, 127(*n*1), 134, 164–65, 168, 171–72, 174, 176, 178, 186(*n*19);
  'battle of ideas' in 5, 105–108, 111–14;
  Din Syamsuddin in 109;
    as chairman of Muhammadiyah (Organisation) 109, 115(*n*19);
    as convenor of the World Peace Forum 109;
    as deputy chairman of Majelis Ulama Indonesia (Indonesian Ulama Council) 109;
    as deputy secretary-general of World Islamic People's Forum 109;
  Indonesian Police 113–14;
  International Crisis Group in 115(*n*21);
  Jakarta 98, 101, 110;
  Jones, Sidney in 115(*n*21);
  Learning Assistance Program for Islamic Schools 106;
  Majelis Ulama Indonesia (Indonesian Ulama Council) 109;
  Muhammadiyah (Organisation) 110, 112;
  Nahdlatul Ulama 110, 113;
  Pancasila, as state ideology of 109
Institute of Southeast Asian Studies (*see under* Singapore)
insurgency 30, 49, 55–56, 76;
  counterinsurgency 55, 57–58, 76

intelligence 7, 14, 17, 19, 56, 76, 93, 105, 113, 143, 147–48, 154
International Criminal Court 73
International Crisis Group (*see under* Indonesia)
International Force East Timor (INTERFET) 155–56, 158, 172, 174
International Institute for Strategic Studies (IISS) 118, 124;
Shangri-la Dialogue hosted by 118, 124
Iran 33–35, 37, 41–42, 50–53, 69, 78–79
Iraq 41, 45, 52, 69, 70, 74–75, 96;
Abu Ghraib prison 76;
Baghdad 76;
(*see also* wars)
Irian Jaya 88–89, 172
Islam 31, 34, 54, 106–114;
fundamentalism in 5, 33, 108, 112;
Muslims 32–34, 50, 106–114;
pluralism and 106, 108–110, 112, 114;
radicalism in 5, 54, 106–110, 112;
salafism as branch of 111–12, 15(*n*21);
sharia law 109, 110–12;
Shia 45;
Sunni 45, 112
Israel 52, 112, 113–14
Italy 46

Jakarta (*see under* Indonesia)
Japan 11, 13, 32, 33, 39–40–42, 43, 46, 61, 63–65, 67–68, 73, 86, 118–21, 123, 125, 127(*n*10), 146, 169, 173, 176–67;
Commander-in-Chief British Commonwealth Occupation Force (BCOF) 146
Jemaah Islamiyah (JI) 105, 106, 111, 113;
Abas, Nasir on 111;
Samudra, Imam 111–12
jihadism 5–6, 30–31, 34–35, 105–116 (*chapter* 7)
Job, Brian 120, 124
Jones, Sidney (*see under* Indonesia)

Kangaroo military exercises (*see under* Australian Defence Force (ADF))
Kaplan, Lawrence 99
Kazakhstan 35
Keating, Michael 155
Keating, Paul 98
Kennan, George 44
Kennedy, John Fitzgerald 40
Keynes, John Maynard 67
Khalilzad, Zalmay 70
Killen, Jim 167
Kiribati 91–92, 94–95
Kissinger, Henry 88
Kitchener, Field Marshal 12
Koran (*see* Qur'an)
Korea (*see* North Korea; South Korea)
Korean War (*see under* wars)
Kraft, Herman 124
Kuala Lumpur (*see under* Malaysia)
Kuomintang 39
Kuwait 68, 70, 152, 156, 168
Kyoto Protocol 73
Kyrgyzstan 35

Lae (*see under* Papua New Guinea)
Laos 54
Latin America 32, 35–36;
(*see also* individual entries for countries of Latin America)
League of Nations (*see under* Wilson, Woodrow)
Leahy, Peter 87, 97
Lebanon 49, 52, 113–14;
Beirut 99
Lenin, Vladimir 106
Leningrad (St. Petersburg) (*see under* Russia)
Leopard tank (*see under* tanks)
Libby, Lewis 'Scooter' 70
Lippman, Walter 69
London (*see under* United Kingdom)

M1 *Abrams* tank (*see under* tanks)
Ma Ying-Jeou 39
MacArthur, Douglas 144, 146
Mackay, Iven 146
Mackay, Ken 144

Majelis Ulama Indonesia (Indonesian Ulama Council) (*see under* Indonesia)
Malaya 11, 13, 127(n1), 146
Malaysia 88–89, 134, 147;
 Kuala Lumpur 124
Malkasian, Carter 55, 59
Manchuria 63
Maphilindo 117, 127(n1)
Maritime Intelligence Centre 153
Marshall Islands 95
McLachlan, Ian 178
McMahon, William 165
McNarn, Maurie 157–58
media 58;
 Cable News Network 69;
 New York Times 68, 71;
 Sheridan, Greg 98
Menzies, Robert 136, 139, 164–65
Mexico 32, 33, 36
Middle East 22, 24, 34–37, 41, 45, 49, 51, 53–54, 125, 157;
 (*see also* individual entries for countries of Middle East)
Millar, Tom 147, 149, 151, 163, 168, 184
Mongolia 63
Moore, John 181
Moore-Wilton, Max 90
Morales, Evo 36
Mountbatten, Louis 144
Muhammad (Sunnah), Prophet 110, 114
Muhammadiyah (Organisation) (*see under* Indonesia)
Multinational Interception Force 156
'multipolar world' 29–30, 34–35, 42;
 (*see also* 'bipolar world'; 'unipolar moment'; 'unipolar world')
Musharraf, Pervez 107
Muslims (*see* Islam)
Myanmar (*see* Burma)

Nagl, John 55, 59
Nahdlatul Ulama (*see under* Indonesia)
Namibia 20, 171
National Security Council (*see under* United States)
National Security Strategy (*see under* United States)

Nauru 89, 91
Nelson, Brendan 24, 85
Nepal 91
Netherlands 46, 62, 63, 86
Network Central Warfare (NCW) (*see under* warfare)
Network of East Asian Think Tanks (NEAT) 118–19, 121, 125
New Caledonia 89;
 Noumea 89
New Guinea 86, 88, 146–47;
 New Guinea Force 146;
 Dutch New Guinea 101 (*see also* Irian Jaya);
 German New Guinea 145 (*see also* Papua New Guinea)
New York Times (*see under* media)
New Zealand 13, 87, 89, 95
Nigeria 32, 33
Nixon, Richard 54;
 as architect of Guam Doctrine 12, 13, 41, 99, 134, 165
North Atlantic Treaty Organization (NATO) 44, 68
North Korea 34, 36–37, 40–42, 50–53, 70, 78–79, 120, 122–23, 126, 173;
 Pyongyang 123
Nott, John 101
Noumea (*see under* New Caledonia)
nuclear 30, 37–38, 41–43, 50–51, 73, 74, 120, 122, 173;
 Nuclear Non-Proliferation Treaty (*see under* treaties);
 nuclear terrorism 50;
 Global Initiative to Combat Nuclear Terrorism 51;
 nuclear weapons 4, 15, 33, 40, 50–2, 54, 62, 67–68, 73, 75
Nuku'alofa (*see under* Tonga)

Oberon-class submarine (*see under* submarines)
Official Development Assistance 90
O'Neill, Robert (Bob) 16, 151, 168;
 Defence of Australia: Fundamental New Aspects 16

Index

Operations:
  Operation *Catalyst* (*see under* wars);
  Operation *Damask* (*see under* wars);
  Operation *Enduring Freedom* (*see under* Afghanistan);
  Operation *Falconer* (*see under* wars);
  Operation *Iraqi Freedom* (*see under* wars);
  Operation *Lagoon* (*see under* Bougainville);
  Operation *Slipper* (*see under* Afghanistan)
Ottoman Empire (*see under* Turkey)
'over-the-horizon' radar 138

Pacific Basin Economic Council 119
Pacific Economic Cooperation Council 119
Pacific Oceans Command (*see under* wars)
Pacific 2020: Challenges and Opportunities for Growth (*see under* AusAID)
Pakistan 33– 35, 43, 107
Palestinian Territories 52, 113–14;
  Hamas, election of, in 52
Pancasila, state ideology of (*see under* Indonesia)
Papua New Guinea (PNG) 15, 19, 88–92, 94–96, 135, 168, 170, 172, 174, 176, 186(*n*19);
  budget of 89;
  Finschhafen on northeast coast of 86, 146;
  Lae in 86, 101–102;
  Port Moresby 89, 92–93, 174;
  Rabaul 145;
  Sandline International crisis in 93, 135, 174
Patey, George 145
'peer-competitors', idea of nations as 30–31, 34–35
Pentagon (*see under* United States)
People's Republic of China 3–5, 30, 32–40, 43–45, 47(*n*9), 61–65, 73, 80, 100, 119–20, 122, 124–25, 165, 169, 171, 173, 176–78, 182–83;
  Beijing 38, 43, 47(*n*9), 119, 122, 173;
  Tiananmen Square incident in 176;
  Tibet, as autonomous region of 63–64;

Xianjiang, as autonomous region of 43
Persian Gulf 20, 32, 43, 168, 172;
  (*see also* wars)
Petraeus, David 54
Philippines 40, 88, 91, 127(*n*1)
Phuoc Tuy province (*see under* Vietnam)
Pinochet, Augusto 36
Population, composition, growth and ageing of 4, 24–25, 29, 32–34, 36, 41, 61, 91, 94–95, 141;
  (*see also* Australian National University, Demography and Sociology Program)
Port Moresby (*see under* Papua New Guinea)
Port Vila (*see under* Vanuatu)
Portugal 46, 63, 86, 89
Potts Point, NSW (*see under* Australia)
Powell, Colin 70, 122–23
'pre-emption', doctrine of 73
PRC (*see* People's Republic of China)
Project for a New American Century (*see under* United States)
Putin, Vladimir 51
Pyongyang (*see under* North Korea)

Qatar 157
Quadrennial Defense Review 2001 (*see under* United States)
Quadrennial Defense Review 2006 (*see under* United States)
Qur'an 110–11, 114

Rabaul (*see under* Papua New Guinea)
RAAF (*see* Royal Australian Air Force)
RAN (*see* Royal Australian Navy)
Rapid Response Command 160
Reagan, Ronald 40, 71
Regional Assistance Mission to Solomon Islands (RAMSI) (*see under* Solomon Islands)
regional security institutions 117–18, 123, 126; (*see also* individual institution headings)
Republic of China (*see* Taiwan)
Review of Australia's Defence Capabilities, 1986 (*see under* Dibb, Paul)

'revolution in military affairs', concept of 72
Rice, Condoleezza 42, 79, 125
Ritchie, Chris 156
Royal Australian Air Force (RAAF) 21, 24, 97, 134, 137–38, 146, 151, 181;
(*see also* Australian Defence Force (ADF))
Royal Australian Navy (RAN) 21, 24, 97, 137–39, 146, 153, 181;
(*see also* Australian Defence Force (ADF))
Royal Navy (*see under* United Kingdom)
Rudd, Kevin 31, 86
Rumsfeld, Donald 34, 72
Russia 29, 32–35, 37, 40–41, 43–46, 51, 63, 73, 80;
St. Petersburg 45;
(*see also* Soviet Union)
Rwanda 20, 135, 172, 177

salafism (*see under* Islam)
Samoa 94–95
Samudra, Imam (*see under* Jemaah Islamiyah)
Sanderson, John 153
Sandline International crisis (*see under* Papua New Guinea)
SARS (*see* Severe Acute Respiratory Syndrome)
Scherger, Frederick 147
sea-air gap 2–3, 7, 87, 97
Second World War (*see under* wars)
Serbia 46;
Belgrade 122
Severe Acute Respiratory Syndrome (SARS) 121–22
Severino, Rodolfo (*see under* Singapore)
Shalders, Russ 143
Shanghai Cooperation Organization (SCO) 35, 118–19, 125
Shangri-la Dialogue (*see under* International Institute for Strategic Studies (IISS))
sharia law (*see under* Islam)
Sheridan, Greg (*see under* media)
Shia (*see under* Islam)

Singapore 40, 86, 88, 118, 123, 134;
Institute of Southeast Asian Studies in 123;
Severino, Rodolfo as member of 123
Six-Party Talks 118
Smith, Ric 23
Solomon Islands 24, 85–86, 89, 90–95;
Honiara 92–93;
Regional Assistance Mission to Solomon Islands (RAMSI) 89, 92
Somalia 20, 135, 153, 172, 177
Somare, Michael 90
Sopie, Noordin (*see under* 'Track 2')
South Africa 32–33
South Korea 39–41, 117–18
Southeast Asia Treaty Organization (SEATO) 117
Southwest Pacific Area (*see under* wars)
Soviet Union 29–30, 35, 41, 44, 68, 71, 119, 169, 172–73, 176, 185(*n*16);
(*see also* Russia)
Spain 46
Special Operations Command 154, 158
St. Petersburg (*see under* Russia)
State Department (*see under* United States)
Strategic and Defence Studies Centre (SDSC) (*see under* Australian National University (ANU))
Strategic Basis of Australian Defence Policy (*see under* Australia)
'strategic guidance' 6, 14, 17, 19, 131–33, 135–41
strategic geography 2, 6, 13–15, 20–21, 24, 55, 86–88, 97, 99, 139
submarines 23, 25(*n*5), 39, 101, 104(*n*46), 120, 137, 159, 169;
Collins-class submarine 166;
Oberon-class submarine 165;
(*see also* warfare)
Sudan 36
Suez, Egypt 12–13, 134
Suharto 86, 165, 171, 176, 178
Sukarno 165
Sunnah (*see under* Muhammad (Sunnah), Prophet)
Sunni (*see under* Islam)
'superpowers', role of 30, 119, 169

surveillance capability 14, 19, 57, 105
Suva (*see under* Fiji)

Taiwan 37–41, 62–65, 122, 126, 173, 179;
Taiwan Strait 122
Tajikistan 35
Taliban (*see under* Afghanistan)
Tange, Arthur 87, 140, 149–50, 166
tanks 22, 57;
M1 *Abrams* tank 42;
Leopard tank 134;
Taylor, Rod 153, 155
terrorism 3–5, 24, 44, 46, 49, 54, 69–70, 74, 76–77, 85, 105–114, 120–21, 124;
counterterrorism 5, 105–108, 110, 113–14, 136;
(*see also* nuclear; United States; 'war on terror')
Tet Offensive (*see under* wars)
Thailand 88, 134
Tiananmen Square incident (*see under* People's Republic of China)
Tibet (*see under* People's Republic of China)
Tonga 91–95
Nuku'alofa 93
Top, Noordin Mohammed 105
'Track 1' (official track) 118, 121;
(*see also* entries for entities such as the ASEAN Regional Forum; Shanghai Cooperation Organization; and East Asia Summit)
'Track 2' (unofficial track) 118, 121–22, 124;
Cossa, Ralph and involvement with 124;
Evans, Paul and involvement with 124;
Hernandez, Carolina and involvement with 124;
Sopie, Noordin and involvement with 124;
(*see also* entries for entities such as the Council for Security Cooperation in the Asia-Pacific; and Network of East Asian Think Tanks)
Transnational Terrorism: The Threat to Australia (*see under* Department of Foreign Affairs and Trade)

treaties 40, 67, 98, 131;
Agreement on Framework for Security Cooperation between Indonesia and Australia 98;
Anti-Ballistic Missile Treaty 73;
ANZUS Treaty 123;
Nuclear Non-Proliferation Treaty 15, 42–43, 73;
Treaty of Amity and Cooperation 123
Treloar, Bob 155
tri-Service officer cadet academy, proposal for 148
Truman, Harry S. 39, 44
Tse-tung, Mao (*see* Zedong, Mao)
Turkey 63;
Ottoman Empire 46, 63
Tuvalu 92, 94
28th Commonwealth Brigade (*see under* war)

'unipolar moment' 5, 29, 68, 76;
(*see also* 'bipolar world'; 'multipolar world', 'unipolar world)
'unipolar world' 4, 29, 30–31, 42, 79, 80;
(*see also* 'bipolar world'; 'multipolar world', 'unipolar moment')
United Kingdom 2, 11–13, 43–45, 49, 55, 62–63, 101, 123, 145–46, 164, 168;
London 106;
Royal Navy 12, 138, 145;
HMS *Invincible* 138;
Thatcher Government (*see under* wars)
United Nations 3, 33, 39, 44–46, 64, 67, 70, 90, 122, 153, 172, 177, 180;
United Nations Security Council 45
United States of America 2–3, 5–7, 11–13, 24, 29–44, 47(*n*9), 49–55, 62–65, 67–80(*chapter 5*), 86, 96–101, 103, 109, 113–14, 118–19, 121–25, 133–34, 136, 146–47, 156–58, 164–65, 167–69, 173, 176–78, 180, 184, 185(*n*16);
Center for Naval Analyses 55;
Central Intelligence Agency 109;
Declaration of Independence 69;
11 September 2001 terrorist attacks on 3, 22, 30–31, 34–35, 41, 51, 73–75, 77–78, 118, 121–22, 156, 184;

199

Guam, as unincorporated territory of 39;
Guantanamo Bay Naval Base, Cuba 113;
National Security Council 42;
National Security Strategy 71;
Pentagon, 43, 79;
    funding of 70–71;
    views and strategy of 30, 33–34, 38, 70–75, 77;
Project for a New American Century 72;
Quadrennial Defense Review 2001 73;
Quadrennial Defense Review 2006 34;
State Department 42, 79, 100;
US Congress 37, 43, 70, 76, 100;
US economy 67;
US military 7, 30, 41, 70, 96–97, 99, 133;
    American Second Field Force 148;
    US Air Force 39;
    US Army 53–54;
        US Army Field Manual 3-24 54, 59;
    US Central Command 158;
    US Commander Pacific Fleet 100;
    US Marine Corps (USMC) 53–55, 100;
US-Australian Joint Facilities 169;
US-Japan-Australia Trilateral Strategic Dialogue 118;
US-Japan-South Korea Trilateral Coordination and Oversight Group 118;
Washington, D.C. policymaking in 31, 34–43, 46(n5), 67–70, 73–77, 101;
(*see also* wars)
uranium, selling of 43
Uzbekistan 36

Vanuatu 89, 91, 94–95, 172;
    Port Vila 92
Venezuela 36, 37
Viet Cong (*see under* wars)
Vietnam 33, 98, 134;
    Bien Hoa province 147;
    Phuoc Tuy province 147;
    Vietnam War (*see under* wars)

Wallace, Jim 98
Wanandi, Jusef 124
wars:
    Boer War 145;
    Falklands War 101, 104(n46), 138;
        General Belgrano incident 101, 104(n46);
        Thatcher Government during 101;
    First World War 12, 41–42, 67, 87, 143, 145;
        Australian Naval and Military Expeditionary Force 145;
    Korean War 39, 146, 173;
        Commander-in-Chief British Commonwealth Force Korea during 146;
        28th Commonwealth Brigade in 146;
    1990–91 Persian Gulf War (including Operation *Damask*) 68, 70, 71, 152–53, 168, 172, 177;
    Second World War 11, 13, 14, 41–42, 61, 63–64, 67, 86–87, 134–35, 139, 144–45, 152, 164;
        Central War Room 145;
        Combined Operational Intelligence Centre 145;
        Coral Sea (battle) 86;
        Northern Territory Force 146;
        Pacific Oceans Command 144;
        Pearl Harbor, attacks on, during 67, 85;
        Southwest Pacific Area 144, 146;
    2003 Iraq War (including Operations *Catalyst*, *Falconer* and *Iraqi Freedom*) 3–5, 7, 30–1, 42, 49, 50, 53, 54, 55, 56, 64, 75–79, 96–97, 99, 114, 136, 157–58, 184;
    Vietnam War 11, 18, 49, 54–56, 68, 87–88, 96, 101, 103(n33), 134–36, 145–48, 165–66, 168, 171–72;
        Australian Army Force Vietnam 146;
        Australian Force Vietnam 146, 148;
        Commander Australian Force Vietnam (COMAFV) 144, 146–47;

Tet Offensive 41;
Viet Cong 56;
(*see also* Cold War; 'war on terror')
'war on terror' 73, 75–76, 105, 108–110, 113–14, 121, 184
Ware, Helen 94
warfare 24, 52, 137, 139, 144;
anti-submarine warfare 24;
asymmetric warfare 30;
mine warfare 24;
Network-Centric Warfare (NCW) 24
Washington, D.C. (*see under* United States)
Weapons of Mass Destruction (WMD) 24, 70, 76
Weinberger, Caspar 99–100
West Papua (*see* Irian Jaya)
White, Hugh 2–3, 23, 124
White Paper Core Group (*see under* AusAID)
White Paper on the Australian Government's Overseas Aid Program (*see under* AusAID)
Whitlam, Gough 134, 167
Wilson, Woodrow 43–44;
League of Nations as Wilsonian system of 43–44
Wilton, John 144, 146–49
Wolfowitz, Paul 70
Woodward, Bob 75, 81(*n*14);
Plan of Attack, book by 75
World Conference on Religion and Peace 109
World Islamic People's Forum (*see under* Indonesia)
'world out of balance', concept of (*see under* Bell, Coral)
World Peace Forum (*see under* Indonesia)

Xianjiang (*see under* People's Republic of China)

Yudhoyono, Susilo Bambang 107
Yugoslavia 64

Zedong, Mao 38, 64
Zemin, Jiang 122
Zoellick, Robert 38, 42, 43, 47(*n*9)
Zulfidar, Abduh 112

www.ingramcontent.com/pod-product-compliance
Lightning Source LLC
Chambersburg PA
CBHW041238240426
43661CB00067B/2910